*Conservation
and
Agriculture*

Conservation and Agriculture

Edited by

Joan Davidson and **Richard Lloyd**

A Wiley–Interscience Publication

JOHN WILEY & SONS LTD

Chichester · New York · Brisbane · Toronto

Library of Congress Cataloging in Publication Data:

Main entry under title:

Conservation and agriculture.

'A Wiley–Interscience publication.'
Includes index.
1. Conservation of natural resources.
2. Agriculture. I. Davidson, Joan. II. Lloyd, Richard.
S944.C65   333.7′6   77-697
ISBN 0 471 99502 9

J. W. Arrowsmith Ltd.
Winterstoke Road, Bristol BS3 2NT

List of contributors

MICHAEL BODDINGTON
BSc(Ag. Econ.), NDA

Principal, Rural Planning Services, Forestry House, Great Milton, Oxford.

IAN BROTHERTON
MA, MSc, PhD

Lecturer, Department of Landscape Architecture, University of Sheffield.

CHRISTOPHER BULL
BA, MPhil

Lecturer, Monkwearmouth College, Sunderland.

JOAN DAVIDSON
MA, MSc

Lecturer in Rural Planning, Gloucestershire College of Art and Design, Cheltenham.

MAX HOOPER
BSc, PhD

Principal Scientific Officer, Institute of Terrestrial Ecology, Monks Wood Experimental Station, Huntingdon.

CLUNIE KEENLEYSIDE
MA, MSc

Senior Countryside Assistant, Durham County Council.

JOHN KING
BSc, PhD

Principal Scientific Officer, Hill Farming Research Organization, Edinburgh.

PATRICK LEONARD
BSc(Agric.), Dip.Ag.Econ.

Principal Research Officer, Countryside Commission, Cheltenham.

RICHARD LLOYD
BSc, MPhil, MRTPI

Principal Research Officer, Countryside Commission, Cheltenham.

NORMAN MOORE
MA, PhD

Chief Advisory Officer, Nature Conservancy Council, London.

CHRISTOPHER NEWBOLD
BSc, PhD

Freshwater Biologist, Chief Scientist Team, Nature Conservancy Council, Huntingdon.

CHRISTINE STOAKES   *Formerly Research Officer, Countryside*
    BSc, MSc   *Commission, Cheltenham.*

HEW WATT   *Farmer, Heath Place, Orsett, Grays,*
    OBE, JP   *Essex; member of the Nature Conservancy*
                                     Council.

GERALD WIBBERLEY   *Professor of Countryside Planning, Uni-*
    CBE, BSc, MS, PhD, Hon. ARTPI   *versity College and Wye College, Univer-*
                                     sity of London; member of the Nature Con-
                                     servancy Council.

The views expressed in this book are not necessarily those of the organizations by which the authors are or were employed.

Contents

Foreword

HEW WATT OBE JP

Conservation has always taken second place in agricultural development because farmers must put the economic needs of a thriving countryside before other interests.

There is no doubt that we now face a multiplicity of often competing demands in rural areas and a scarcity of means to meet them. Since 1970 there have been many reports which highlight rural problems from a particular viewpoint. Farmers are often made to feel that they are the enemy in the countryside whereas in most cases they have created it.

This book describes in detail many agricultural changes that must concern all thinking people. In future, it will be difficult to produce more food from our own soil yet satisfy the increasing demands upon the countryside for leisure and recreation and for the conservation of landscapes and wildlife. These problems concern farmers very much. We are determined to continue to produce that part of the nation's food that the government requests of us; but at the same time we want to leave the countryside in good heart for those that follow. This means that conflict must be replaced with consensus. Only by examining the situation in a calm and detached way are we likely to make the right choices and decisions about the management of agricultural land to satisfy all the interests involved. It is the aim of this book to help us make the right decisions.

Later chapters discuss ways of securing the enhancement of landscape and wildlife values along with efficient food production and forestry. These cover a range of possibilities from persuasion to compulsion, from carrot to stick. All industries have their 'cowboys' and we in farming are not without ours; but the great majority of farmers, as confirmed by a recent Ministry of Agriculture survey of attitudes, are open to advice on wildlife and landscape matters. Even so, the countryside is our factory floor and therefore our economic base must come first.

Incentives to farm in a particular way are, in my view, a method much surer of success than more statutory controls. If a farmer is to be persuaded, for example, that draining a certain marsh will lead to an irreplaceable loss of plant and animal species, then society must make up his economic loss in retaining the marsh. With all large schemes of land reclamation for food production, I believe there should be much closer cooperation between the Ministry of

Agriculture as the grant-aiding agency and conservation bodies who can negotiate management arrangements.

In the past, owners of large estates have cooperated in negotiating management agreements to safeguard areas of scientific, access and landscape value but recent fiscal measures are now beginning to take their toll. It seems to me essential that *all* traditional estate owners who have done so much to maintain an attractive countryside should have relief from capital transfer tax, provided that they do not use the money in ways that will eventually lead to the destruction of rural values. It is obvious that the land user who inherits his enterprise free of debt finds it more economically possible to cooperate with conservation and landscape demands than a young farmer, fresh out of agricultural college, trying to make every square metre of land service his mortgage. Additional sources of income from recreational and leisure enterprises are to be welcomed. Many farmers are able to continue on a small acreage because of income from a caravan or fishing enterprise. Only if farmers are prosperous will they be able to adopt landscape and wildlife conservation measures.

'Redistribution of wealth' is a cry almost as popular as 'giving the land to the people' but in my view none of those countries who have tried to put these two aims into practice, principally by doctrinaire methods, have achieved a more attractive countryside with a higher quality of life for all. It is my view that statutory controls to achieve conservation objectives over the whole countryside are likely to rouse the wrath of all land users.

For generations farmers have so arranged their daily work to suit the vagaries of weather and the changing economic climate that they will be loath to accept the delays of government controls. Only in wartime has their necessity been accepted. New regulations now could encourage such a movement of non-cooperation as to bring about more harm to conservation interests than any other single act.

What then does the future hold?

I doubt whether there will be a fast expansion of home food production. Much more likely is a change in production patterns with economic pressures forcing us to live within our means and to accept a plainer diet with a reduced consumption of animal products. The European Economic Community as a whole is already over 90 per cent self-sufficient in temperate foods. Britain is the odd man out, so it may be that the export of people rather than industrial products could be the best contribution to conserving our countryside.

These are changes for the long term; in the meantime we have to deal with existing problems and this book discusses a range of alternative possibilities. It should not be beyond the wit of us all to find a workable system that could achieve both the aims of increased food production and the maintenance of a thriving and attractive countryside. As a farmer, I believe moral persuasion rather than coercion will provide the solution to our conservation problems.

Preface

This book is one of a series which deals with the development and management of natural and semi-natural habitats. The focus of this volume is the environment of agriculture, in the uplands and the lowlands, and its associated habitats of hedgerows, woods and wetlands, which are all increasingly influenced by modern farming practice. These habitats, cutting across the traditional structure of ecosystems, may seem an odd choice for study. Yet they represent an important spectrum of wildlife localities, including communities of species richness and rarity found only in association with agricultural activities. All have been, and continue to be, highly modified by man; indeed some have been greatly impoverished by their recent regimes of management.

The idea for a book on this theme grew out of three main issues: the progress of modern agriculture; growing pressure for action to conserve the rural environment; and the lack of effective communication between those whose activity is the economic development of rural resources and those whose concern is with their protection for aesthetic and scientific reasons.

Conservationists are increasingly realizing that since some 80 per cent of the land surface of Britain is farmed, much of it intensively, it is unwise to ignore the wildlife interest over so large an area. On many criteria, modern agriculture poses the most extensive threat to wildlife values, at a time when areas of value to wildlife are also being destroyed or modified by a growing number of urban and industrial processes in a period of renewed emphasis upon natural resource exploitation. Farming can no longer be considered the natural custodian of rural areas, as it was two decades ago. Chapter 1 shows how its practices are becoming less and less influenced by the constraints of natural systems and more and more capable of inducing major and permanent change in them. The future suggests that agriculture, like many other industries, will operate in an even more highly controlled and uniform environment.

Chapters 2–7 in Part I of the book look at some of the effects of changing agricultural practices on the major ecosystems of the farmed countryside, and try to assess what are likely to be the more damaging consequences of further intensification and technical developments in agriculture.

There is growing concern about the environment of both town and country. In the countryside, it is the survival or re-creation of wildlife resources, particularly of diversity, which are basic to the continuation of a varied and attractive environment. At the prospect of accelerating change and not just the decline, but the extinction of some species and landscapes, there has been growing pressure for action from public and private conservation groups. Yet the measures required in detail, the priorities, and the means of achieving them are proving less easy to specify. This is made more difficult because there is conflict not only between agriculture and conservation but within the conservation movement itself. There are differences in the aims and the solutions proposed by those whose concern is with a particular species of plant or animal and those who value whole landscapes; between those who research and those who teach; between those who want greater segregation of protected areas and those who seek a new partnership with farming.

Chapters 8–11, the bulk of Part II of the book, look at some alternative ways in which the wildlife and landscapes of the farmed countryside might be conserved. They range from the promotion of more voluntary conservation activity, through the greater use of financial and other incentives to the introduction of legal controls upon some farming activities.

Chapter 12 considers the prospects for implementation in a time of uncertainties—about the economic future and in attitudes towards the countryside—where the conflict between agriculture and conservation is sometimes more illusory than real. There is a lack of mutual understanding, borne as much of inadequate knowledge as of prejudice. Too little information is often unwittingly the cause of environmental damage and of failures in effective remedial action. The languages and locations of discussion in farming and ecology are separate. Farmers are probably as suspicious of ecologists as they are of planners; they do not understand the relevance of research findings. Research workers are often naive and unsympathetic about the practical needs of modern agriculture.

It is the aim of this book to reach both groups, as well as the students of disciplines concerned with rural resource management. We have tried to cast a bridge between the academic and the practical. Our authors represent a wide range of practitioners in the realms of agriculture, ecology and planning; they are drawn from central and local government, from universities and private practice and they are experienced in both research and policymaking.

We are grateful to all of them for their contributions and for suffering patiently the often strange and idiosyncratic demands of their editors. A number of busy people have found time to read drafts of the book at various stages: we are particularly grateful to Ann Lloyd and John Davidson for their valuable comments upon its structure and content. Its errors and omissions remain our own.

J.D.

November 1976   R.L.

PART I

ENVIRONMENTAL IMPLICATIONS OF AGRICULTURE

Chapter 1

Agricultural change

R. J. LLOYD AND G. P. WIBBERLEY

Since the beginning of the last war, the expansion of output has been a major goal for agriculture and this remains the cornerstone of present policy, for Britain's food demands are still greater than her food production and the balance of requirements must be made up by increasingly expensive imports.

Until the early 1800s Britain was largely self-sufficient in food. But then, despite some improvement in home output, rapid population growth in the nineteenth and early twentieth centuries led to a situation of increasing dependence on imports to the extent of 70 per cent of consumption by 1939. However, since food could be imported freely and cheaply during the 1920s and 1930s there was little incentive for improvement and home agriculture operated well below maximum efficiency. It was the emergency of the Second World War which stimulated a drive for increased farm efficiency and output in the interests of import saving.

Agricultural expansion has been brought about by improvements in techniques and strong government intervention in the industry in the form of price supports for the main agricultural products and grants and subsidies to encourage better farm practice and re-equipment. The technical and structural developments in farming over the last 30 years have produced significant increases in the output of all major foodstuffs; for example, in England average wheat yields rose by more than 50 per cent between 1949 and 1972[1] (Figure 1), and yields in many other products such as eggs, milk, sugar-beet, potatoes and poultry meat rose by a similar order. The contribution of this increased productivity to import saving has been impressive. By 1971, despite a rise in population since the war of over 6 million, Britain produced about half of all her food needs and two-thirds of her temperate food requirements.[2] This has been achieved with 6 per cent less land as, between 1945 and 1971, about $1\frac{1}{2}$ million acres of farmland were lost to other land uses, mainly urban development and afforestation.

THE IMPLICATIONS OF AGRICULTURAL CHANGE

Increases in production have not been achieved without considerable changes in the fabric of the countryside. Many landscape elements, and their associated wildlife, have been removed; others have been so modified that their

3

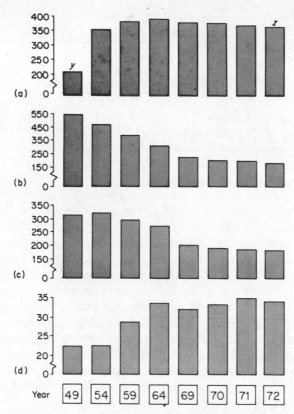

Figure 1. Agricultural change: Selected statistics—
England. (a) Number of tractors ('000). (b) Whole
time workers (family and hired) ('000). (c) Number of
holdings ('000). (d) Wheat yields (cwt per acre).
$y = 1948$; z = figures underestimated compared with
1971 owing to change of timing in collection.
(Source: Ministry of Agriculture, Fisheries and Food
(published annually). *Agricultural Statistics: England
and Wales.* London, HMSO)

values, in non-agricultural terms, have been reduced. Seven features of recent
agricultural change have had particularly important implications: increasing
mechanization; reductions of farm manpower; the amalgamation of holdings;
concentration of production and specialization; modifications of farm practice;
changes in land ownership; and fluctuating land values. Each of these changes
is considered in turn, together with additional factors which have encouraged
the removal of hedges and trees.

Mechanization

Between 1949 and the late 1950s the number of tractors[3] in England
increased by over 75 per cent to about 370,000[1] (Figure 1) entirely replacing

the horse in agriculture[4] and Britain now has the highest tractor density in the world with 1 tractor to 36 arable acres.[5] Although the number of tractors has remained relatively stable since the late 1950s, the stability is illusory for the available horsepower has been rising steadily as tractor replacements have been made with larger and more powerful machines.[6]

Mechanization permits considerable gains in labour productivity and the cost of labour is a major factor influencing the scale of mechanization. Hedge maintenance provides a good example of this. When hand trimming is replaced by mechanical cutting there are savings in maintenance time, and therefore in labour costs: Hooper and Holdgate quote 75p as the cost per chain of trimming by hand compared with only $7\frac{1}{2}$p by machine,[7] where hedges are cut every year.

Of all the agricultural trends, increasing mechanization has probably had most impact upon the fabric of the countryside. To obtain a satisfactory return on investment in tractors and combine harvesters, non-productive time must be reduced to a minimum. When fields are amalgamated time spent on turning and changeover operations can be saved and, in the case of distributive operations such as sowing and fertilizing, wastage of material through overlap on turns can be avoided. Even so, there is probably an optimum field size for distributive and harvesting operations determined mainly by the need to minimize travelling time to and from loading or unloading points. Edwards[8] considers there is little operational advantage to be gained from exceeding row lengths of 500 yards and this implies square fields of about 50 acres which would allow machinery to work efficiently in both directions.

The trend towards more powerful and efficient machinery, particularly tractors, coupled with high cereal prices, is also encouraging the drainage, ploughing and arable cultivation of areas formerly thought suitable only for permanent pasture. The proportion of farmland subjected to the landscape and other changes associated with intensive arable cultivation is thus increasing.

Traditionally hedges were maintained by hand trimming, supplemented periodically (at roughly 20-year intervals) by laying. But this is a rapidly dying craft and most hedges are now mechanically trimmed. Where it is inconvenient to manoeuvre hedge-cutting equipment around them many sapling trees, which might once have been selected for growing on, are now removed and in the long term this will mean the loss of most hedgerow trees as mature ones die and are not replaced. Hedges are now kept lower and narrower and in this condition they are less valuable in the landscape and as habitats for wildlife. Without periodic laying it is difficult to keep hedges stockproof and many in livestock areas now need reinforcing with wire.

Reduction in farm manpower

The reduction in manpower requirements has been spectacular. In 1949 there were over 540,000 full-time farm workers (family and hired) in England. By 1959 this total had fallen below 400,000 and by 1971 to less than 200,000[1] (Figure 1). This fall in labour demand, coupled with rising farm output, has resulted in an average annual rate of increase in labour productivity of 6 per cent over the last ten years, an increase in productivity per man of twice that of the rest of British industry.[9] The reduction in manpower and increases in labour productivity can largely be attributed to the exploitation of economies of scale. Dexter[10] cites examples from both arable and livestock enterprises which imply that there are substantial economic advantages to be gained from increasing farm acreages by amalgamating holdings, and from specialization in production. Reductions in manpower mean that there is now little labour available to undertake tasks such as hedge maintenance which are peripheral to the main business of running a farm. Where hedges have lost their agricultural function, as in arable areas which no longer need stockproof field divisions, many have been removed to reduce the burden of maintenance.[11] They have also been removed in livestock areas and replaced by post and wire fencing which is more flexible and easier to maintain, though of rising cost in erection and repair.

Amalgamation of holdings

The number of farm holdings in England fell by almost half between 1954 and 1972, from just over 320,000 to less than 190,000[1] (Figure 1 and Table 1).

Table 1.   Number of agricultural holdings in England*

Year (June)	Total	Less than 20 acres	20–50 acres	50–100 acres	100–300 acres	300–500 acres	500–1000 acres	over 1000 acres
1949	312,364	138,654	54,524	49,174	57,695	8825	3020	472
1954	320,419	148,511	53,483	48,638	57,159	9003	3098	527
1959	299,312	133,453	49,735	47,136	55,536	9301	3432	619
1964	274,520	119,832	44,216	43,433	52,503	9658	4065	813
1969	204,209	64,700	37,740	37,757	48,307	10,064	4851	1100
1970	194,340	60,622	35,114	35,805	46,432	9997	5106	1264
1971	189,835	58,459	33,885	35,009	45,868	10,039	5244	1331
1972	182,853	53,879	32,876	34,053	45,280	10,068	5293	1404

* Analysis by size of holding.
Area is that of crops and grass (excludes rough grazings).
Source: Ministry of Agriculture, Fisheries and Food (published annually).
    Agricultural Statistics: England and Wales, HMSO, London.

The reduction was most marked in the case of those farms of less than 50 acres and was accompanied by a rise in the number of large holdings (over 1000 acres). The amalgamation of holdings frequently results in a rationalization of field layout with enlargement of fields and the removal of many former boundaries. Coppock[6] suggests that as a general rule field size is directly related to farm size with small farms tending to have a smaller average size of field and a higher proportion of small fields. Thus, as farm sizes increase, often as a result of large-scale farmers buying up small inefficient farms, field sizes will grow, particularly on the land newly acquired.

Concentration of production and specialization

As farms have increased in size there has been a greater degree of geographical concentration of production and more specialization at the farm level. Evidence for the trend towards specialization is shown by a fall in the number of mixed holdings, from 14 per cent in 1963 to 8 per cent in 1968[12] and by an increase in crop acreages and herd sizes on individual farms.[13]

Since the war there has been a gradual shift towards a greater concentration on arable production. In 1949 50·5 per cent of the agricultural acreage in England was arable land; by 1971 the proportion was 54·2 per cent.[1] This change had taken place largely at the expense of the area of permanent grassland, which has fallen steadily. Although the changes at national level may appear small, in several regions major changes have occurred. Smith[14] suggests that agricultural change still falls comparatively lightly upon most of western and northern England, but in the east it is a different picture. In the west and north in 1966 there were nine counties with over 60 per cent of their agricultural acreage under permanent grassland and rough grazings and another seventeen with between 40 and 60 per cent. In the east and southeast, however, there were ten counties with less than 40 per cent and nine with less than 20 per cent, the last group comprising the East Riding of Yorkshire, all three parts of Lincolnshire, Huntingdonshire and the Soke of Peterborough, Cambridgeshire, Norfolk, Suffolk and Essex. Nearly all these counties had shown an annual loss between 1963 and 1966 of between 4 and 6 per cent of their previous years' acreage of permanent grassland.

There has been an increasing polarization of farming types, with livestock enterprises predominating in the west and north, and arable enterprises increasing in the southeast and, particularly, in the east. The effect of this geographical concentration in farming types is to produce a more dramatic difference in regional landscapes. A mixed pattern of farming can be integrated with the traditional landscape of small enclosures but specialization, whether in arable or livestock production, leads to modernization of structure and to rationalization of farm layouts with many field boundaries removed. The concentration of all-arable enterprises in the east and southeast of Britain poses special problems of landscape conservation, while the continuing loss of permanent grassland, in areas where the total acreage is already low, has important implications for wildlife conservation.

Changes in farm practice

In arable areas, the discipline imposed by rigid systems of rotational farming has been eased by the increasing use of artificial fertilizers to maintain soil fertility, and of selective herbicides, fungicides and insecticides to control weeds and to prevent crop disease. Where variations of the famous Norfolk four-course rotation were common, they have now been largely replaced by intensive cropping systems. There seem to be no limits to continuous cropping;

an example from Salisbury Plain is of barley being grown in the same field for eleven years in succession.[5] In the past, fields were a convenient way of managing rotational farming. Intensive cropping provides further justification for amalgamating fields and otherwise rationalizing farm layouts.

Even where hedges and trees are retained they are often damaged by herbicide spray drift or by careless straw burning after harvest, problems which have assumed increasing importance in recent years. Straw-burning in particular is now more widespread, especially in eastern England where the concentration of cereal growing means that in most years there is straw surplus to agricultural requirements.

A further problem in arable areas is the increasing use of deep ploughs which can damage field monuments.[15] Deep ploughing close to hedges and the roots of hedgerow trees may also be partly responsible for the increasing incidence of 'die back' which is now affecting large numbers of trees in the east and southeast.[16] An additional cause is likely to be the lowered water table which results from drainage improvements. Figure 2 shows that the rate of drainage has increased sixfold since 1950. In the year ending March 1973 nearly a quarter of a million acres of agricultural land in England and Wales were drained, a record figure for one year.[17]

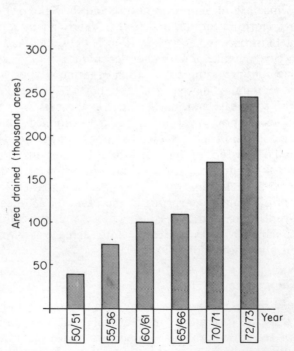

Figure 2. Agricultural land drainage in England and Wales. (Source: Carter, C. (1973). An article on drainage in *Power Farming*, **51** (2))

In livestock areas the trend is towards more intensive grazing management involving the ploughing of permanent pasture which is replaced by shorter term grass leys, or its improvement with fertilizers (especially nitrogen) and herbicides. Such applications severely change the flora of old grasslands and decrease their floristic variety. There is also a change towards housing livestock indoors all year round. In this situation of 'zero grazing' the grass crop is cut rather than grazed and brought to the stock as silage. Even where stock are allowed to graze in fields the new regime is one of strict rotational grazing with the animals moved periodically to avoid trampling and fouling of the pasture. Fairbrother[5] points out that grass may not be the best forage crop although it is relatively tolerant to trampling; thus with zero grazing we may see the increasing use of lucerne as food for stock, or cereals may be cut at their early 'grass stage'.

Strict rotational grazing demands the creation of small, equal-sized enclosures. Existing field shapes frequently do not lend themselves to easy subdivision so that progressive farmers are removing internal hedges and creating temporary paddocks with post and wire fencing. Where animals are housed indoors all year round stockproof field divisions are redundant, and there is yet another justification for hedge removal.

Changes in land ownership

This century has seen a large increase in the amount of farmland which is owner-occupied, the area of rented land in England and Wales falling from 88 per cent in 1910 to 46 per cent in 1969.[12,18] The tendency is for smaller farms to be owner-occupied and larger ones to be rented. Much of the swing to owner-occupation can be attributed to the fragmentation of estates brought about by high taxation and the burden of estate duty and, before the 1958 Agriculture Act permitted farm rents to be raised, insufficient rent income.

Further fragmentation of ownership is expected to result from the operation of capital transfer tax and to be accelerated if the proposals for a wealth tax are implemented.[19] Capital transfer tax replaces estate duty which could be avoided if estates were transferred seven years or more before death. Thus, although farming is favourably treated under capital transfer tax with tax assessed on only 50 per cent of the value of the land and buildings and 70 per cent on livestock and machinery,[20] the tax cannot be avoided and must place additional burdens on owner-occupiers. Under the proposed wealth tax, owners of chargeable assets (including land) valued at over £100,000 will be subject to an annual tax, probably at the rate of 1 per cent. This tax would also impose additional burdens on the owner-occupied sector of farming.

Westmacott and Worthington[11] suggest that the majority of recent land purchases have fallen into three distinct categories: purchases by 'commercial' farmers who have sold land elsewhere for development; purchases by 'institutions' who are buying land for investment purposes but will expect a good income meanwhile; and purchases by non-farming individuals who are seeking capital growth but also a pleasant place to live in the country and whose income is derived mainly from non-farming activities. A further category has been the land speculator who buys land, often at the urban fringe, in the hope of realizing its value as developed land. However, the recently introduced Community Land Act[21] should discourage speculation and ensure that the enhanced value of developed land is retained by the community.

Part-time farming is of growing significance, particularly within commuting distance of the main conurbations. A sector survey of southeast England between London and the Kent coast found that no less than 30 per cent of all agricultural land was owned by 'part-time' farmers in 1964, most of this in smaller holdings, often of less than 20 acres.[22] Mixed tenure is also growing and though this helps the provision of capital and land to individual farmers, it further complicates the management of the landscape.

The effect on the fabric of the countryside of these various types of land purchase is difficult to assess but certain trends might be predicted. The commercial farmer, reinvesting the proceeds of a land sale for urban development, would be well placed financially to modernize his new holding, which may involve removing much of the existing fabric. Institutional landlords are usually absentees committed to goals of capital safety, appreciation and profit maximization; they are unlikely to be concerned about amenity values. Land speculators may, as in the past, allow land to become derelict. Only the part-time farmer, looking for a country retreat, is likely to be much concerned with the general amenity of his land.

Changes in agricultural land values

From 1945 until 1972 agricultural land prices rose slowly but at rates generally exceeding the loss in money values, thus making farm land a good investment. In 1950 average values in England and Wales were about £60 an acre and in January 1972, £300 an acre.[23] 1972 saw an unprecedented rise in values, the average sale price rising to £750 an acre by September. In 1973 values reached about £800 an acre but fell again during 1974 and early 1975, levelling out at about £550 an acre.[24] By the middle of 1975 prices had again begun to rise and this rise is expected to continue.[25] A major cause of rising sale prices during 1972 and 1973 was probably the repurchase of land by farmers who sold land for building at rapidly rising values.[25] These farmers had to re-invest to qualify for roll-over relief on capital gains tax.

There are regional differences in land values and also differences between farms of different sizes and between land with or without vacant possession. Regional differences represent variations in land quality and farming potential but also, increasingly, the demand for land by part-time 'hobby' farmers and by land speculators. The highest average sale prices are found south and southwest of London where part-time farming and speculation are common. The lowest prices are in Wales where land capability is often poor.[23] Small farms command larger prices per acre than larger holdings probably because most owner-occupiers cannot afford the total outlay on the larger holdings which are being bought with largely city-based finance. Land with vacant possession also attracts a premium.

High land values have severe implications for the fabric of the countryside. Farmers who wish to expand but who find that land costs prohibit extensions of their holding are likely to intensify the use of their land. It is under these circumstances that farm woodland may be cleared, hedgerows removed, ponds filled and land reclaimed which was previously considered too marginal to farm. It is this land, which is often steep or poorly drained, that may be especially valuable in terms of wildlife or landscape interest. Likewise, farmers who have bought expensive land with borrowed capital will have to farm it intensively if they are to achieve a sufficiently high return to service the interest payments. Finally, high land values increase the problems of disposal of estates on the death of the owner which may lead to their fragmentation as already discussed. Expensive land cannot be wasted: many hedges and their associated ditches have been removed to gain extra workable land, incidentally also eliminating two maintenance tasks. However, the case for removing hedges alone to gain more land is less attractive since to gain one acre of land would mean the removal of 110 chains of six-foot wide hedge or 200 chains of well-trimmed three-foot hedge.[26] In arable areas the average width is about four and a half feet and thus about two miles would need to be removed to gain one acre of land.[11]

The removal of hedges and trees

The loss of hedgerows and trees has been a consequence of almost all the agricultural changes so far discussed. They have also been removed to improve vermin and weed control, to simplify drainage operations and to allow greater crop flexibility. The last reason is an important one. Fixed field sizes may hamper changes in cropping patterns; thus, the removal of internal boundaries and their replacement, where necessary, by marker posts or 'temporary' fencing can increase efficiency. In all-arable areas there are probably no agricultural reasons for retaining hedges. Indeed, only in areas of high-value horticultural crops, where hedges have some value for shelter, can their retention be justified. Elsewhere the value of the land they occupy and the cost of their maintenance exceeds any possible increase in yield brought about by the shelter they offer.[11] Moreover, there is little evidence to support the widely held view that hedges can prevent soil erosion. Wind erosion appears to be more effectively controlled by special methods of crop husbandry and by the better timing of spring cultivations than by retaining hedges.

Trees, whether in hedges, shelterbelts, plantations and small woods, or parkland, are generally a problem for farmers in arable areas because they interfere with crop growth.[27] By creating shade they may slow down the drying out of the land in spring and so delay cultivation, and they may delay germination and the ripening of the crop, which may also be damaged by wind turbulence. Low branches can interfere with agricultural operations while roots may damage equipment and compete with the crop for moisture and nutrients. In all farming areas trees are removed where they interfere with the maintenance of hedges or ditches or because they harbour pests. Trees also have a capital value and have often been felled in times of low farming profitability.

Attitudes

All these reasons for change in the fabric of the farmed countryside have been economic in nature as they relate to efforts to increase output or to reduce operating costs. An important additional cause of change is the personal preference of farmers. Many hedges and trees, once they have lost their agricultural functions, have been removed because farmers would prefer to work their farms without them, even though they may be the very features which others would like to see retained. Similarly, tidiness is the reason for destroying nettle patches, for mowing closely the verges of farm roads and for spraying hedge bottoms. All these areas are important for wildlife, but good farming practice is judged, by fellow farmers, according to productivity and tidiness.

Government intervention in agriculture

The government first became significantly involved in agricultural affairs with the introduction of a protective agricultural policy in the early 1800s.[28] Protection, in the form of guarantees for particular crops, was reintroduced during the First World War in order to boost farm output[29] and help for some individual commodities was again introduced in the 1930s during the general depression, when the government saw the need to protect British agriculture during a period of falling world commodity prices. Marketing Boards for individual farm products were established to help maintain the prices received by producers and in the late 1930s modest grants were made available to encourage desirable farm practices such as the use of fertilizers. Government research increased with the establishment of the Agricultural Research Council in 1930.

The Second World War, like the First, prompted major government involvement in agriculture to ensure increased home production. Price incentives and subsidies were offered to farmers, together with inducements to improve their efficiency. There were grants for land drainage, reclamation and the ploughing of permanent pasture; in return, farmers had to accept a considerable degree of control over their operations by the wartime County Agricultural Executive

Committees. Government intervention in agriculture up to this point was piecemeal and designed to meet particular situations rather than as part of any consciously developed overall agricultural policy. The Second World War, however, demonstrated the extreme vulnerability of Britain to interruptions in her food supplies from abroad and provided a major stimulus to the 1947 Agriculture Act which promised positive and continuing support for the industry.

The 1947 Agriculture Act[30] speaks of promoting and maintaining a stable and efficient agricultural industry capable of producing at home whatever proportion of Britain's food is in the national interest, having regard to the desirability of producing it at minimum prices consistent with proper remuneration and living conditions for farmers and agricultural workers and an adequate return on capital invested in the industry.

Before Britain entered the European Economic Community in 1973, the policy was operated through a system of guaranteed prices for the major products, the prices being set annually after a review of the economic conditions in the industry by the government and representatives of the producers. The way in which this system of support is now being modified as Britain harmonizes her agricultural development with the Common Agricultural Policy of the six original members of the EEC is discussed later in this chapter.

Farm improvement has been encouraged by grants, incentives and technical advice from the Agricultural Development and Advisory Service (ADAS: the field organization of the Ministry of Agriculture). Since 1970 some advice on conservation issues has also been available following some extra training of ADAS officers. The main current aid programme comprises the Farm Capital Grants Scheme 1973, the Farm Amalgamation Scheme, and the Farm and Horticultural Development Scheme.[31]

Under the Grants Scheme expenditure on a wide range of items, such as farm buildings, yards and roads, field drainage and orchard grubbing, is eligible for grant aid[32] while under the Amalgamation Scheme farmers are offered grants to encourage the voluntary amalgamation of uncommercial units to create or enlarge profitable holdings. A parallel Payments to Outgoers Scheme offers payments to occupiers of uncommercial units who sell them for an approved amalgamation or in certain circumstances for afforestation or for public use. Those who amalgamate can also obtain loans to help finance the purchase of additional land. The Farm and Horticultural Development Scheme puts into effect an EEC Directive on Farm Modernization[33] and is partly financed by the Community Agricultural Fund. It is designed to enable farmers whose incomes are below the average in non-agricultural industry to achieve comparability. Applicants for grant are required to put forward a long-term development plan (up to six years) showing that at the end of the plan period their farm will be able to support at least one full-time worker at the comparable income. The range of items eligible for grant is wider than under the Farm Capital Grants Scheme and includes hedges and shelterbelts.

FUTURE AGRICULTURAL CHANGE

There are two groups of factors which will affect the way in which British agriculture will change in the future: those resulting from events unique to Britain; and those which arise from changes taking place in Europe and in the world as a whole.

British factors

The current (1976) British balance of payments problem, caused largely by a fourfold increase in the price of imported oil, has greatly increased the importance of home-grown agricultural produce. Food prices for produce imported from outside the European Economic Community have also risen substantially. Both factors will ensure that an expansionist agricultural policy, designed to increase self-sufficiency in food supplies and reduce imports, will continue. In January 1974 the National Farmers' Union called for a five-year expansion programme to reduce the then annual sum of £1600m spent on temperate food imports and the government have since pledged themselves to a policy of expansion where this can be achieved efficiently and economically.[34] The need for import-saving measures should, however, be reduced when North Sea oil begins to make a major contribution to British energy needs.

Although population forecasts have been revised to take account of a falling birth rate, it has been predicted that population growth will continue, with the population of the United Kingdom rising from 56 million in 1973 to about 59 million in 2001.[35] Even if only the present ratio of home-grown to imported food is maintained, this population growth will require increased output from British agriculture. More houses, probably at higher space standards, means that agricultural land will continue to be required for urban uses. The Department of the Environment has suggested that by 2001 11·9 per cent of Great Britain will be urbanized compared with 9·1 per cent in 1970.[36] This represents a growth in urban area of over 30 per cent and a loss of more than $1\frac{1}{2}$ million acres of productive agricultural land.[37] If an agricultural expansion programme is to be successful, the remaining agricultural acreage must be made to yield a greater output.

External factors: the Common Market

The EEC Common Agricultural Policy is designed to increase agricultural productivity; to ensure a fair standard of living for farmers; to stabilize markets; to guarantee regular supplies; and to ensure reasonably priced supplies for consumers. At present these objectives are being promoted through systems of market support and guidance. Although the whole structure of the Common Agricultural Policy is now in debate, Common Market entry has already affected the pattern of British agriculture.

Under the market support system, the European Council of Ministers sets an optimum[38] level of prices for most individual products in advance of each marketing year. Two methods are used to ensure that market prices approximate to these levels: a variable levy is applied to imports from non-member countries and an 'intervention price' is fixed just below optimum price levels. If the market price drops below the intervention level, national agencies enter the market to buy the product, which may be resold within the Community if the price recovers, or exported or otherwise removed. An 'Intervention Board for Agricultural Produce' has been set up to administer the system in Great Britain. Optimum price levels and intervention levels for farm produce in the EEC have been generally higher than the equivalent British guaranteed prices (Table 2); thus, for British farmers, the gross receipts for most agricultural products will increase in the EEC, although such increases will be partly or wholly offset by increased costs. During a transition period (to 1978) Britain is free to fix her own basic and intervention prices, raising them in six annual steps to reach EEC price levels. As the market prices are increased so the deficiency payments paid to British farmers are being phased out.

Table 2. EEC target and intervention prices and UK guaranteed prices 1972/73

	Wheat £ per ton	Barley £ per ton	Fat cattle £ per live cwt	Milk p per gallon
EEC target price	47·41	43·44	15·63	23·0
EEC basic intervention price	43·65	39·88	–	–
UK guaranteed price	34·40	31·20	13·20	20·6

Source: Davey, B. H. (1973). Supplies, Income and Structural Change. In Rogers, S. J. and Davey, B. H. (eds.) (1973). *The Common Agricultural Policy and Britain*, Saxon House, Westmead.

Davey[37] has suggested that during the transition period price relativities between different commodities could well be altered in an attempt to influence the pattern of production. Thus, British farmers could receive substantial increases in farm-gate prices for cereals, beef, pigs and milk and smaller increases for eggs, poultry meat and sugar beet while the market price for sheep could rise following the phasing out of the deficiency payments on this product. Costs, however, will also rise sharply, particularly for concentrate feeding stuffs and for fertilizers as the current British fertilizer subsidy must be removed under EEC rules. The result by 1978/79 is likely to be a reorientation of British agriculture on the lines suggested by Davey[39] and recorded in Table 3. His main prediction is that the high cost of concentrate feeding stuffs will increase the emphasis on producing livestock from grass. Gardner[40] suggests that this trend, coupled with a concern in intensive arable areas about possible long-term damage to the soil from the husbandry techniques and heavy machinery now used,[41] could increase the scale of livestock rearing in areas which are now

Table 3.   Change in production patterns in UK agriculture by 1978/79

Dairy Farms	Some expansion in the size of the dairy herd can be expected, accompanied by an improvement in the standard of grassland management
Livestock Farms	Greater emphasis on cattle and less on sheep and a more effective utilization of grassland
Mixed Farms	No change in cropping pattern, but a greater emphasis on beef with an improvement in the standard of grassland management
Cropping Farms	Little scope for expanding acreage but with some expansion of cereals at the expense of potatoes

Source: Davey, B. H. (1973). See source to Table 2.

predominantly arable. This charge is likely to be reinforced by the higher prices now paid for beef and lamb.

In this way, there may be a return to a system of mixed farming in Britain but this is unlikely to be on traditional lines. A more probable development is the intensive rearing of livestock using zero grazing techniques, with grass produced from short-term leys as part of a rotation in the same way as any other crop. Gardner suggests that this system could have the added advantage of making crop farming easier, reducing cereal diseases and improving the long-term fertility of the soil.

The EEC guidance system of agricultural support is designed to encourage structural reform including farm amalgamation, farm modernization and a progressive reduction in the agricultural labour force. Much of the community is agriculturally self-sufficient and to prevent food surpluses resulting from increased output (giving lower market prices and farm incomes) some of the less productive land may have to be retired from agriculture and used mainly for forestry and recreation.[42]

Structural reform will be on a voluntary basis. To encourage farmers to leave the industry it is proposed that those over 60[43] should be offered early retirement pensions, with compensation paid in proportion to the amount of land surrendered. But such payments will only apply in particular circumstances: where the land will add to a potentially or presently economically viable farm; where it contributes to a land bank; or where it can be used for recreation, forestry or some other public use. Farm modernization will be encouraged by a system of subsidies on the interest paid on borrowed capital for investment in farming, the payments being varied to take account of the present and potential viability of the holdings.

Over much of Europe, the main aim of structural reform and modernization is to improve the living standards of the agricultural community by reducing the size of the agricultural labour force, thereby increasing the incomes of those remaining. In Britain, with one of the most efficient agricultural industries in Europe, structural reform is almost complete; EEC membership will simply ensure that agricultural improvement will continue. Analyses of the comparative advantages held by the British agricultural industry in relation to its entry into the EEC have stressed the better physical structure of British farms: larger in size, better laid out and better equipped.

Over the next decade, agricultural change in Britain will probably follow closely the trends already established. A further decline in the agricultural labour force may be expected, brought about by rising wage rates and by the counter-attractions of industry. Farm amalgamations will continue, though probably at a slower rate since higher land values make it impossible for small farmers to buy land, and desirable for many landowners to retain it. A growth in institutional holdings may also be expected because of the investment value of agricultural land. But the major development is likely to be a further increase in mechanization and it is this trend which will have the most impact on the fabric of the countryside. As Nix has suggested,[44] fewer men and an anticipated reduction in the cost of machinery relative to labour means that the rate of mechanization will continue to increase—more powerful tractors and larger machines will be the order of the day. In arable areas, more attention will probably be paid to the timeliness of operations to reduce the problems of soil damage from heavy machinery and soil blow. Thus, practices as well as machines will alter, with chemical warfare on weeds and stubbles and minimal cultivations becoming more and more the rule rather than the exception.

All this will mean that landscape and other features which hinder farming operations will be under increasing pressure for removal and the change will not be confined to arable areas. Increased emphasis upon livestock production and improved grassland management with a more widespread use of paddock grazing systems will result in a further loss of hedges and trees. Fertilizers will be used more extensively, and steep slopes, wet areas and scrub will be reclaimed to increase the cultivatable area. Some of the implications of these developments for the landscape and its wildlife are discussed in the following chapters.

External factors: world food prices and food availability

Rising world food prices provide a further incentive to increase the output from British agriculture. In 1973 Britain spent over £500m more in foreign exchange on food than in 1972,[45] partly because of devaluation of the pound but mainly because of a shortage of many products in world markets. While the current shortages and high prices may be only a short-term problem, they may recur if world population continues to grow at the present rate (from 3600 million in 1970 to an estimated over 7000 million by the end of the century).[46] If output does not keep pace with this growth, much of the food now imported into Britain will be required to feed increased populations in the exporting countries. Alternatively, where food is still available for export, any increase in prosperity of those Third World countries (such as India) who now have food deficits would enable them to bid for any surplus food. The conclusion must be that, by the end of the century, Britain may no longer be able to rely on imported food from many of her current sources.

THE PROSPECTS FOR OUTPUT FROM BRITISH AGRICULTURE

Since 1945 Britain has increased the proportion of temperate food grown at home from about 50 per cent to 70 per cent. Although output in 1976 was depressed following an unprecedented drought (the driest twelve months in many areas since records began), it has been suggested that during the next decade continued farm modernization will further improve agricultural efficiency, bringing, as in the past, a growth in output. Even without technical advances in machinery, chemicals, in crop varieties and animal breeds, Davey[39] believes there is scope for a considerable improvement in performance simply by better management and wider use of the best practices now available, for national levels of crop and stock yields are well below the best yields achieved by progressive farmers.

Ultimately, there must be a limit to the growth in output per acre of land, yet, despite the reservations about the possible long-term effects on soil fertility of some present practices, most agricultural experts believe that the limit to growth is a long way off. Blaxter[47] for example, while accepting that the law of diminishing returns must apply, believes that we are nowhere approaching ultimate yields, or even reaching a point at which returns are negligible for effort.

Davey, extrapolating past trends, suggests that between 1969/70 and 1978/79 yields of many of the major products will increase by up to 14 per cent (details are given in Table 4). In the case of livestock, the increases in yield quoted do not take into account the higher stocking densities made possible, for example, by improved grassland management, and thus the total increase in production of milk and meat per unit area will be considerably higher, representing an annual growth rate for all agricultural produce of about $1\frac{1}{2}$ per cent per annum compounded. With higher investment in the industry an even greater rate of growth might be expected and a figure of $2\frac{1}{2}$ per cent per annum has been suggested in the White Paper 'Food from our own Resources'.[34]

Not everyone accepts that this is a realistic goal for British agriculture in the context of recent events. Many farmers, especially livestock farmers, have suffered from the uncertainties of British entry into the Common Market while the combined effects of inflation and new forms of capital taxation have contributed to a reduction of confidence in the industry. In consequence, farmers, although they have the technical ability, may be less willing than in the

Table 4. Selected performance measures for UK agriculture in 1969/70 and extrapolations to 1978/79[a]

Performance measure	Unit	1969/70	1978/79	Increase %	Increase % per annum simple rate	Increase % per annum compound
Milk yield per cow[b]	gallons	850·0	892·0	5	0·55	0·53
Lambing percentage[b] (lowland flocks)	lambs/ewe	141·0	151·0	7	0·79	0·76
Egg yield per hen	doz. eggs	18·9	21·3	13	1·41	1·34
Pigs reared per sow[b]	pigs/annum	15·5	17·5	13	1·43	1·36
Sugar beet yield	tons/acre	15·5	17·5	13	1·43	1·36
Main crop potato yield	tons/acre	10·5	12·0	14	1·59	1·49
Spring barley yield	cwt/acre	29·0	33·0	14	1·53	1·45
Winter wheat yield	cwt/acre	33·0	37·2	13	1·41	1·34

[a] Calculated by the Agricultural Adjustment Unit from past trends.
[b] The increase in yield does not take into account increased stocking densities (see page 18). .
Source: Davey, B. H. (1973). Supplies, Income and Structural Change. In Rogers, S. J. and Davey, B. H. (eds.) (1973). *The Common Agricultural Policy and Britain*, Saxon House, Westmead.

past to respond to a call for rapid expansion in the short term. The costs of the recent drought will also mean that less capital will be available for investment over the next year at least.

The prospects for expansion in the longer term may be more certain. During the mid-1960s there was concern about the rate of urbanization of rural land which would result from the population growth then projected and from rising space standards. The likely effects of this urbanization and population growth upon the ability of Britain to produce a 'reasonable' proportion of her own food supplies was studied by Edwards and Wibberley who tried to answer the question 'How much land will be needed for food production in England by the end of the century?[48] They made projections, on the basis of past evidence and future prospects, of the probable yields of agricultural produce at the end of the century, and compared production levels with the agricultural land area likely to be available and the projected level of population.

A decade ago it was expected that the population of Britain would increase very considerably by the end of the century;[49] Edwards and Wibberley, in their calculations, used figures ranging between 67·3 million and 69·7 million. Yet, even at this level of population and with a 10 per cent loss of agricultural land, they concluded that Britain could actually increase the proportion of food grown at home if there could be an annual increase in total agricultural output per unit area of between 2 and $2\frac{3}{4}$ per cent compounded.

Since their study, population projections have been revised downwards by a substantial amount and recent projections suggest an end-of-century total of only about 59 million. A reworking of the calculations made by Edwards and Wibberley using these population projections, a lower figure for land take (that suggested by the Department of the Environment),[36] and a range of growth rates for agricultural output from $1\frac{1}{2}$ to $2\frac{1}{2}$ per cent per annum compounded, suggests that even at the $1\frac{1}{2}$ per cent growth rate Britain could steadily increase the proportion of home-grown produce, raising this to over 85 per cent of temperate produce by the end of the century. With a $2\frac{1}{2}$ per cent growth rate it is conceivable that Britian could become totally self-sufficient in temperate foods during that period.

Therefore, although there may be continued pressure over the next few years to maximize agricultural output at any price to aid the balance of payments (a problem that may be solved by the end of the decade), in the longer term there should be less and less need to farm every acre intensively. The implications of this for wildlife and the landscape could be considerable and must strengthen any case for positive conservation measures.

NOTES AND REFERENCES

1. Ministry of Agriculture, Fisheries and Food (published annually). *Agricultural Statistics: England and Wales*, HMSO, London.
2. Coppock, J. T. (1971). *An Agricultural Geography of Great Britain*, Bell, London.
3. Includes tracklayers.
4. There were still over 435,000 farm horses in Britain as late as 1946.
5. Fairbrother, N. (1970). *New Lives, New Landscapes*, Penguin, Harmondsworth. The number of combine harvesters has also increased from just over 3000 (1949) to nearly 60,000 by 1965.
6. Coppock, J. T. (1969). Land-Use Changes and the Hedgerow. In Hooper, M. D. and Holdgate, M. W. (eds.), *Hedges and Hedgerow Trees*, Proceedings of Monks Wood Experimental Symposium No. 4, pp. 19–27, The Nature Conservancy, London.
7. Hooper, M. D. and Holdgate, M. W. (eds.) (1969), *Hedges and Hedgerow Trees*, p. 96.
8. Edwards, A. J. (1969). Field Size and Machine Efficiency. In Hooper, M. D. and Holdgate, M. W. (eds.), *Hedges and Hedgerow Trees*, pp. 28–31.
9. Ministry of Agriculture, Fisheries and Food (1973). *Annual Review of Agriculture 1973*, Cmnd 5254, HMSO, London. Labour productivity is measured in terms of the volume of gross produce per head.
10. Dexter, K. (1967). Productivity in Agriculture. In Ashton, J. and Rodgers, S. J. (eds.), *Economic Change and Agriculture*, pp. 66–84. Papers presented at an Agricultural Adjustment Unit Symposium, Oliver and Boyd, Edinburgh.
11. Westmacott, R. and Worthington, T. (1974). *New Agricultural Landscapes*, publication CCP76, Countryside Commission, Cheltenham.
12. Ministry of Agriculture, Fisheries and Food/Department of Agriculture and Fisheries for Scotland/Ministry of Agriculture, Northern Ireland (1970). *The Changing Structure of Agriculture*, HMSO, London.

13. During the period 1960 to 1965 the number of dairy herds of over 50 cows and pig herds of over 50 sows increased by 4·5 per cent and 8·5 per cent respectively, while the number of farms growing over 100 acres of wheat increased by 7·6 per cent per ·annum. Source: Sykes, J. D. and Reid, I. G. (1967). The Development of British Agriculture—Its Prospects and Problems. *District Bank Review*, No. 161, March 1967.

14. Smith, A. E. (1970). Sites of Ecological Interest. In Sheail, J. and Wells, T. C. E. (eds.), *Old Grassland—Its Archaeological and Ecological Importance*, Proceedings of Monks Wood Experimental Station Symposium No. 5, pp. 6–11, The Nature Conservancy, London.

15. Saunders, A. D. (1970). Sites of Archaeological Interest. In Sheail, J. and Wells, T. C. E. (eds.), *Old Grassland*, pp. 1–5.

16. Forestry Commission (1972). *A Hedgerow Tree Survey in the East Region Conservancy*, unpublished Report.

17. Carter, C. (1973). An article on Drainage in *Power Farming*, **51** (2), August 1973.

18. Ministry of Agriculture, Fisheries and Food/Department of Agriculture and Fisheries for Scotland (1968). *A Century of Agricultural Statistics: Great Britain 1866–1966*, HMSO, London.

19. Government Green Paper (1974). *Wealth Tax*, Cmnd 5704, HMSO, London.

20. As amended under the Budget, April 1976.

21. Under the Act local authorities will ultimately have the duty to acquire development land at current use values.

22. Gasson, R. (1969). *The Influence of Urbanization on Farm Ownership and Practice*. Studies in Rural Land Use, Report No. 7. Department of Agricultural Economics, Wye College (University of London).

23. Munton, R. J. C. (1973). Recent Trends in Farm Land Prices in England and Wales. *Estates Gazette*, **227**, 29 September 1973, 2162–2165.

24. Figures from *The Farmland Market*, No. 4, July 1975. A joint *Estates Gazette/Farmers Weekly* publication.

25. Building land values reached a median value of over £25,000 an acre in 1972 but values have fallen recently by up to 40 per cent. Nevertheless, the sale of farm land for building still represents a very large capital gain.

26. Edwards, A. J. (1966). Some Theoretical Considerations of Field Size and Shape. *National Agricultural Advisory Service Quarterly Review*, No. 72, pp. 162–168.

27. The problem is discussed in detail in the Merthyr Committee Report, Forestry Commission (1955). *Report of the Committee on Hedgerow and Farm Timber*, HMSO, London. See especially Appendix C.

28. Under the Corn Law Act of 1815, to encourage expansion to meet the needs of a rapidly growing population, a ban was imposed on wheat imports until the price of the home-grown product reached 80 shillings a quarter. This protection was replaced in 1826 by a sliding scale but then abolished totally from 1846 when the Irish potato famine, rapid urbanization and the opening up of the 'New World' encouraged the import of large quantities of food.

29. The Corn Protection Act of 1917 guaranteed minimum prices for wheat, oats and potatoes. These guarantees were abolished in 1921.

30. Agriculture Act, 1947, Chapter 48, HMSO, London, Section 1(1).

31. Details of the schemes are given in *At the Farmer's Service*, Ministry of Agriculture, Fisheries and Food (published annually).

32. The standard rate of grant is 20 per cent but up to 55 per cent is available for expenditure on drainage. Higher rates of grant are available for some improvements in the uplands under the Farm Capital Grants Scheme 1970.

33. Directive 72/159/EEC. The standard rate of grant is 25 per cent but higher rates of grant are available for some items in the uplands.

34. Government White Paper (1975). *Food from our own Resources*, Cmnd 6020. HMSO, London.
35. The Registrar General's Quarterly Return, July 1974.
36. Department of the Environment (1971). *Long-Term Population Distribution in Great Britain—A Study*, HMSO, London. The figures include 'development' in rural areas, for example, mineral workings and reservoirs.
37. Productive agricultural land is taken to comprise arable land and permanent grassland and to exclude rough grazings. It is assumed that all urban expansion will be at the expense of productive agricultural land. There were about 28 million acres of productive agricultural land in Great Britain in 1972.
38. Referred to as the target, guide or basic price according to commodity.
39. Davey, B. H. (1973). Supplies, Incomes and Structural Change in UK Agriculture. In Rogers, S. J. and Davey, B. H. (eds.) (1973), *The Common Agricultural Policy and Britain*, Saxon House, Westmead, pp. 95–111. A collection of papers presented at an Agricultural Adjustment Unit Symposium in July 1972.
40. Gardner, B. (1973). Traditional Farming Makes a Comeback. *New Scientist*, 26 July 1973, 193–194.
41. This led the Strutt Committee to recommend the restoration of grass breaks on unstable soils. Agricultural Advisory Council (1970), *Modern Farming and Soil*, the Report of the Strutt Committee.
42. The so-called 'Mansholt Plan'. Under the original plan, published as a Memorandum in 1968, it was envisaged that $12\frac{1}{2}$ million acres of land would be retired from agriculture. It is now considered unlikely that this figure will be achieved in the foreseeable future.
43. Fifty-five in the case of member states where more than 15 per cent of the economically active population are engaged in agriculture: i.e. Eire and Italy.
44. Nix, J. (1973). Paper given at the National Power Farming Conference, *Power Farming*, **50** (4), April 1973.
45. *The Economist* (1973). Can that Import Bill Ever Come Down? *The Economist*, 17 November 1973, 96–97.
46. Meadows, D. H., Meadows, D. L., Randers, J. and Behrens, W. W. (1972). *The Limits to Growth*, a Report for the Club of Rome's Project on the Predicament of Mankind, p. 34.
47. Blaxter, K. (1974). Power and the Agricultural Revolution. *New Scientist*, 14 February 1974, 400–403.
48. Edwards, A. M. and Wibberley, G. P. (1971). *An Agricultural Land Budget for Britain 1965–2000*. Studies in Rural Land Use, Report No. 10, School of Rural Economics and Related Studies, Wye College (University of London).
49. The 1964-based projection was of a population of 74·8 million by the year 2000.

Chapter 2

Arable land

N. W. MOORE

Arable means capable of being ploughed; but when we talk of arable land we normally mean tillage, which is usually defined as land which has been ploughed within seven years of the point of observation. In 1971, 28 per cent of Great Britain was arable in this sense (Figure 3).

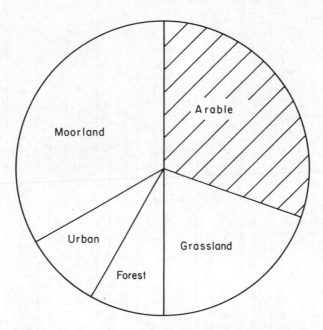

Figure 3. Arable land and other land uses in Great Britain, c.1971. (Source: *Agricultural Statistics United Kingdom, 1969–71*, HMSO, and other sources)

The percentage of arable land has fluctuated over the centuries from small beginnings on the lighter soils in the Neolithic Age until today when more land is under the plough than at any time since the 1880s, except for a short period in the Second World War (Figure 4). Originally, the acreage of arable land was

23

roughly proportional to the size of the population, but as time progressed it was increasingly affected by both the export and import trades. By Tudor times, English corn was exported extensively to Norway and the Netherlands, and this export trade lasted for another 200 years. Until the recent expansions, the greatest extent of arable farming came in the mid-nineteenth century just before the repeal of the Corn Laws in 1846. After that date the population depended increasingly upon imports from overseas and the area of arable land, particularly after disastrous summers in the 1870s, declined as more and more of it went down to grass (Figure 4). Since the nineteenth-century, towns and roads have taken up increasing amounts of land (Figure 3): urban development

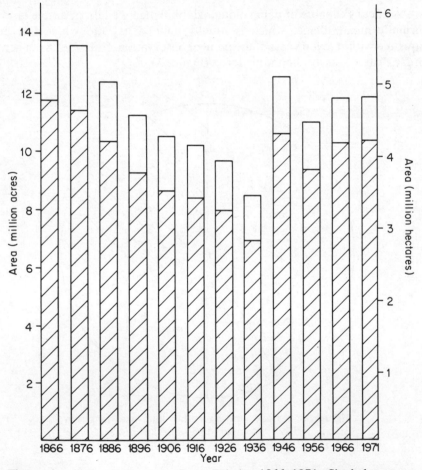

Figure 4. Area of tillage in Great Britain, 1866–1971. Shaded area = England and Wales; whole area = Great Britain. Figures for 1866, 1876 and 1886 include lucerne. (Data from *A Century of Agricultural Statistics Great Britain 1866–1966*, Table 43, London HMSO, 1968, and *Agricultural Statistics United Kingdom 1969–1971*, Table 3, London, HMSO, 1973)

in particular is often located on arable land since this is usually flat, well-drained and ideal for building. However, development has not affected the total acreage of farmland significantly because the reclamation of wasteland has partially compensated for losses to towns and roads.

Agricultural statistics were not available before 1866, but we can be certain that arable land has been a feature of the British landscape for at least 4000 years and has probably accounted for about a quarter of our land surface during the last 1000 years. Thus, it is an important and long-standing ecological element in this country.

ARABLE LAND IN ECOLOGICAL TERMS

Before man became an abundant species in the British Isles, most of the surface of Britain was covered by forest and marsh. Patches of bare soil must have been very small and doubtless were quickly colonized by plants: trees, uprooted in gales, left small patches of soil in the forest, as did the activities of some mammals, notably moles and wild boars. Rabbits can produce quite large areas of bare soil round their burrows, but they were introduced in Norman times long after arable land had become an important feature of the British Isles. The only large natural areas in the temperate zone which remotely resembled arable land were the shores of rivers, lakes and the sea, and bare ground on the edge of ice sheets and glaciers. Tischler[1] has suggested that these were the original habitats of many organisms now found in crop habitats. Thus, arable land is a highly artificial ecosystem and has no real counterpart in the systems which existed in this country before man became the dominant species.

In arable farming, land is ploughed to enable crops to fill the role of pioneer species on bare soil. The actual process of ploughing is a violent one; it kills or damages plants already growing in the area, and changes a relatively stable soil system into one where temperature and humidity become much more variable. After ploughing the flora and fauna consist almost entirely of soil organisms. These are affected to varying degrees by the nature and growth of the crop and then by all the physical and chemical treatments to which a ploughed field may be subjected—harrowing, rolling, irrigation, the use of fertilizers, herbicides and insecticides. In many areas the land is also affected by straw or stubble burning after cereals have been harvested. Very little is known about the exact effects of all these procedures; clearly they differ according to the species of crop, the type of instrument used for ploughing and harrowing, and the chemical nature of fertilizers and pesticides. But it is not surprising that the fauna of soils in arable areas are impoverished compared to that of woodlands and grasslands.

The arable ecosystem is characterized by a marked seasonal sequence from *bare ground*, through *growth* to the *post-harvest* period, although the duration of each stage will depend on several factors, of which the farming system is the most important.

In the bare ground stage, after ploughing, the living part of the system is virtually confined to soil plants and animals. In the growth stage the weeds and their associated fauna colonize the crop and compete with it, and the crop, with or without the aid of hoeing or the application of herbicides, becomes dominant and eventually matures. This stage can be divided into two types of crop ecosystem. The living elements of type *one* consist of:

1. the crop species;
2. weeds;
3. animals and fungi dependent on the crop;
4. animals and fungi dependent on the weeds;
5. soil flora;
6. soil fauna.

Of course the boundaries are not rigid. For example, the roots of the crop and weeds are part of the soil system, and many beetles and other arthropods live in the soil by day and on the crops and weeds by night. Rather few animals are specific in their feeding habits and so some which feed on the crop may also feed on some of the weeds. The living elements of type *two* consist of:

1. the crop species;
2. animals and fungi dependent on the crop;
3. soil flora;
4. soil fauna.

This type of ecosystem occurs when the crop shades out all competitors, or when a selective herbicide is used which kills all plants other than the crop, as for example, when simazine is used on maize (examples are given in Table 5). Again, in practice, there are intermediate situations. A field of type two will often be type one before cover is formed or the herbicide applied.

In the post-harvest stage the crop has been removed, and any weeds which may have survived the farming operations in stage two become dominant. Until quite recently this stage, as fallow or stubble, could remain for several months, and so some weeds were able to germinate and produce seed before harvest and the onset of winter. However, today the farmer usually ploughs the field as soon as conditions allow.

It is obvious that the arable ecosystem undergoes a much more radical change than most natural ecosystems. The only comparable natural change is that caused by fire. Fire destroys most living matter above ground but its effects below ground are usually less severe than those caused by ploughing, especially deep ploughing.

In addition to the effects of ploughing, there are those brought about by changes in cropping: plants and animals colonize one crop in one season and may then be confronted with quite a different crop in the following year, or later in the same year. Great changes in species do occur in seral successions in natural systems, but they are much more gradual than this. Not surprisingly, relatively few species can adapt to life on arable land. The life cycles of those that do have to be short enough to make use of the special features of the crop's regimes, and they have to possess efficient means of dispersal so that they can exploit new habitats provided by farming. It is impossible to give a statistic of plant and animal species found on arable land. There are about 150 important insect pest species of arable crops in Great Britain; but there are very many more species on arable land which are not pests.

Very few vertebrates are able to subsist entirely on arable land, although many can and do use crops and their weeds and associated fauna for shelter or food as well as the flora and fauna of hedges and ditches. In Britain no mammal is confined to farmland, much less to arable land. However, two species are very abundant here. It appears to be the preferred habitat of the hare, which can live in the total absence of woody cover, and cropland also appears to be the second-best habitat for the wood mouse. Pollard and Relton[2] have shown that the wood mouse ranges widely in hedge and field habitats. Apparently it can live in the absence of woody cover but it seems to prefer hedges and woods. Jefferies, Stainsby and French,[3] from their study on the effects of dieldrin and mercury cereal seed dressings on small mammals, suggested that there may be two populations of wood mouse: one which is based on the hedges and does not move far from them into the crop and one which is a true field population based on the crop itself. This may prove to be an example of an essentially woodland species becoming adapted to living in the new open systems provided by man. The red deer is another example; originally a forest species, it now lives mainly on moorlands.

Of the 50 or so more common terrestrial breeding birds in Great Britain, the partridge, the red-legged partridge, the lapwing and the skylark are capable of living in arable crops with no woody cover.[4] The meadow pipit does not need trees or bushes but is a breeding species of rough grasslands rather than arable land. The corn bunting can also live on arable land provided song posts are available and these need not be trees. Among rare species, the stone curlew and the quail can live in purely arable areas. The yellow wagtail, normally a bird of water and flood meadows, can also live on arable land while the yellowhammer, the reed bunting, the sedge warbler and the whitethroat are common on farmland but dependent on associated ditch vegetation. Numerous species, for example the blackbird, song thrush, dunnock and rook, depend on woody cover for breeding but feed on arable land.

If we take another well-known group of animals, the butterflies, only three of our 56 breeding species, the Large White, the Small White and the Green-veined White can breed in the arable system. All are dependent on cabbage, rape and other brassicas. Clearly, the arable system is characterized by a relative paucity of species, but the species which are present may be abundant, especially those which can exploit the abundance of the crop species itself.

Table 5. Herbicides used on arable land

Common name	Chemical group	Mode of action (see note 1)	Used against (see note 2)	Principally in (crop)	Acute oral LD50 to rat (mg/kg) (see note 3)	Other features (see note 4)
Aminotriazole	Heterocyclic nitrogen	T	BLW, grass WO, BG	Many	1100–2500	
Barban	Carbamate	T		Wheat, peas, sugar beet	600	
Bromoxynil	Benzonitrile	C	BLW	Cereals	190	In mixtures with MCPA, Ioxynil, Dichlorprop
Chlorpropham	Carbamate	SA	BLW	Peas	5000–7500	±Diuron, Fenuron, Monolinuron
Chlortoluron	Substituted urea	T, SA	BG, BLW, WO	Cereals	>10 000	
2,4-D	Phenoxyacetic acid	T	BLW	Cereals	375	
Dalapon	Halogenated aliphatic acid	T	Grass	Many	9330	
2,4-DB	Phenoxyacetic acid	T	BLW	Cereals	700	±MCPA, 2,4-D
Desmetryne	Triazine	T, C	BLW	Brussels sprouts, cabbage, kale	1390	
Di-allate	Thiolcarbamate	SA	BG, WO	Brassicas, sugar beet	395	
Dicamba	Benzoic acid	T	BLW	Cereals	2900	±Dichlorprop, MCPA, Mecoprop, etc.
Dichlorprop	(Phenoxy) propionic acid	T	BLW	Cereals	800	±2,4-D, MCPA, Mecoprop.
Dimexan	Dithiocarbonyl	C	Seedlings	Many	340	±Chlorbufan and Cycluron
Dinoseb	Dinitrophenol	C(SA)	BLW	Peas, beans, cereals	58	±Monolinuron
Diquat	Quaternary ammonium	T	BLW	Desiccator of potato, peas, etc.	231	

	Chemical group	Action	Weeds	Crops	LD50	Mixtures
Endothal	Cyclic-dicarboxylic acid	SA	Seedlings	Sugar beet	51	
EPTC	Thiolcarbamate	SA	BLW, grass	Potatoes	1630	
Ioxynil	Iodo-benzonitrile	T	BLW	Cereals	110	±Bromoxynil
Lenacil	Uracil	SA	Seedlings	Sugar beet	>11,000	
Linuron	Substituted urea	T, SA	BLW	Many	4000	±Lenacil, Monolinuron
MCPA	Phenoxyacetic acid	T	BLW	Cereals	700	
MCPB	Phenoxybutyric acid	T	BLW	Cereals	680	±MCPA
Mecoprop	2-(Phenoxy)propionic acid	T	BLW	Cereals	930	±2,4-D, Fenoprop
Methabenzthiazuron	Substituted urea	T, SA	BG	Cereals	>2500	
Metobromuron	Substituted urea	SA	BLW	Potatoes	>5000	
Metoxuron	Substituted urea	T, SA	BLW, BG	Cereals	3200	
Monolinuron	Substituted urea	T, SA	BLW, grass	Potatoes	2250	
Paraquat	Quaternary ammonium	C, T	BLW, grass	Many	150	
Prometryne	Substituted triazine	T, SA	BLW	Peas, carrots, potatoes	3150–3750	Prometryne
Propachlor	Amide	SA	Seedlings	Brassicas	1200	
Pyrazon	Diazine	SA	Seedlings	Sugar beet	3300	
Simazine	Triazine	SA	BLW	Beans, maize	>5000	
Sodium monochloroacetate	Halogenated acetic acid	C	Seedlings	Brassicas	650	(sodium chloroacetate)
2,3,6-TBA	Substituted benzoic acid	T	BLW	Cereals	1500	
TCA	Halogenated aliphatic acid	SA	Couch, WO	Many	3200–5000	
Terbutryne	Triazine	SA	BG	Cereals	2400–2980	
Tri-allate	Thiolcarbamate	SA	BG, WO	Cereals, peas	1675–2165	
Trietazine	Triazine	SA	BLW	Potatoes	2830	
Trifluralin	Trifluoromethylaniline	SA	Seedlings	Brassicas	>10,000	

1. C = Contact; SA = Soil acting, pre-emergence; T = Translocated.
2. BG = Black grass; BLW = Broad-leaved weeds; WO = Wild oats.
3. Acute oral LD50 refers to the single dose of the pesticide administered orally which kills 50% of the experimental population. It is expressed in mg of pesticide to kg of experimental animal. Low figures indicate high toxicity.
4. Several herbicides are only used in mixtures containing other herbicides. Bromoxynil is only sold in mixtures.

The wildlife value of arable land is twofold. First it provides the principal habitat of plant species which are confined to disturbed ground; many of our weed species are in this category. Secondly it provides unstable systems which give admirable opportunities to study the ability of species to adapt to new conditions and the competitive relationships between species. Studies on the wildlife of arable land, together with those made in other habitats, sometimes give us warnings about the unforeseen hazards of pollution, climatic change and other factors.

Among natural systems, those which are species-rich, for example rainforest and temperate broadleaved forest, contain species which tend to have relatively stable populations, whereas the populations of those systems which contain few species, for example tundra, tend to be subject to considerable fluctuations. In other words, stability is associated with diversity, although the two are not necessarily causally related. Therefore, one would expect plants and animals in arable systems to fluctuate considerably, and initially this is often the case.

When a species increases to such an extent that it has an economically significant effect on the crop, we call it a pest. Many of the characteristic features of arable systems reflect activities undertaken by man to control pests. Such activities are essential and are made inevitable by growing the crop in the first place, because once a complex system has been replaced by a simple one, instability is likely to follow. Modern agriculture cannot fail to produce monocultures; indeed its high productivity depends upon them. Crop monocultures tend to be less stable than more 'advanced' natural systems such as grasslands, marshes and moorlands; however, the farmer reimposes a new form of stability by using crop protection methods. Eventually it may prove possible to reduce some of the more serious effects of the instability of crop monocultures by introducing appropriate forms of complexity in the first place, but it is important to realize that by growing crops at all we make the need for crop protection inevitable. Pesticides have enabled farmers to do without crop rotations, but the simplification of the new systems increases the need to control the environment of the crop by the greater use of pesticides. World food shortages, combined with rising land prices, force farmers to increase productivity in the short term if they are to remain in business. Thus the economic factors of the present time are forcing farmers to make their crop ecosystems less and less like natural ecosystems or even the semi-natural ones which we have associated with farming in the recent past.

EFFECTS OF MEASURES TO INCREASE YIELDS

Crop yields can be increased in six main ways by:

1. reducing competition between the crop and other plants: that is weed control;

2. reducing competition between man and other organisms which feed on the crop; that is insect pest control;
3. rectifying any soil deficiencies of those substances which are essential for growth;
4. raising the temperature so as to increase the rate of metabolic processes and hence growth;
5. preventing physical damage by, for example, providing shelter against wind, and drainage to prevent waterlogging;
6. breeding forms with higher yields, forms which are less susceptible to physical damage (for example short-stalk cereals which are less easily damaged in storms), and strains which are more resistant to attack by fungi and insects.

All these activities have an effect on the total arable land ecosystem as well as on the crop itself, for the crop is only part of the system in which it is grown. Some of these activities are elaborated below.

Improving the chemical environment of the crop

Chemicals are applied to provide nutrients such as phosphates or nitrates, to reduce the acidity of soils, and to provide trace elements which may be deficient. These chemicals affect weeds as well as crops, beneficially in some cases, detrimentally in others. For example, the recent increase in nettles on the edges of fields may be largely due to the increased use of fertilizers. On the other hand, the decline of several weeds of acid soils, such as the corn marigold, may be due to liming, when it is not due to herbicides. The nature of the soil fauna depends to a large extent on its pH, so that changes brought about by liming alone are considerable.

Pest control

Pesticides include all chemical agents used by man to control organisms of different kinds, and thus the term covers herbicides, fungicides, insecticides, acaricides (which kill mites) and rodenticides. These chemicals were little used until the middle of this century when under the pressures generated by the Second World War they became one of the principal means of increasing food production. Their use is now an integral part of modern farming in all parts of the world. Pesticides can be inorganic or organic, naturally occurring or synthetic, but the vast majority are synthetic organic substances and as such no plant or animal species has had evolutionary experience of them in the past. None are wholly specific and so all kill organisms other than the pest against which they are used. Their effects on organisms are of two kinds: direct toxicological where the pesticide kills or damages the organism under consideration; and indirect toxicological where the pesticide kills or damages other species whose absence or reduction alters the ecological pressures on the organism concerned. For example, a pesticide may destroy an animal's habitat, reduce its food supply, favour or disfavour a competitor, or reduce the population of a predator. The net result of the application of a pesticide is bound to be very complicated since it changes so many ecological relationships.

Herbicides

Weeds compete with the crop for nutrients, water and light, although sometimes they may help it by providing shade and shelter during an early stage of development. Weeds harbour both pests and beneficial animals: as we shall see, the damage to Brussels sprouts by the caterpillars of the Cabbage White butterfly can be prevented by certain ground predators and therefore the number of predators may be increased by allowing weeds to grow among the crop. Thus, if the weeds could be manipulated so that they supported enough predators to obtain good control of the pest without damaging the crop by competition, then they would no longer be weeds—'plants in the wrong place'—but an agent of crop protection.

But in general it is advantageous to grow 'clean crops'. This can be achieved in several ways: by cultivation at times of the year which will favour the crop rather than the weeds; by hoeing; by using clean seed; and by the use of herbicides; and all these methods are used. However, the use of herbicides has become the main method of weed control owing to its simplicity and because it saves manpower and hence money. Herbicides range from total to selective. Selective herbicides are applied to the growing crop with no or only slightly harmful effects on the crop itself. The growth-regulating herbicides, such as MCPA and 2,4-D, are widely used and have greatly reduced the numbers of poppies, charlock and other weeds which have been abundant for centuries. Their decline must have led to the reduction of animal species dependent upon them. However, other plant species, with which these weeds competed successfully in the past, have greatly increased. This process has favoured the species which most resemble the crop: thus the wild oat and black grass are now among the most important weeds in cereal districts of England today. But even these species can be controlled by herbicides such as Barban and Tri-allate, although treatment is relatively expensive.

Practically all arable fields in Great Britain have been treated with herbicides at one time or another; most are treated at least once a year and many more frequently than this. Some of the consequences are plain to see—a field red with poppies or blue with cornflowers is now a relatively rare sight while a yellowing cornfield topped with an upper layer of pale green wild oats has become a much commoner occurrence. However, not all attractive weed species have declined as a result of herbicides: the disappearance of the corncockle is largely due to the use of cleaner cereal seed in recent years.[5] These huge floristic changes, which are being studied in the Botanical Society of the British Isles/Weed Research Organization Survey,[6] must have had immense effects on arthropod populations, but apart from a preliminary study by Potts,[7] little is known about them. The most detailed study of the indirect effects of herbicides also by Potts,[8] is on the effects of herbicides on the partridge. This bird has declined over the last decade and a half, and Potts gives good evidence to show that this is partly due to herbicide use. The adult partridge is a vegetarian, but the chicks need insect food. Previous work had shown that there were fewer insects on fields treated with herbicides than on those which had not been treated. When bad weather coincides with the time that the partridge chicks need protein the shortage of insects in sprayed fields becomes critical and many chicks die.

A list of the more commonly used herbicides, with a guide to their use and toxicity, is given in Table 5. It will be seen that they include a wide range of chemicals and that most are not very toxic.

Fungicides

Fungicides are used extensively against blight and other fungal diseases of vegetables and corn seed. In Britain the use of organo-mercury seed dressings is nearly universal. Jefferies, Stainsby and French[3] have shown how mercury levels in wood mice increased eleven times after their habitat had been drilled with winter wheat dressed with mercury. However, the amount found (0·39 ppm wet weight) did not indicate acute hazard. Pigeons, which have fed on spilled dressed corn, sometimes contain much larger residues. Nevertheless, so far as is known, no species has been severely affected by the agricultural use of mercury in Great Britain, although there continues to be much concern about mercury poisoning on account of events in Japan and Sweden. A list of the more commonly used fungicides is given in Table 6. It will be seen that apart from mercury, most are not very toxic substances.

Insecticides

Insecticides are used to kill insect pests but they are also likely to kill other animals in the crop ecosystem. The more toxic ones, such as dieldrin and certain organophosphorus insecticides, may kill vertebrate animals as well as invertebrates. Those insecticides that are not broken down quickly but persist in the soil or in plant and animal tissues for a long time and are fat-soluble present special problems because they can accumulate in fat and be passed from prey to predator. Dempster[9] has shown that the Cabbage White butterfly on Brussels sprouts can be controlled by ground-living predators, notably the beetle *Harpalus rufipes* and the arachnid *Phalangium opilio*, both of which feed on the larvae at night. When a Brussels sprout crop is sprayed with DDT, the butterfly larvae are killed but so are these predators. Therefore when immigrant Cabbage White adults lay more eggs on the sprouts, the larvae which

Table 6. Fungicides used on arable land

Common name	Chemical group	Mode of action (see note 1)	Used against	Principally in (crop)	Acute oral LD50 to rat (mg/kg) (see note 2)	Other features (see note 3)
Captafol	Thiodicarboximide		Blight	Potatoes	5000–6200	
Captan	Thiodicarboximide		Seed disease	Seed dressings	9000	
Carboxin	Thiocarboxanilide	S	Loose smut	Cereals	3820	
Drazoxolon	Isoxazolone		Damping off	Peas	126	
Ethirimol	Pyrimidine	S	Mildew	Spring barley	4000 (♀)	
Fentin	Organotin		Blight	Potatoes	125 (acetate) 108 (hydroxide)	±Maneb
Mancozeb	Dithiocarbamate		Blight	Potatoes	>8000	±Zineb
Maneb	Dithiocarbamate		Blight	Potatoes	6750	±Zinc oxide, zineb
Mercury	Organomercury		Seed diseases	Seed dressings, cereals	20–1140	
Nabam	Dithiocarbamate		Blight	Potatoes	395	With zinc and manganese sulphates
Propineb	Dithiocarbamate		Blight	Potatoes	8500	
Quintozene	Chloronitrobenzene		Damping off, etc.	Brassicas	>12,000	
Thiram	Thiuramdisulphide		Seed diseases	Seed dressings	375–865	
Tridemorph	Substituted morpholine	S	Mildew	Barley, oats, wheat	1250	
Zineb	Dithiocarbamate		Blight	Potatoes	>5200	

1. S = Systemic.
2. As note 3 to Table 5.
3. Several fungicides are only used in mixtures containing other fungicides.

hatch are less subject to control and so can increase without hindrance. The situation becomes worse after the second year of spraying because the population of predators is further depressed owing to the persistence of DDT in the soil. In this instance, from the pest's point of view, the advantageous indirect ecological effect of the pesticide outweighs the harmful direct toxicological effect and so the application of the insecticide causes an increase in the pest. This type of situation probably arises frequently but it has been little studied. In perennial crops like orchards continuous use of persistent insecticides has produced new pests. Perhaps the most famous case is that of the fruit tree red spider mite and related species which have become pests of orchards throughout the world mainly because the predatory mites and other arthropods which used to control their numbers have been reduced by the use of DDT and related compounds. A list of the more commonly used insecticides is given in Table 7.

Control of pesticides

The need to control pesticides in order to protect farmworkers, the consumers of treated food, domestic animals and wildlife is obvious, and in most countries there is a complicated system of control to this end. In the United Kingdom it is called the Pesticides Safety Precautions Scheme and is operated by an interdepartmental and interdisciplinary Advisory Committee, which, with its Scientific Subcommittee and helped by specialist panels, decides whether each new pesticide and each new use of old ones can be permitted. The decision of the committees is based on data about the nature of the pesticide and its metabolites, methods of chemical analysis, residue studies on treated crops, acute oral and dermal toxicity and chronic toxicity studies on mammals, acute oral toxicity studies on birds, fish and bees, and on other work requested by the Scientific Subcommittee. Despite the thoroughness of testing, an absolute assurance that the chemical will be safe can never be given because the multitudinous field situations contain factors which may interact with the pesticide and cause some unforeseen effect. Nevertheless, during the 13–16 years that the scheme has been in full operation, none of the pesticides approved has produced serious side-effects as far as is known. On the other hand, some of the uses of pesticides introduced beforehand have had to be withdrawn—notably many uses of persistent organochlorine insecticides. Initially, the consequences of the combination of persistence and fat solubility were not realized, but when it was demonstrated that these chemicals were becoming distributed throughout the world, could become concentrated in aquatic animals, and could be transferred in food chains, restrictions were made on many of their uses. Monitoring studies on man, on his food, and on wildlife indicator species have shown subsequently that the restrictions have been successful in reducing the amounts of these substances in the British environment.

Table 7. Insecticides and other pesticides used on arable land

Common name	Chemical group (see note 1)	Mode of action (see note 2)	Used against	Principally in (crop)	Acute oral LD50 to rat (mg/kg) (see note 3)	
Aldicarb	OC(P)	S	Soil nematodes	Sugar beet	1	
Aldrin	OC(P)		Cabbage root fly	Cabbage	67	Uses reduced because of persistence as dieldrin
BHC	OC(P)		Many, including wheat bulb fly	Many	125–200	
Carbophenothion	OP		Wheat bulb fly	Winter wheat	32	
Chlorfenvinphos	OP		Wheat bulb fly, etc.	Wheat, cabbage, carrot	10–39	
DDT	OC(P)		Many	Many	113	Uses reduced because of persistence
Demephion	OP	S	Aphids	Sugar beet, brassicas, beans, etc.	<1	
Demeton-S-Methyl	OP	S	Aphids	Many	57–107	
Dizinon	OP		Aphids, cabbage root fly, carrot fly	Cabbage, carrot	150–600	'Metasystox'
Dichloropropene	OC		Eelworms	Potatoes, sugar beet	250–500	'D–D'. ±Dichloropropane
Dieldrin	OC(P)		Cabbage root fly	Cabbage	46	Uses reduced because of persistence
Dimethoate	OP	S	Cabbage root fly, aphids	Brassicas	320–380	
Disulfotan	OP	S	Aphids, carrot fly	Brassicas, beans, carrot	13	
Endosulfan	OC(P)		Pollen beetle, seed weevil	Rape	5–220	

			Pest	Crop	
Ethoate-Methyl	OP	S	Aphids	Brassicas, potatoes, sugar beet, etc.	340
Fenitrothion	OP		Weevils leatherjackets	Peas, cereals	250–500
Fonofos	OP		Cabbage root fly	Brassicas	8–18
Fomothion	OP	S	Aphids	Many	375–535
Malathion	OP		Many	Many	2800
Menazon	OP	S	Aphids	Brassicas, sugar beet, potatoes	1950 (♀)
Metaldehyde			Slugs	Many	1250 (rabbit)
Mevinphos	OP	S	Aphids	Beans, peas sugar beet	4–12
Oxydemeton-Methyl	OP	S	Aphids	Many	65
Phorate	OP	S	Aphids, carrot root fly, etc.	Many	4
Phosphamidon	OP	S	Aphids	Many	28
Tetrachlorvinphos	OP		Lepidoptera, beetles	Brassicas, peas	4000–5000
Thiometon	OP	S	Aphids	Potatoes, sugar beet, beans	120–130
Thionazin	OP		Carrot root fly	Brassicas	12
Trichlorphon	OP	S	Cabbage root fly, lepidoptera	Brassicas	630

1. OC(P) = Persistent organochlorine, OP = Organophosphorus.
2. S = Systemic.
3. See note 3 of Table 5.

While the Pesticides Safety Precautions Scheme and similar schemes can protect consumers and workers from acute and subacute poisoning, it cannot predict the complicated indirect effects of using a pesticide. This is beyond the scope of any registration scheme. Only experience in the field can determine whether a pesticide really does increase crop yields, and if it does, that this benefit exceeds any harmful 'side-effects' which it may have. Ordinary economic pressures eventually determine the short-term value and hence the use of a pesticide—if it is not effective or it is too expensive it will not be used. Unfortunately pesticide use is nearly always only looked at from a short-term point of view, because there is no easy way by which long-term considerations can be taken into account. Restrictions on the use of persistent organochlorine insecticides is one of the few cases where consideration of possible long-term harmful effects were allowed to override the short-term advantages of using DDT, aldrin, dieldrin and heptachlor. While it would be difficult to improve the testing before registration of a new pesticide, much could and should be done to look for unforeseen hazards in its first years of use. There are administrative difficulties for both Government and Industry but they could be overcome.

It is important not to take a parochial view of the matter because requirements vary from country to country. For example, it is right for countries in the temperate regions to restrict the use of persistent organochlorine insecticides in order to safeguard fish supplies and other wildlife, but it would be wrong to prevent the use of DDT in houses in many tropical countries where DDT is the only practical method for the control of malaria.

Straw-burning

In many countries fire has been an important agricultural tool for centuries. It is used as a means of clearing forest by farmers who engage in shifting cultivation in Africa and southern Asia. In Britain, swaling is traditionally carried out on rough grassland to obtain an early bite for stock and to control scrub growth, as on the slopes of the Purbeck Hills in Dorset and the Cotswolds, and on moorlands to provide young growth of heather as a food for grouse. However, until recently it was not an integral part of arable farming practice, and only during the last 15 years or so has it become a feature of arable farming, particularly in southeast and eastern England. The reasons are these: much of East Anglia and the East Midlands used to contain mixed farms, in which straw was valuable for the stock, but over the last 20 years cereal growing has become predominant and so there is a surplus of straw locally; but it is not economic to export it to the West Country where there is a shortage. Further, the combine leaves straw in a form which is not easily used. If straw is left on the ground it encourages fungal diseases. These reasons provide a strong case for burning. On the other hand, where straw is chopped up and returned to the land it supplies nutrients which otherwise would have to be provided by fertilizers.

Little work has been done on the effects of straw- and stubble-burning on the flora and fauna of arable land. As with heather-burning, the effect will depend on the strength of the fire but what little information is available suggests that it has little direct effect on soil plants and animals. In one preliminary study[10] straw-burning reduced populations of insects living above ground by 85 per cent, the numbers of insects emerging in the following year by 71 per cent and the species present by 61 per cent. The indirect effects of straw-burning on mammals and birds through changes in available food supply are quite unknown. Where there is much woodland, waste and permanent grassland, the effects are likely to be small, but in the barley prairies of East Anglia and the East Midlands, where nearly all the land is under the plough and a large proportion of it is burned each year, the effects could be significant. Perhaps the most important effects are aesthetic and sociological. Hedges and trees damaged by fire are eyesores whether or not the damage is lasting. They give the impression that the farmers are either incompetent or do not care about the land they farm or the feelings of their neighbours. Both impressions are unfortunate because they reduce the sympathy of towndwellers for the farming community. Incidentally straw-burning does far more damage to hedges than herbicide drift. While herbicide drift from fields to gardens has sometimes caused damage to garden plants and hence has led to litigation, the effects on wild species do not appear to be very great. More damage is done by the deliberate use of wide spectrum herbicides to hedge margins. This kills the more attractive species and after an initial setback deep rooted weeds such as couch grass and nettles become dominant. In other words the herbicide has the exact opposite effect to that which was intended by its use.

INTERACTION OF ARABLE LAND WITH OTHER ECOSYSTEMS

Arable land in Britain does not cover very large continuous areas; while average fields are much larger than they were 30 years ago owing to the use of modern machinery and to the labour costs involved in maintaining hedges and open ditches, fields greater than 50 hectares are still unusual although they are likely to be more common in the future. In other words, arable land is broken up by a network of hedges and ditches whose flora and fauna are essentially 'natural', although the hedge shrubs in all but the oldest hedges were planted in the first place. As a result, the flora and fauna of an ordinary arable farm are a great deal richer than those of the arable land itself because they contain both the species supported by arable land as well as woodland species found in the hedges and the grassland species found at the bottoms of hedges and on the edge of ditches.

During the last 30 years many hedges and hedgerow trees have been taken out and so the biomass of the species found in hedges and ditches relative to the biomass of the species found on arable land must have declined. However, hedge removal has not been total and so very few species have been lost on most farms. The destruction of numerous hedges has made many people ask whether the loss of wild plants and animals from them has had any significant consequences for agriculture and wildlife conservation. To answer this question we must know something about the relationship between the flora and fauna of hedges and those of the fields. Until recently little research had been undertaken on this subject. It was known however that spindle bushes in hedges provided host plants for the bean aphid. It was obvious that rabbits living in hedges and ditches caused damage to growing crops in their vicinity. It was also clear that many beneficial or potentially beneficial species, for example bumblebees, predatory and parasitic insects, were dependent on the hedges rather than on the crops themselves.

From his work on carabid beetles, Pollard[11] has shown that species on farmland can be divided into three groups: field species; hedge species and those species which are associated with the hedge but are not restricted to it. Hedge species may be of conservation value but are unlikely to have much effect on agriculture, but those which depend on hedges and also occur widely in crops might be important to agriculture. The extent to which they are economically important depends on their abundance in relation to pest species. Local conditions are likely to determine the economic significance of these animals and generalizations about their value cannot be expected. However, there are no obvious differences in the pest situation between arable areas where there are no hedges, for example the Fens and parts of Bedfordshire, and those areas which are well-hedged. This suggests that hedges are unlikely to be very important either in providing refuges for pests or for crop protection, whatever other values they may have as windbreaks, fences and refuges for wild plants and animals. As agriculture becomes more intensive, interaction between arable land and interstitial habitats will change in character and the two types of ecosystem are likely to diverge yet further. At present hedges are much less important for conservation than small woods, but if the total acreage of the latter were to decline significantly the value of hedges would increase correspondingly (see Chapter 3).

Road verges

Arable land is intersected by roads and lanes as well as by hedges and ditches, and the interaction between the flora and fauna of road verges and arable land is another subject of debate. For many years the vegetation on road verges was so similar to that of permanent pasture on the neighbouring farms that it was not often considered in its own right. But in recent years a large proportion of permanent pasture has been ploughed and turned into grass leys or arable land and most of the grassland which has not been ploughed up has been treated with fertilizers and herbicides so that its floristic characteristics have been changed. As a result, road verges tend to be much richer in species than most meadowland and hence are of great interest and value as reservoirs for wild plants and animals. On the other hand, the farmer tends to think that any plant which he has not planted is a weed and he is therefore concerned about the colonization of arable land by species living on road verges. This fear is groundless in most cases since, as Way has shown,[12] the species on road verges are nearly all grassland ones which are unable to live under arable conditions. It is unlikely, therefore, that the road verge flora provides arable land with a source of noxious propagules. There are a few exceptions such as some thistle species and couch grass;[13] however, most of these occur on road verges as the result of temporary disturbance caused for example by laying pipes. Conversely, most of the weeds on arable land are not able to colonize undisturbed road verges.

Arable land as a source of pollution

The increase in pesticide and fertilizer use on arable land means that the latter has increasingly become a source of environmental pollutants. Fertilizers may pass from arable land into drainage ditches and so cause eutrophication in them or in the ponds and lakes into which they flow. However, all the available evidence suggests that effluents from intensive animal units provide a much more significant source of unwanted nutrients than does the ordinary application of fertilizers. Similarly, if partially empty pesticide drums are dumped in ditches or spraying machinery is cleaned out in them, these malpractices can cause serious direct and indirect damage to fish populations, and threaten water supplies for drinking or irrigation downstream.

The persistent pesticides pose a special problem. They can disperse from arable land by volatilization, by being attached to particles in water and by being stored in the bodies of animals. The use of aldrin and dieldrin as cereal seed dressings against wheat bulb-fly has been studied extensively in recent years. Until 1962 a large proportion of all the corn sown in the 9 million acres under cereals in Great Britain was treated with these chemicals. Although the application rate was very low (about 2 ounces of active ingredient per acre) and the pesticide should not have been available to animals living above ground as it was only applied to seed corn, nevertheless it had an important ecological effect. In practice, enough corn was left on the surface to kill numerous pigeons, game birds and song birds. Many predators, especially foxes, badgers, peregrines, kestrels and sparrowhawks died from eating contaminated prey. Many of the deaths occurred quite long distances from arable land, demonstrating that an agricultural practice confined to arable land could have effects on species living in other habitats. The acute toxicological effects and the subacute effects on reproduction, were sufficient to cause serious population declines in the three birds of prey. Following restrictions on the use of aldrin and dieldrin as seed dressing in 1962, all the bird species affected are now showing signs of recovery. The organophosphorus substitutes for aldrin and dieldrin are much less persistent, and while a few cases of acute poisoning of birds and mammals are to be expected since they are also very toxic compounds, these chemicals are unlikely to cause serious secondary effects.

THE FUTURE

The world population continues to rise as do standards of living. This will make it harder for the United Kingdom to buy its food abroad, and so intensification of agriculture is likely to increase in this country as chapter 1 argues in detail. The main pressures will be on the fertile lands of the southeast half of the country, but doubtless much marginal land will be reclaimed as well. At a time when more people than ever are concerned about the conservation of wildlife and an attractive environment, agriculture ceases to provide these as an unplanned by-product, as it did in the past. The possibility of combining efficient agriculture and conservation in one operation in the future, as occurred until recently almost without design, seems remote. The only effective compromise will be provided by a mixture of intensive agriculture and intensive conservation.

At present modern farms can be modified to a small extent in order to increase populations of wild plants and animals. In nearly all cases this involves taking small areas of land out of agriculture. In many farms this is possible without serious loss of production, since many farms have patches of steep ground, marshy hollows, old pits and ponds which would be expensive to reclaim, and if reclaimed would not add greatly to revenue. Sometimes small areas of a farm can be farmed less intensively than the rest. For example, a farm with hundreds of acres of pasture can usually afford to leave a few acres untreated with fertilizers or herbicides. Most of the species of wildlife on farmland are dependent on the small woods, hedges, ditches and ponds and not on the arable land itself, and so alterations in farming practices are generally much less useful in conserving wildlife than not farming parts of the land. The restriction of hazardous pesticides is an exception to this, but the decision not to use a pesticide is in the hands of the Advisory Committee on Pesticides and other Toxic Chemicals, which determines which pesticides may be used, and is not in the hands of the farmer. On the other hand only the farmer and his contractors can prevent the misuse of pesticides. Where game is considered as a crop, a farmer may be willing to modify both his farm and his farming practices very considerably in order to favour pheasants and partridges, for example, by taking marginal land out of cultivation in order to provide food and cover and by undersowing cereals to provide food. If he does these things many other wild species benefit from his measures. This is discussed further in Chapter 11.

The maintenance of our agricultural resources will depend on our ability to conserve the better land by adopting sound planning and ecological principles. Much can be learnt from natural systems but it is quite wrong to think of the arable system as if it were a simple variant of a natural system. It is *sui generis* and requires its own branch of ecology. For example, while the study of population dynamics and evolutionary changes in natural ecosystems can tell us much about the nature of interactions of species within the arable system, an inherently unstable monoculture treated with a range of totally new mortality factors which exert immensely powerful selective pressures is quite unlike any natural system. The natural system is full of feedbacks, but the arable one is largely determined by economic forces external to it. The time has come to look at the problem of the biology of arable land in its own right and studies should include economics as well as ecology. The underlying purpose should be the same as it always has been for responsible farmers—the maintenance of the highest sustainable yield. This aim should be pursued in parallel with other social aims such as the conservation of wildlife and the creation and maintenance of fine landscapes. These two types of activity will compete for land, but as long as we think of the final result as a 'mixture' rather than a 'compound', then both aims can be achieved and harmonized.

If we take a very long view the situation may change radically: proteins may be synthesized industrially and carbohydrates produced in tanks and greenhouses rather than in fields. Many of the weed and pest species which have plagued mankind in the past will probably become much rarer and confined to disturbed ground on the coasts, and by buildings and roads and in gardens. Then, the extent to which we have wildlife on the land which used to be arable, will depend on the size of the human population and its environmental needs.

NOTES AND REFERENCES

1. Tischler, W. (1948). Biozonotische Untersuchungen an Wallhecken. *Zool. Jb. Abt. Systematik, Okologie und Geographie der Tiere*, **77**, 284–400.
2. Pollard, E. and Relton, J. (1970). Hedges V: a Study of Small Mammals in Hedges and Cultivated Fields. *Journal of Applied Ecology*, **7**, 549–557.
3. Jefferies, D. J., Stainsby, B. and French, M. C. (1973). The Ecology of Small Mammals in Arable Fields Drilled with Winter Wheat and the Increase in their Dieldrin and Mercury levels. *Journal of Zoology*, **171**, 513–539.
4. Murton, R. K. (1971). *Man and Birds*, Collins, London.
5. Fryer, J. D. and Chancellor, R. J. (1970). Herbicides and our Changing Weeds. In Perring, F. H. (ed.), *The Flora of a Changing Britain*. Report of the Botanical Society of the British Isles, No. 11.
6. Chancellor, R. J. (1975). Report of the Botanical Society of the British Isles/Weed Research Organization Survey of Arable Weeds, No. 1. *Watsonia*, **10**.
7. Potts, G. R. (1970). Recent Changes in the Farmland Fauna with Special Reference to the Decline of the Grey Partridge. *Bird Study*, **17**, 145–166.
8. Potts, G. R. (1971). Agriculture and the Survival of the Partridge. *Outline on Agriculture*, **6**, 267–271.
9. Dempster, J. P. (1968). The Control of *Pieris rapae* with DDT: II. Survival of the Young Stages of *Pieris* after spraying. *Journal of Applied Ecology*, **5**, 451–462.
10. Vickerman (personal communication).
11. Pollard, E. (1968). Hedges IV: A Comparison between the Carabidae of a Hedge and Field Site and those of a Wooldland Glade. *Journal of Applied Ecology*, **5**, 649–657.
12. Way, J. M. (1970). Roads and the Conservation of Wildlife. *Journal of the Institute of Highway Engineers*, **17** (7), 5–11.
13. Two species of thistle, two of dock, and ragwort are noxious weeds and steps to prevent them invading agricultural land are required by law.

Chapter 3

Hedgerows and small woodlands

M. D. HOOPER

On the evidence of pollen analysis, woodlands have existed in these islands since the ending of the last ice age 10,000 years ago. Hedges, 'little lines of sportive wood run wild', are much more recent. The Romans wrote of them before Christ, but the first documentary evidence of their existence here is a Saxon reference to northern England in the sixth century. The laws of Ine of Wessex suggest that by the seventh century hedges were an established feature of the landscape and served the function of stopping stock from straying.

From then until this century, the area of woodland has decreased and the number of hedges increased. Sometimes trees were cleared for agricultural production but quite often the woodlands had already been devastated. The need for large timber for building houses and ships, together with demands for smaller wood for charcoal or as faggots for heating and cooking, all took their toll. In these latter cases it seems that as the resource began to dwindle the nature of the management changed to maintain the supply of wood by coppicing. In areas where woodlands had been extensively cleared before the advent of cheap coal, the growing number of hedgerows were often managed in this way to provide the smaller timber, even up to cordwood size. Even so, the main function of hedges remained as a stock barrier. The increasing frequency of hedgerows reflected first, the profitability of sheep in Tudor times and later, the improvement brought about in farming by the practice of rotation, where the distribution of stock around the holding made hedges necessary adjuncts to the new farming systems.

These changes and their causes varied from place to place throughout the centuries. Woodland removal to create a Roman farm often took place on land recorded again as woodland in the Domesday Book. That land may still be wooded now. However, trees may have given place to open fields before the compilation of the Hundred Rolls (1279 A.D.) later perhaps to become a Tudor sheep ranch with large closes and few hedges. These closes might have been divided subsequently with new hedges to create a mixed farm under the new systems of the nineteenth century, only to have all the hedgerows swept away for a modern arable farm of the twentieth century. In some cases, new woods were planted for game birds and as fox coverts in the eighteenth and nineteenth centuries. Those too may survive today or have been swept away in the recent changes. Figure 5 shows the pattern of hedgerow change from the eleventh century to the present day in part of Cambridgeshire.

Traditionally, England is said to have a landscape created in the eighteenth century, the outcome of new agricultural techniques, of the ideas of gardeners such as Repton and Brown, and of the Enclosure Acts in the reign of George III. All these processes reshaped perhaps a third of the landscape in a relatively short time. Elsewhere, in much of the southeast, west and southwest, for example, changes were taking place more slowly; indeed in some areas there has been little change since the sixteenth century. The countryside can therefore be viewed as a patchwork of continuous change within which major patterns emerge and disappear through time. This mosaic can be frozen at various points in time on maps and photographs and in statistical compilations. One particular point in time seems pre-eminently suitable for present purposes—the years after the last war between 1945 and 1947. The general patterns of the landscape had changed relatively little over the previous two generations and aerial photographs taken at that time have caught the landscape before the pressures of the last 30 years. The Forestry Commission carried out sample surveys of woodlands in 1947–1949[1] and hedgerow trees in 1951[2] and these provide evidence of changes in cover since the early post-war years.

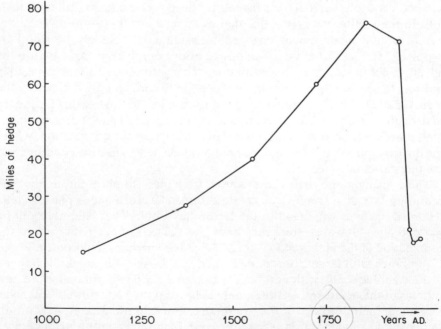

Figure 5.   Hedgerow acquisition and loss on 4500 acres of Cambridgeshire

THE PATTERN OF HEDGES AND HEDGEROW TREES

Precise figures for total length of hedgerows are not available. The Forestry Commission recorded hedges in sample plots from eleven counties in England, Scotland and Wales in 1954–1957.[3] They estimated the total length of boundaries as 950,000 miles and suggested that about two-thirds were hedgerow boundaries, that is some 620,000 miles of hedge. From a series of aerial photographs taken in 1946 and 1947[4] in various parts of England and Wales it is possible to see that, on average, a square mile of farmland had about thirteen miles of hedgerow. If there were then some 38,000 square miles of farmland with hedges, the total hedge mileage would be about 500,000 miles. Since Scotland was not included this seems a comparable figure to that found by the Forestry Commission.

The general distribution of hedgerows at that time was not uniform. Arable eastern England had larger fields and fewer hedges than the mixed farms of the centre, while areas in the southwest with tiny fields had a very high mileage of hedgerows. In Norfolk about 10 to 12 miles of hedgerow were to be found on a square mile of farmland, with 16 miles in Leicestershire, while in Devon 32 miles was by no means unusual. The large mileage of hedgerows in Devon has excited comment for over 100 years. John Grant, writing of the district around Exeter in 1844, found that nearly 8 per cent of the land area was covered by hedges; this amounted to 1651 miles of hedge or about half as long again as the 'Great Wall of China'.[5]

Over this varied pattern of hedgerow distribution were superimposed other patterns determined by the type of hedgerow management (or mismanagement), or by the constituent shrub species. The hedges of Devon, for example, are often planted on banks, are well-managed as befits stock country and usually consist of a variety of shrubs. But there are exceptions, as in those areas of moorland which were reclaimed for agriculture in the nineteenth century where pure beech hedges were planted on the flat. In arable country hedges have often been neglected where they serve no agricultural function; elsewhere, secondary functions, such as the provision of cover for game birds, have ensured the continuation of management.

Thus both general views and detailed pictures can be built up for hedgerows, but this is not the case with hedgerow trees. The Forestry Commission did survey trees in 1938, in 1942, in 1951 and in 1965[6] but, as they included park timber and sometimes woods under one acre and varied the recording categories from time to time, the fine detail is obscured. Local surveys of trees in hedgerows have also been made periodically by schools and amenity groups but these rarely appear in the literature. The most comprehensive source of information on hedgerow trees for the early post-war years is a 1951 Forestry Commission Census.[2] This was carried out using random sampling methods and although the sampling frequency was low (only about one acre in every 8000 was examined) the methods do allow some estimate of the degree of possible error. The total number of hedgerow and park trees came to over 73 million, of which 55 million were in England, 11 million in Wales and 7 million in Scotland. These trees were classified in various ways by quality of timber and by species so that we can say, for example, that 4·8 million of the trees in Scotland were fit only for firewood. More importantly, the figures suggested that at some time in the future hedgerow trees would begin to play less part in the landscape through insufficient recruitment of young trees. Around 90 per cent of these trees were native broadleaves (a third were oak) and they represented a fifth of the total volume of standing timber in Great Britain at that time.

To examine the position further, the Merthyr Committee was set up in 1953 to advise whether or not timber trees could be grown effectively in farm hedges in compatibility with good agricultural practice and if so how this should be promoted. Reporting in 1955,[7] the Committee suggested many ways by which the growing of trees on farms could be encouraged, involving action by government departments, local authorities, and landowners themselves. Today, more than 20 years later, few of their recommendations have been actively pursued.

WOODLANDS

The post-war position for the smallest woods, those under five acres in extent, is also to be found in the 1951 Census.[2] They covered some 180,000 acres (of which 120,000 acres were in England) representing about 5 per cent of the total woodland area of Britain.

An assessment of the condition of the remaining 95 per cent of the woodland cover in the post-war years is to be found in the earlier Forestry Commission Census of 1947–1949.[1] Every wood of five acres or more in extent was classified by type and age, and the principal and subsidiary species recorded. The total area of British woodland was found to be approaching $3\frac{1}{2}$ million acres but, like hedges, the distribution was not uniform. Sussex, Surrey and Hampshire, with 15 per cent of their surface covered by woods, led the English table with only three other counties (Kent, Berkshire and Herefordshire) above 8 per cent. At the other end of the scale were counties such as Cambridge, Huntingdon, Lincoln and the East Riding of Yorkshire—all fertile agricultural areas. About half the woodland area was classified as high forest, almost equally divided between conifer and broadleaved forest, 10 per cent was coppice and 15 per cent was scrub.

Such was the position at the end of an era. Now the number and distribution of hedges, trees and woods have changed.[8-13]

CHANGES IN HEDGES AND TREES

There has been a continuing loss of hedges, starting slowly at first in the early post-war years, gathering momentum through the nineteen-fifties to reach a peak in the sixties, followed by a decline in the last few years. In addition to the temporal pattern, there is a spatial pattern too. Arable areas have lost more hedges than the zones of mixed farming; stock farming areas have lost least of all.[14]

As a crude estimate overall, we may say that 5000 miles of hedge were removed from farmland in England and Wales each year between 1945 and 1970, that is a loss of a little under 1 per cent each year for 25 years. But these figures disguise the wide variations in space and time. Norfolk lost half its hedges between 1946 and 1970. Rutland, on a line between arable and mixed farming, lost a quarter of its hedges on the arable but less than 10 per cent from areas predominantly in grass. In terms of yards of hedgerow removed per acre, the average annual rate of removal was about half a yard on arable, a quarter of a yard on mixed farms and perhaps one-tenth of a yard on stock farms. This is supported by Westmacott and Worthington[11] who found that about half a yard of hedge was removed annually on arable land in Huntingdonshire, a quarter of a yard in an area of mixed farming in Hertfordshire but only a sixth of a yard in a grazing area of Warwickshire. The loss of hedges from arable land is shown dramatically in Figure 6 which records their pattern near Hitchin (Hertfordshire) in 1947, 1961 and 1970.

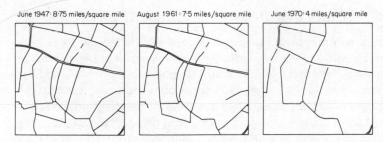

June 1947: 8·75 miles/square mile   August 1961: 7·5 miles/square mile   June 1970: 4 miles/square mile

Figure 6. The pattern of hedges near Hitchin, Hertfordshire, in 1947, 1961 and 1970

Westmacott and Worthington have established that hedgerow trees, like the hedges they stand in, are also disappearing but generally at a faster rate. While the annual overall loss of hedges was recorded as just less than 1 per cent, the loss of hedgerow trees was nearer 2 per cent. But there were regional variations; some areas had lost nearly 90 per cent of their trees while in the Warwickshire study area there was an increase.[15] Again there was an association between arable farming and the greatest rate of loss but in contrast to the major differences in hedgerow density it seems that in all areas hedgerow trees were equally common, at about 50 to 60 per 100 acres in 1947.

Both the New Agricultural Landscapes Report and the earlier Forestry Commission studies demonstrate that the most significant factor affecting the immediate future of hedgerow trees is their age distribution. If trees are classified in four age classes—sapling, young, middle-aged and mature—it can be seen that the proportion in each group is changing in the following way:

$$1938 - 33:21:19:27$$
$$1942 - 24:30:22:24$$
$$1951 - 42:19:19:20$$
$$1965 - 24:29:24:23$$

The minor variations may be readily explained. The high number of saplings in 1951 probably reflects the lack of routine hedge trimming in the war years, and the recruitment of these to the tree classes gives the increase in the young and middle-aged trees in the 1965 figures. But the really significant point is the reduction in saplings. In the 1972 figures from the New Agricultural Landscapes Study, only one area had more saplings than semi-mature trees. To ensure replacement and to allow for mortality, the number of saplings should about equal the number of trees in all other classes; the Merthyr Report, for example, suggested a ratio of $6:3:2:1$ for the age distribution. Clearly there are insufficient saplings to make good the losses now occurring. It is also significant that many of the saplings comprise elm and ash: elm is susceptible to disease, and Westmacott and Worthington suggest that ash is short-lived in arable areas because it is surface rooting and may be damaged by ploughing.

CHANGES IN THE WOODLAND PATTERN

In sharp contrast to the losses in hedges and hedgerow trees, the area of woodland has increased markedly by nearly 1 per cent per annum or 15 per cent between 1947 and 1965. The most dramatic figure in lowland England is a 78 per cent increase in Forestry Commission woodlands, much of this by the afforestation of heathland although a proportion results from the acquisition of woodland from private owners. Looking into these increases more closely it is found that, in lowland England, while conifer high forest has about doubled in extent, broadleaved high forest has increased by only 14 per cent. It may be suspected that a considerable part of this latter increase has come about by the transfer of woodlands from the coppice and scrub classes to the high forest class. In other woods, coppice has continued to decline while conifers have become much more common.

Oak is still the major component in the woods of lowland England and figures for changes in East Anglia suggest that there has been little alteration in recent times.[16] To extrapolate from the changes between 1947 and 1965 shown by the Forestry Commission Census figures may be dangerous. The increase in Forestry Commission woodlands and in conifer plantations during this period reflects older policies of building up strategic reserves of timber and a commercial attitude which emphasized a maximum return on investment. In recent years the emphasis has switched to social and amenity considerations and it seems unlikely that much of the remaining broadleaved woodland will be replaced by conifers, although the current uncertainty over Capital Transfer

Tax does not help accurate forecasting. However, there do seem to be certain trends which can be stated—an overall increase in woodland area, a concentration on conifers with the larger plantations on poorer soils, and some decline in the frequency and perhaps the size of broadleaved woods.

IMPLICATIONS FOR THE LANDSCAPE AND WILDLIFE

The motive for all these recent changes has been economic; hedges, for example, have been removed in the search for greater efficiency in the use of land, machinery and manpower. There is, however, a growing awareness that changes which produce short-term monetary gains can have adverse environmental effects which often cannot be evaluated financially.

Such research as has been done suggests that the environmental implications are of three kinds. Firstly, there are unforeseen local effects which could be measured in monetary terms. Hedge removal, for example, modifies the microclimate, increases wind speed and the possibilities of soil erosion, and alters the populations of beneficial insects, both predators and pollinators. In addition, the long-term flexibility of farm operations may be reduced. With the rising cost of creating stockproof field boundaries, a farmer who removed all his hedges some years ago may now find a return to stock impracticable. Secondly are the unforeseen effects whose significance can only be expressed in subjective opinions. New conifer plantations in an expanse of upland heather may reduce the population of golden eagle, raven, buzzard and red deer but in turn increase black grouse, hen harriers and roe deer. The significance of these side-effects must be based upon a personal view of the relative values of these species and this in turn may depend upon their frequency elsewhere. Finally, there are long-term implications for the landscape and for wildlife of a continued decline in the cover of hedges, woods and trees.

Removal of any of the components of a landscape, whether related to the topography or to the vegetation, will have some impact. In an area of marked contrasts of relief, the creation of an open landscape by the large-scale loss of hedges and trees probably does not reduce significantly the quality of that landscape although its character will change. In the flatter areas, however, where the majority of landscape changes are currently taking place, large-scale hedge and tree losses are having a serious visual consequence through the loss of vertical elements and the exposure of manmade 'intrusions' such as poles, wires and poorly designed buildings which in areas of greater relief would not appear so prominent.

Unlike components of the landscape which can be recreated, features of wildlife value, such as ancient (primary) woodland, cannot be replaced adequately by the establishment of new woodland. Rackham points out that secondary woodland may remain floristically impoverished for many centuries;[17] thus, it is important that as much as possible of the remaining area of primary woodland in lowland Britain, which includes many of the small woods, be preserved and appropriately managed.

Hedges represent an extension of the woodland-edge habitat into open country and are important for wildlife since they enable woodland species to survive in more open areas. Their total area is considerable. Based on the 1962 estimate of 616,000 miles[3] and assuming an average width of two yards, there are 436,000 acres of hedges in Britain, an area greater than all present national nature reserves. Caborn[18] considers that, from an ecological viewpoint, hedges should be viewed in relation to the total area of cover available for wildlife. Thus, their removal would be of lesser consequence in areas with a high proportion of the land under broadleaved woodland or scrub (such as Sussex) and of greater consequence in sparsely wooded areas (such as Lincolnshire).

The effects of hedgerow loss on plants are substantial. About 250 species occur frequently enough in hedges to be regarded as hedgerow plants and hedge removal would affect the total population of 20 species very seriously, a further 20 species quite seriously and another 30 to 40 species to a marked extent, possibly leading to the extinction of species in some counties.[19] The consequence for hedgerow fauna are even more severe. Moore[20] shows that a highly significant proportion of our total terrestrial species breed in hedges although none, or very few, are confined to them (Table 8). The species include those of open country, scrub and woodland (Table 9) and if hedges were

Table 8.   Distribution of fauna

Taxon	Total British lowland terrestrial species	Total breeding in hedges	Commonly breeding in hedges	Confined to hedges
Mammals (less bats)	28	21	14	0
Birds	91	65	23	0
Butterflies	54	23	15	0

Table 9.   Number of species breeding in hedges: total number of species from habitat type

Taxon	Open country	Scrub	Woodland
Mammals (less bats)	3 : 3	–	17 : 24
Birds	4 : 14	17 : 18	43 : 54
Butterflies	7 : 22	1 : 1	15 : 31

Tables 8 and 9 based on Moore, N. W. (1969). The Conservation of Animals. In Hooper, M. D. and Holdgate, M. W. (eds). *Hedges and Hedgerow Trees*, Proceedings of Monks Wood Experimental Station Symposium No. 4, pp. 53–57, The Nature Conservancy.

eliminated their populations would be greatly reduced. If destruction were to coincide with the loss of woodland or a large-scale change from hardwoods to conifers, much of our woodland fauna would be at risk. For many species, particularly birds, there is evidence that they can live at a higher density if only some of the hedgerows are removed. Thus, the important consideration is not the absolute mileage of hedge removed but the mileage expressed as a proportion of the total length of hedge in any area.[21] For example, five miles of hedge removed from an area containing twenty miles would be less serious for wildlife than the removal of five miles of hedge from an area containing only six miles.

PROSPECTS FOR CONSERVATION

Although there is some unanimity of view about the need to retain hedgerows and small woods, there is a conflict in objectives between individual conservationists: between those interested in birds and those in plants, between those interested in wildlife and others in landscape. There is conflict between all these and the economic land manager. The problems and the possibilities for conservation arise at two levels: in the local management of particular woods and hedgerows, and in the protection and creation of a network of cover across agricultural land.

Chapter 1 demonstrated that modern farming imposes limits upon the time and manpower available and skilled enough for traditional hedge maintenance. The comparative costs of hand and mechanical trimming are also significant: Caborn[18] in 1971 quoted £48 to £320 per mile for hand trimming as against £5 to £15 for mechanical trimming, while to cut and lay by hand would cost from £320 to perhaps £1120 per mile.

Machine cutting and the use of chemicals are often equivalent to removal in their destruction of wildlife habitats. The ideal hedge management regime for wildlife may well be to maintain an A-shaped cross-section and to lay the hedges periodically (perhaps every 15 years) in rotation to encourage vigorous growth. But such practices may be impractical in farming terms since the A-shaped hedge, because it tapers at the top, must be left taller to keep it stockproof.

Perhaps surprisingly, with mechanical trimming and periodic laying, the relative costs of hedge management to produce stockproof boundaries and of post and wire fencing are not dissimilar, with a slight advantage in favour of the hedge. The British Trust for Conservation Volunteers suggest the following figures:[22]

The costs of maintaining an existing mature hawthorn hedge
It is assumed that the hedge is laid at 15-year intervals and trimmed annually except for the first two years after laying and the three years prior to laying when it 'lies fallow'. This management regime may be taken as typical.

Item	£ per chain
Laying at years 1, 15, 30, 45 and 60 at £8.00	40.00
Trimming for a total of 40 years at £0.10 per year	4.00
Total cost after 60 years	£44.00

Pro-rated annual cost about 73p per chain

The costs of cattleproof fencing
It is assumed that the fence must be replaced at 20-year intervals. If sheep netting, rabbit netting etc, are added the cost is somewhat higher.

Item	£ per chain	
Erection (year 1)	15.00	
Annual maintenance	nil	
Replacement at years 20, 40 and 60 at £15.00	45.00	
Total cost after 60 years	£60.00	
Total cost after 80 years	£60.00	(before next replacement)

Pro-rated annual cost to the end of the fence's life at year 80 about 75p per chain.

While the hedge may be comparable in terms of maintenance costs, the fence provides considerable additional benefits in terms of convenience and flexibility and it is these factors above all others which are the main determinants of the future of the hedge in stock-rearing areas. In most arable areas hedges now have no function whatsoever.

But not all hedgerows are equally important from the conservation point of view. From a wildlife standpoint it may be desirable to define a minimum density of hedges to maintain viable populations of plants and animals. There would also be value in identifying the older hedges as conservation priorities, not only from an historical viewpoint but also since the older the hedge the greater appears to be its wildlife value, the number of plant species being directly related to age.[23] Westmacott and Worthington[24] have suggested that it is feasible for hedges, trees and shrubs to be retained or planted on the naturally or artificially unproductive areas of a farm, such as those slopes too steep to plough, and along the boundaries of ownership. Such features may also be retained or planted where they provide essential cover for game.

Since the significance of hedgerow loss varies with the total amount of vegetative cover in any area, the replacement of hedges by clumps of trees and shrubs may be an adequate substitute. However, many ecologists believe that the continuity of habitat which hedges provide may be essential to ensure migration of species and that clumps of woodland alone could not allow maximum diversity. In essence we are asking questions about the number and stability of populations of plants and animals in patches of habitat of different sizes. Are two trees twice as good as one? Is one large wood better than several small ones with the same total area? Does it matter if the trees and woods are far apart?

The general theory which covers this domain was put forward some years ago by two American scientists concerned with islands in the sea.[25] They assumed the number of species on an island is a balance between immigration and extinction. The smaller the island the higher the rate of extinction, and the nearer the source of immigrants the higher the rate of colonization. A small island near its source will have more species than a distant one, and a large island will have more species than a small one the same distance away from the source. An important corollary is that a small island will have a high turnover rate and will be in a greater state of flux than a large one.

These generalities can be translated directly into the woodland situation. A small wood will have fewer species than a large one and two woods will be better if they are close together rather than far apart. We can be more specific in terms of area: as a rule of thumb, to double the number of species in a wood the area must be increased tenfold. Even the nature of the species can be predicted from what is known of their dispersal powers and territorial behaviour. Naturally, there are ecological considerations as well as geographical ones: obviously, however large a broadleaved wood, it is unlikely to contain species dependent on conifers.

Such a combination of ecological and geographical theory might also be applied to fields. For example, the larger a field of wheat the more species it will contain but these species will be those that can survive in such a situation—indeed those best fitted to exploit the situation, that is the weeds and pests of wheat. This could mean an economic upper limit to field sizes and a preferred distance apart between two fields of the same crop, for essentially similar situations are already known in agriculture. Strains of vegetative crops are often bred far from their main growing areas for fear of disease and seed crops for certification must be grown away from possible contaminant pollen.

These ideas may also contribute to fresh views on the management of the landscape. The landscape has always been a mosaic of uses and it appears that a particular pattern of the mosaic probably has particular effects. Any outline plan for land should not be based on using one piece of land for several things at once but on juxtaposing the many uses in space and time, creating a mosaic rather than a plan for multi-purpose use.

The most limiting dimension of the woodland mosaic can therefore be seen to be not space but time. The broadleaved woods, beloved by conservationists, could be recreated but it would take time. The fewer and further apart the relicts, the greater the length of time it would take, even with efforts to facilitate colonization by introducing seed or vegetative propagules. It takes several centuries for plant species to colonize a new wood and therefore for a naturalist what exists now is of paramount importance. For those interested in landscape the time scale is much shorter, perhaps only 50 years. But what kind of accountant or politician plans for such a period?

NOTES AND REFERENCES

1. Forestry Commission (1952). *Census of Woodlands 1947–49: Woodlands of Five Acres and Over*, Forestry Commission Census Report No. 1, HMSO, London.
2. Forestry Commission (1953). *Hedgerow and Park Timber and Woods under Five Acres 1951*, Forestry Commission Census Report No. 2, HMSO, London.
3. Locke, G. M. L. (1962). A Sample Survey of Field and Other Boundaries in Great Britain. *Quarterly Journal of Forestry*, **56**, 137–144.
4. Pollard, E., Hooper, M. D. and Moore, N. W. (1974). *Hedges*, Collins, London.
5. Grant, J. (1844). Hedges and Enclosures of Devonshire. *Journal of the Royal Agricultural Society*, **5**, 420–428.
6. Forestry Commission (1970). *Census of Woodlands 1965–67*. HMSO, London. See in particular Chapter 12, Comparisons with Earlier Surveys.
7. Forestry Commission (1955). *Report of the Committee on Hedgerow and Farm Timber* (The Merthyr Committee Report), HMSO, London.
8. How they have changed can be stated only at a general level since although all have been surveyed, differences in sampling methods obscure fine details. The most coherent story can be told of the removal of hedges. There are three or four wide-scale surveys available: that done for the old Nature Conservancy (note 9), some data from the BTO Common Bird Census (note 10), and data in the *New Agricultural Landscapes* Report (note 11). These are supported by local studies such as Baird and Tarrant's (Norfolk) (note 12) and Cowie's (Yorkshire) (note 13).
9. Hooper, M. D. (1969). The Rates of Hedgerow Removal. In Hooper, M. D. and Holdgate, M. W. (eds.), *Hedges and Hedgerow Trees*, Proceedings of Monks Wood Experimental Station, Symposium No. 4, pp. 9–11, The Nature Conservancy. Additional survey information is described on pages 94–95.
10. Williamson, K. (1967). The Bird Community of Farmland. *Bird Study*, **14**(4), 210–226.
11. Westmacott, R. and Worthington, T. (1974). *New Agricultural Landscapes*, Chapter 3. Countryside Commission publication No. 76.
12. Baird, W. W. and Tarrant, J. R. (1973). *Hedgerow Destruction in Norfolk 1946–1970*. University of East Anglia, School of Environmental Studies.
13. Cowie, J. D. (1973). *Rates of Hedgerow Removal*. Research Group, Land's Arm, Ministry of Agriculture, Fisheries and Food, Leeds.
14. These variations in space and time make quoting rates somewhat hazardous—the time and place must always be specified and because of the differential distribution of hedges at the beginning it is always as well to quote rates in terms both of length of hedge removed and percentage loss. Two places, one in the west and one in the east, may both lose five miles of hedge—in the west this may be a seventh of the total, in the east it is more likely to be half.
15. The majority of the trees in the Warwickshire Study area were elms, which increase rapidly through suckering. Since the study elm disease has taken its toll in this county.
16. Peterken, G. F. and Harding, P. T. (1975). Woodland Conservation in Eastern England. *Bird Conservation*, **8**, 279–298.

17. Rackham, O. (1971). Historical Studies and Woodland Conservation. In Duffey, E. and Watt, A. S. (eds.), *The Scientific Management of Plant and Animal Communities for Conservation*. Proceedings of the 11th Symposium of the British Ecological Society, 563–580. Blackwell, Oxford.
18. Caborn, J. M. (1971). The Agronomic and Biological Significance of Hedgerows. *Outlook on Agriculture*, **6**(6), 279–284.
19. Hooper, M. D. (1969). The Conservation of Plants. In Hooper, M. D. and Holdgate, M. W. (eds.), *Hedges and Hedgerow Trees*, pp. 50–52.
20. Moore, N. W. (1969). The Conservation of Animals. In Hooper, M. D. and Holdgate, M. W. (eds.). *Hedges and Hedgerow Trees*, pp. 53–57.
21. Hooper, M. D. (1970). Hedges and Birds. *Birds*, **3**, 114–117.
22. British Trust for Conservation Volunteers Ltd (1975). *Hedging: A Practical Conservation Handbook*, pp. 21–22.
23. Hooper, M. D. (1970). Dating Hedges. *Area*, No. 4, 1970.
24. Westmacott, R. and Worthington, T. (1974). *New Agricultural Landscapes*, Chapter 8.
25. MacArthur, R. M. and Wilson, E. O. (1967). *The General Theory of Island Biogeography*. Princeton University Press, Princeton, New Jersey.

Chapter 4

Wetlands and agriculture

C. NEWBOLD

Wetlands have been arbitrarily defined as all areas of marsh, and all stretches of water, including coastal water, less than six metres deep, temporary or permanent, static or flowing.[1] Such areas have been exploited and modified by man for many centuries. Some have been drained to eradicate the breeding grounds of the malarial mosquito; peatlands were, and still are, a valuable source of fuel in many areas of the world; and farmers, attracted by the high fertility of the soil, have drained other wetland areas.

It is the demands for increased food production which continue to threaten the survival of many remaining wetlands. The nature reserves of the Carmargue and the Coto Donana will be fundamentally changed if crops such as rice are grown there. The Somerset Levels, drained many centuries ago, contain small fields often of poor agricultural quality divided by drainage channels which are of considerable scientific and biological interest. These dikes are relict sites giving some indication of the biological interest of the former wetland but, with the proposed improvements in drainage which will lower the water table, many will be filled in. Larger but far fewer dikes will continue to drain the area, and the biological interest must suffer. In other areas of Britain, drainage channels and water meadows are similarly threatened either by intensive management of the watercourses or by fertilizer application to the meadows.

The water meadow, of which a few still survive in England, has been a wetland type of particular agricultural significance. It makes use of subterranean water which, in chalk and limestone areas, wells up after winter rain to fill surface rivers. Coming from far underground, the water is at a higher temperature than the surrounding land. When flooded on to the meadow the water has two functions: it prevents frost and aerates the soil, thus encouraging an early spring flush of grass. Yet water meadows are no longer required by the modern farmer although they abound with herb-rich plants of considerable biological interest. The conflict of interest between, on the one hand, an increase in production for the farmer and, on the other, a biological interest with no economic gain means that many water meadows have been lost.

Paradoxically, the natural biological productivity of many wetland areas is considered to be as high or even higher than the most intensively farmed arable land. A farmer converts this potential into crops which are more easily marketable, but the management of wetlands for livestock, wildfowl, fish, timber, reed and even for fur can allow these naturally highly productive areas to yield crops of great benefit to man and with little modification of the environment. The amenity value of wetland areas is also being increasingly recognized, and although intensive recreation could disrupt their scientific interest, there is now greater potential for their protection. Despite increased awareness of the need to retain and manage wetlands for economic and amenity purposes, such areas continue to be lost to meet the demands of agriculture.

WILDLIFE VALUES

The biological interest of wetlands results from the numerous habitats available for wildlife. Some habitat types are distinct ecosystems, for example, certain kinds of raised bog. Others, like reedswamp or the littoral zone of a seashore, may be classified as 'ecotones' or transition environments separating two distinct ecosystems. All wetlands represent some stage in the active and directional process of plant succession and the following discussion looks at some of the major wetland habitats which are valued for their biological interest along the succession from open water, through fringing vegetation, marsh and fen, to woodland.

Open water

Some stretches of open water poor in nutrients (oligotrophic) may remain unchanged for centuries, but habitats can become artificially enriched, passing eventually to a nutrient-rich or eutrophic state. The main nutrients causing enrichment are nitrogen and phosphorus and these determine the level of plant growth or productivity of the water body. The input of external nutrients depends on land use within the catchment area: a mountain or moorland lake will generally be oligotrophic because the farmland surrounding it will be poor in nutrients. But modern fertilizers which enrich the run-off water may increase the nutrient status of water bodies; they could also change an acid lake into an alkaline one, thus causing a decline in acid-loving plant communities. A lake in lowland Britain is likely to be mesotrophic, eutrophic or highly eutrophic according to the land use and the amount of fertilizer applied to the soil. Farming practice can therefore alter substantially the character of a water body, although urban activities also affect even the most remote rural areas and it is often difficult to separate the two causes of nutrient enrichment.

Fringing vegetation

Plant communities which develop in wetlands depend partially upon the nutrient balance in the water, but also upon the degree of silting, the soil type, the shoreline pattern, and the distribution and flow of water. Open water becomes invaded by fringing vegetation as silting increases and a reed swamp may be produced which is the base upon which, according to soil type, marsh or fen vegetation develops.

Reed swamp is formed from the decay of such common plants as the reed (*Phragmites communis*) and tall grasses such as *Phalaris arundinacea*. A marsh can develop if the soil is either organic and mineral-poor (leading to an acid marsh) or inorganic and mineral-rich (forming an alkaline marsh). In marshland, the water table is below the soil surface during the summer although water movement may be apparent. Fen will develop if the soil is organic in nature, composed of alkaline peat and mineral-rich, and the water table is at the surface throughout the summer, although there may be little water movement. Common marsh plants are sedges, rushes, meadowsweet and species of *Sparganium*. Decay of the sedges can lead to the formation of an organic peat characteristic of a fen, but the sedge peat may be acid. Grasses such as *Molinia caerulea* and the shrub bog myrtle (*Myrica gale*) may colonize, to be followed later by ling (*Calluna vulgaris*), as the organic layers are built up above the water table. Alkaline fens develop rapidly when the saw sedge (*Cladium mariscus*) colonizes waterlogged reed swamp as it has in many of the fens of East Anglia where it has been used extensively for thatching. Continual cutting weakens the sedge and *Molinia caerulea* often enters the community. The litter from this type of fen has been cut and used by the fen farmers as bedding for cattle, so that both forms of fen have obviously been considerably modified by man.

Woodland

Accumulations of fen peat effectively lower the water table, and if this remains just below the surface at the wettest time of year (normally the winter) then woody plants can colonize, forming what is known as carr. Alder may dominate this stage of the succession, but if it is cleared a true 'mixed' fen develops which will contain rich and varied plant communities.

Salt marsh

Salt marsh represents yet another stage in a wetland succession as silt, trapped by vegetation, slowly reclaims land from the sea. Salt-loving plants can sometimes be found inland where salt concentrations are high. More commonly, salt marsh develops on inorganic muds and silts, between low water and the level of the highest spring tides. Sea grass (*Zostera nana*) and algae often dominate the lower zones, while *Salicornia* spp., the scrub *Halimione portulacoides* and the grass *Spartina anglica* are often found in the middle zone. The drier areas, where cattle and sheep grazing is possible, are often dominated by the grass *Festuca rubra*.

Wetlands in the uplands

Wetland types found in the uplands of Britain, such as blanket, raised and valley bogs, and wet heaths, generally develop acid-loving plant communities which differ greatly in their structure and origin from the fenland vegetation of lowland Britain.

A normally oceanic cool temperate climate with a high humidity provides ideal conditions for the development of the flat or hummocky blanket bogs common in the Pennines, Dartmoor, western Scotland and the west of Ireland. These bogs are dominated by *Sphagnum* spp. and other mosses, and by rough sedges. Raised bogs, most common in Ireland and west Scotland, develop under drier conditions than those associated with blanket bogs, but in a more humid climate than in the fenlands of East Anglia. They are topographical in origin, being built up from lakes which have disappeared through the development of fen peat, marsh or valley bog. Valley bogs, composed mainly of *Sphagnum* spp., develop where acidic water from streams and small rivers stagnates within hollows or shallow basins in valley bottoms. Although these bogs are again a characteristic of highland Britain, a few are found in lowland areas such as the New Forest. Wet heath communities, similar to those of the bogs, develop in the permanently wet zones of dry upland heath.

The fauna of wetlands

Greenshank and wood sandpiper nest on the marshes and bogs of montane Britain and dunlin and redshank on areas of wet heath. Coastal marshes and inland lakes are the preferred wintering and breeding areas of numerous wildfowl species and of waders, while the uncommon red-necked phalarope breeds in the Western Isles and western Ireland on the fringing vegetation of lake shores. The fens of eastern England with their once extensive reedbeds made the marsh harrier, bittern and bearded tit a common sight in the last century. Now these birds breed mainly in coastal marshes which are protected by conservation groups.

Many local or rare moths and butterflies are also found in wetlands but widespread drainage has led to the complete extinction of some species. For example, the drainage of the East Anglian fens, particularly Whittlesey Mere in the nineteenth century, resulted in the extinction of five species of moth.[2] The Large Copper butterfly, once locally abundant on many of the East Anglian fens, is also now extinct although a small population of an imported Dutch subspecies is maintained artificially at Woodwalton Fen National Nature Reserve through the efforts of the Nature Conservancy Council. The Swallowtail butterfly similarly must once have been locally abundant over the fens and broads of East Anglia; while not extinct, this species is now found only on the Norfolk Broads.

Wet zones on farmland

Just as water meadows have all but disappeared, so has the intensification of agricultural management extinguished the micro-wetlands once common on farms. Extension of field drainage, the ability to plough steeper and more uneven ground, and the wider use of pasture improvement methods has meant the removal of many ponds and ditches once valuable for stock watering, together with patches of marshy ground which are themselves remnants of more extensive wetlands. In those areas where stock have been replaced by arable farming, or where the grazing system is based upon the permanent housing of animals fed on grass cropped from improved pastures, wetlands are no longer needed as they are considered wasteful of land and costly to retain. Even if they are not deliberately extinguished on a particular holding, these micro-wetlands are difficult to maintain as the water table falls over surrounding agricultural land.

It is not easy to assess the wildlife values of these micro-wetland habitats of farmland. Some may contain valuable relict species of plants and animals once common on the fens and marshes of the region, while others may serve the purpose of ecological 'stepping stones' between existing larger water bodies. But the habitats are ecologically unstable. Drainage and irrigation can mean a damaging fluctuation of the water table while, if the areas escape drainage, their values may be threatened in other ways. For example, nutrients, mainly nitrogen, from fertilizer applications to adjoining land will run off into dikes and ponds, thus altering the nutrient balance; sewage, rich in phosphates from intensive dairy and pig farming, is often openly drained into farm watercourses; pesticide and herbicide run-off could affect plant production and photosynthesis; dumping of pesticide containers and any consequent leakage could mean locally high and lethal levels to many vertebrates, invertebrates and plants; the use of some molluscicides could affect plant growth on marsh systems; and direct applications of aquatic herbicides to keep drains free from 'weeds' all reduce the chance of survival of any relict flora and fauna. Plants more able to adapt to the changing environment and increasing artificiality of the habitat could easily replace any surviving relict species.

FORCES FOR CHANGE IN WETLANDS

Land drainage

In the early nineteenth century the Oxford clay scarp of southern Huntingdonshire was heavily wooded and some of these woods merged into the vast reed beds of Whittlesey Mere. In the summer, bittern would boom, marsh harriers would be seen silently quartering their hunting ground, while buzzards and red kites, both woodland species, would circle in the rising warm air currents along the scarp. Sparrowhawk and hobby, nesting in the woodland, would prey upon the tits and warblers in the reeds or, in the case of the hobby, the rich invertebrate fauna which must have existed. Wildfowl—gadwall, mallard, teal, pintail, shoveller, tufted duck and pochard—were also abundant; indeed Ramsey, a market town on the edge of the mere, was famous for the sale of wildfowl.

Most of the birds have now disappeared from this area. A number of wetland butterflies and moths are also now extinct with the exception of the Rosy Marsh moth rediscovered in Wales and the Swallowtail butterfly confined to the Broads. The loss of some of these species is undoubtedly due to shooting and to clearance of woodland but the disappearance of many species came about with the drainage of Whittlesey Mere in the mid-nineteenth century. Other fens in East Anglia suffered the same fate, and a flat, hedgeless, almost treeless, but highly fertile farmland remains.

Documented evidence of the drainage of wetlands appears to date from the Romans. Drainage continued in the following centuries as the major river valleys of the southeast of England were settled, but in the east of the country, including south Yorkshire, extensive drainage of the meres and fens was begun only in the seventeenth century.

Until the eighteenth century all drainage schemes relied on surface or field drains. Watercourses were straightened, dikes were dug, and the ridge and furrow pattern, formed during the middle ages through communal strip farming, was often retained because it facilitated surface run-off. By the 1840s tile drains could be manufactured cheaply and under-drainage then increased dramatically although with some decrease during and following the agricultural depression of the 1880s. It was not until 1941 that the rate of tile and mole drainage increased again, helped later by government grants of 50 per cent of the cost of schemes. The annual acreage of land drained has increased sixfold since 1950 (Figure 2 and Figure 7) and from 1969 to 1971 the increase in the number of tile drains laid is especially noticeable; Green attributes this not to greater general wetness of the climate but to an increase in relatively heavy rainfall over short periods of time.[3]

Under-drainage not only facilitates an increase in the rate of rainfall runoff but it is almost certainly a contributory cause of the lowering of the water table. Existing surface drainage channels—often sufficient to prevent flooding—have to be deepened to below the tile drain outlet. In eastern England, the drying up of many farm ponds can probably be attributed to the deepening of watercourses.

Administration of land drainage policy

There are about 101,000 miles of watercourses in Britain, including 2000 miles of canal, 19,000 miles of main river, 20,000 miles of smaller watercourses, and 60,000 miles (more than half the total) of private ditches, dikes and the smaller drains of agricultural land.

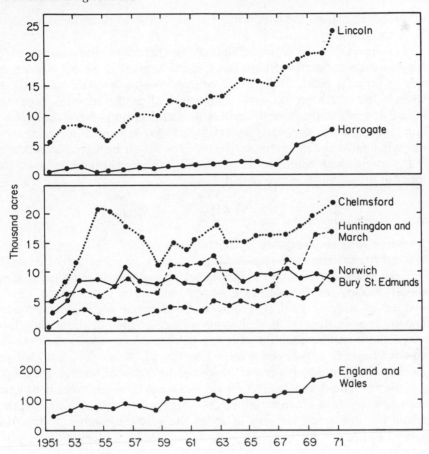

Figure 7. Progress in under-drainage. Area drained in each year. Figures for England and Wales and certain divisional areas of the Ministry of Agriculture. (Source: Green, F. H. W. (1973). Aspects of the Changing Environment: Some Factors Affecting the Aquatic Environment in Recent Years, *Journal of Environmental Management,* **1**, 377–391)

Weed control and the maintenance of riverside banks is now the responsibility of Regional Water Authorities and about 30 per cent of rivers are actively managed in this way. Smaller watercourses and private ditches are managed by 267 Internal Drainage Boards which exist where land drainage and flood prevention are particularly important. Landowners dominate representation on these Boards and voting strength depends upon the percentage of land owned.[4] The drainage policy of about 80,000 miles of waterway is thus, in large measure, the responsibility of farmers and other landowners. The Drainage Boards are completely autonomous: Water Authorities have the power to intervene only when pollution occurs or when any malpractice in management is apparent. The larger the landowner, the more dominant can be his effect on local drainage policy.

The decisions made by Internal Drainage Boards are of vital importance for the conservation of wetlands; but there are clearly other factors besides the needs of farming practice which are contributing to lowered water tables. Demands for water for all uses, domestic and industrial, are rising and abstraction from underground aquifers as well as from rivers could lower ground-water and surface-water levels still further. Farming itself is using more water in irrigation and for intensive livestock systems. It seems paradoxical that faced, perhaps, with future water shortages, farmers continue to give such priority to the under-drainage of their land.

Ecological implications of drainage

Drainage schemes can indirectly affect a large area. Even if an ecologically important area is not itself reclaimed, the 'sphere of influence' of drainage works can cause detrimental changes to water regimes. But the main effect obviously occurs on those areas of marsh and open water which will be converted to farming land. The only wetland remaining will be drainage channels. Species-richness as well as abundance of the aquatic flora will be affected: both will be reduced with the habitat effectively confined to the drainage channels and fewer species able to adjust to the new changed conditions. Perring[5] has attributed the loss of a number of flowering plants to the impact of land drainage (Table 10). The areas in which farming practice relies upon drainage schemes are largely confined to southern and eastern England but this is just the area in which the greatest number of flowering plants occur (Table 11).

Table 10.   Causes of decline of plant species

	Arable change	Ploughing	Drainage	Habitat destroyed	Collecting
Extinctions	1	0	4	4	2
Very rare	7	6	5	0	5
Rapid decline	3	4	7	0	0
Total	11 (15%)	10 (14%)	16 (22%)	4 (5%)	7 (9%)

	Forestry	No management	Natural causes	Total
Extinctions	1	0	8	20
Very rare	2	1	8	34
Rapid decline	3	0	3	20
Total	6 (8%)	1 (1%)	19 (26%)	74

Source: Perring, F. H. (1970). The Last Seventy Years. In Perring, F. H. (ed.) (1970). *The Flora of a Changing Britain,* Report of the Botanical Society of the British Isles, No. 11

Table 11. Geographical distribution of plant species in the British Isles

Plant group	North and west only	South and east only	Universal	Total
Pteridophytes	29	3	30	62
Gymnosperms	1	0	3	4
Angiosperms (flowering plants)	226	351	995	1572

Source: Woodman, M. (personal communication).

The persistence of a relict flora in a drainage channel appears to depend primarily on the height of the water table and this is dictated by the farmer. A high water table is found in the marsh grazing areas of Norfolk, Romney Marsh and the Somerset Levels and a low water table in arable areas such as the East Anglian fens. Marsh grazing areas still have many interesting plants and animals in the drainage channels, but arable areas often contain dikes dominated by reed (*Phragmites communis*), a plant which provides a poor environment for aquatic invertebrate populations. The survival of a relict flora on a modified wetland depends ultimately on the management of the drainage channels, which is discussed later in this chapter.

In all, the drainage of wetlands poses the greatest direct threat to their wildlife value but there are other indirect ways in which these areas can be damaged.

Fertilizers and their effects

Traditionally, farmers depended for improvements to soil fertility on the use of farmyard manure, leguminous crops, seaweed and, locally in the fens, fish. These, freshly caught from the dikes, were placed in rows and soil dug over them. However, since the beginning of this century, artificial fertilizers, particularly those containing nitrogen, potash and phosphates, have been used in increasing quantities. Although potash and phosphate fertilizer use has grown only slightly over the last 20 years, there has been a marked increase in the use of nitrogenous fertilizers over the same period (Figure 8). Under-drainage has increased the rate of rainfall run-off into drainage channels and this is correlated with increased fertilizer applications. The nutrient balance of many watercourses may have been drastically altered in this way.

Nitrogen

Any nitrogen which is applied to the land is subject to variable losses due to run-off. The amounts found in a drainage channel depend on several factors with soil type, land use, varying rates of fertilizer application, rainfall, soil water content, all affecting the rate of run-off. Furthermore, levels of nitrogen are affected by the intensity of urban development and the amount of sewage effluent discharged into rivers.

In rivers like the Great Ouse, which primarily drain agricultural land, run-off is the major source of inorganic nitrogen, and some dramatic increases in the nitrogen load of such rivers have occurred, usually following the springtime fertilizer application. Levels soon fall however. Conversely, in urbanized areas, such as the margins of the River Trent, effluents become the major source of inorganic nitrogen. Even so, the loads of nitrogen in 'urban' and 'agricultural' river systems have not increased significantly at any flow rate as a yearly mean over the last 20 years.[6] These yearly means make no distinction between the input from agricultural sources (including intensive animal husbandry) and urban sources, so that the impact of agriculture on water quality can rarely, if ever, be separated from the effects of the urban environment. On present evidence the normal nitrogen load in a river seems to be relatively independent of the quantity of fertilizer applied to the catchment. Owens et al.[7] estimated that inorganic nitrogen run-off in Britain increased on average from 9·0 to 12·6 kg/ha/year as the amount of nitrogenous fertilizer applied increased from 16 to about 100 kg/ha/year. Clearly, some 80 kg/ha/year of nitrogen is not finding its way into the watercourses. A large percentage will either be taken up by the plants or will be directly volatalized. Some will be utilized by bacteria and some will find its way into the ground water, but the relative amounts will be variable according to the crops, soil type and many other factors. Run-off, for example, is known to be dependent on land use. Owens found that the mean quantities of nitrogen derived from arable, grassland and rough grazing within different counties were 13, 8 and 4 kg/ha respectively. This suggests that intensive arable areas will have a higher nitrogen level in their watercourses than those of intensively farmed grassland areas.

In general, fertilizer run-off seems less important as a source of nitrate pollution compared with the large amount released from industrial or urban sewage effluent. It is more probable that many of the problems of eutrophication and algal blooms stem from this source of nitrogen, except in very intensively farmed arable areas of low population density such as the East Anglian fens, and in grassland and rough pasture areas such as Wales and Scotland.

Nitrogen levels in ground water

The levels of nitrogen found in ground water are now exceptionally high. Untreated water can cause diseases such as methaemoglobinimea but thorough treatment reduces the level of nitrogen to acceptable limits. The source of this nitrogen pollution in rural areas is almost certainly modern agriculture. Increase in the level of fertilizer applications can be correlated with the increase in nitrogen in ground water, but a major source of excess nitrogen arises from the creation of arable land from grassland. The nitrogen in the soil becomes mineralized by aeration and inorganic nitrate leaches down into the ground water. The exact contribution artificial fertilizers have made to groundwater levels is not known.

Phosphorus

Phosphate usage has doubled in the last 20 years, but phosphate, unlike nitrogen, binds to the organic matter in the soil with only small amounts leaching out into watercourses and the high phosphate levels in our rivers arise largely from urban sewage outfalls. Silage effluents and intensive animal husbandry effluents in non-urban areas, with their often poor sewage disposal facilities, will make a significant but only local contribution to the phosphate load in a river.

Again it seems that modern agricultural practice is not as detrimental to the biological interest of an area as are the effects of the urban environment.

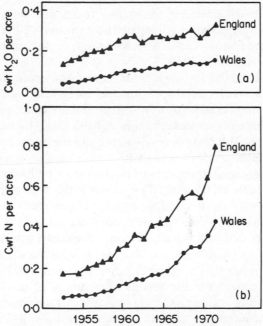

Figure 8. Growth in rate of fertilizer application. (a) Hundredweights of potash applied per acre under crops and grass. (b) Hundredweights of nitrogen applied per acre under crops and grass. (Source: Green, F. H. W. (1973). Aspects of the Changing Environment: Some Factors Affecting the Aquatic Environment in Recent Years, *Journal of Environmental Management*, **1**, 377–391)

Unfortunately it is not possible, even in remote areas like Scotland and Wales, to isolate the effects of agriculture. Caravanning, camping and the necessary service facilities in these remote areas, all confuse any relationship between agricultural practice and nutrient levels in water. What is clear, however, is that the amounts of phosphorus and nitrate required to bring about a gross and detrimental biological change are small. According to one classification of waters ranging from ultra oligotrophic to polytrophic (a polluted water) the phosphorus levels only need to increase from 0·005 to 0·10 mg/litre and the nitrogen levels from 0·2 to 1·5 mg/litre to cause such a change.[8] Such an increase is possible from agricultural pollution but there is no evidence to support any biological change solely attributable to this source.

Wetland management

Insecticide effects

It is extremely difficult to quantify the effects of run-off containing agricultural pesticides and herbicides on aquatic fauna and flora although some research has investigated the effects of the high use of the organochlorine chemicals DDT, aldrin and dieldrin[9] before the voluntary restrictions imposed after the Wilson Report in 1969.[10]

Pesticides and herbicides may enter rivers and watercourses indirectly through rain, inaccurate aerial spraying and spray drift, surface run-off, and from sewage and industrial wastes. In agricultural areas surface run-off used to be considered the most important source of the DDT found in the water of many British rivers. But DDT is very volatile and the greater proportion left in the soil after application will be lost to the air so that, excluding industrial wastes and sewage, rainfall appears to be the major pathway for DDT and its breakdown products DDD and DDE to enter the water of a river system. Other pesticides may act in a similar manner. In one study, dieldrin could not be detected in the muds of many Huntingdonshire ponds even though adjacent fields had been treated with the compound.[11] Similarly, Edwards *et al.*[12] could detect only small amounts in the muds of two ponds even when the application rate was 10–20 times that of normal farming practice and dieldrin was not detected in the water. Yet the results of a survey of pesticide residues in samples of fish, water and mud from six agricultural rivers in southeast England showed that the concentrations were approximately 50 ng/litre[13] for dieldrin, DDT and γ-BHC.[14] High peaks of 170 ng/litre were occasionally detected but these were attributed to accidental discharges. Generally these concentrations were considerably lower than those detected by a previous survey in 1965–66,[15] which may reflect the voluntary restrictions on use after 1969.

Much greater contamination of rivers results from some industrial processes, such as moth-proofing, which can give concentrations of dieldrin or γ-BHC in excess of 500 ng/litre.[16] In agricultural areas where the maximum level of 170 ng/litre for DDT, dieldrin and γ-BHC has been detected, ecological effects on wetlands are likely to be minimal. It is only in areas where industry and agriculture mix that pesticide residues could exert some ecological effect on wetland sites.

The ecological effects of the high contamination levels that are found in some industrial rivers are not fully known but it is very likely that even one of the most sensitive of British fish, the rainbow trout (*Salmo gairdnerii*), would be unaffected. Owens[15] suggested that levels between 1000 and 10,000 ng/litre of either DDT or dieldrin maintained for three months would be required before these chemicals would be lethal to trout, and γ-BHC has a similar toxicity. Possibly the greatest ecological effects may occur through the algae. Wurster[17] showed that concentrations of DDT in excess of 10,000 ng/litre inhibited photosynthesis in several kinds of marine algae, while concentrations of only 300 ng/litre inhibited growth and induced morphological changes in the very common fresh water alga *Chlorella*.[18] In these studies the pesticide was concentrated by the algae with transference from one food organism to another. Moriarty,[19] however, considers that food plays a minor role in determining the sublethal levels found in fish; direct uptake of the pesticide from the water is thought to be the major pathway here. Even so, the low breeding success of herons (*Ardea cinerea*) has been attributed to organo-chlorine residues accumulating in the bird through an aquatic food-chain effect.[20]

Organophosphorus compounds do not persist in water for more than a few weeks and pesticide and herbicide residues in water from applications to the land often cannot be detected. These compounds are likely to exert no permanent effect on aquatic plants and animals. However, the increasing use of highly toxic carbamate compounds in agriculture means that an indirect application from spray drift to a watercourse could have short-term lethal effects on the fauna.

With all pesticides there is always the chance of an accident. Locally high levels of any pesticide often result in fish deaths and can cause a great deal of damage to wetlands. The dumping of old pesticide containers is potentially as dangerous as the accidental spillage since these containers slowly rust and small perforations in the drum could mean that high concentrations are released over a long period of time.

Alkyl-mercury-dressed seed was also used by farmers during the mid-to-late 1960s but use has declined since harmful environmental effects were reported from Sweden,[21] although mercury is still used for bulb dips in the Spalding area of East Anglia. There is no information on background mercury levels in the water of British rivers but Parslow[22] has shown that wading birds, such as the knot (*Calidris canutus*) can accumulate mercury 10–20 times above their normal liver load of 1 mg/litre whilst overwintering on the Wash.

Molluscicide effects

Molluscicides are the first group of chemicals to be considered which are applied directly to wetlands. Rough pasture and wetlands in the northern and western regions of the British Isles are areas where there is often a high incidence of liver fluke infestation in sheep and cattle; molluscicides are used to eradicate the aquatic snail *Lymnaea truncatula* which is the intermediate host for the liver fluke *Fasciola hepatica*.

Copper sulphate was at one time the only suitable molluscicide but it has several undesirable effects. As the normal treatment level is 30 mg/litre for snail control any surface run-off from wet pastures to lakes and streams would be at possibly toxic levels to many plants and animals including zooplankton, insect larvae and fish. One study, for example, found that *Daphnia* were completely eliminated after 10 days with a dose rate of 20 mg/litre.[23] Copper sulphate has also been used for other purposes. As a fungicide it was used to control bunt in wheat but it caused damage to the seed so that germination as well as plant vigour could be affected when a rough pasture was treated. The toxic part of the compound is the cupric ion, and any excess of copper causes necrosis, wilting, reduced growth and the eventual death of plants, especially those which are narrowleaved. In this way copper sulphate could affect the survival of many wetland plants. It is also active in water as an algicide at the low dose of 1 mg/litre. Copper sulphate has a high toxicity for fish (especially rainbow trout)[24] and has been used as a piscicide. It is more toxic in acid waters and the compound is most likely to be used on the acid soils and water of upland pastures where liver fluke infestation is common. Copper sulphate, used as a molluscicide, presents a real threat to the survival of the flora and fauna of wetland sites. Fortunately, it is not used as extensively as it was, mainly because it has been superseded by the molluscicide trifenmorph.

Trifenmorph controls two aquatic snails: *Lymnaea truncatula* and *L. pereger*. Plants and fungi appear to be unaffected by treatment and there is no evidence to suggest that trifenmorph is toxic to the aquatic invertebrate fauna, other than snails. The chemical is not persistent so that the impact of trifenmorph on wetland habitats is probably slight. Even so, any species dependent on snails for food are likely to be affected. A study on Shapinsay Island in the Orkneys where trifenmorph is used is being undertaken by Aberdeen University so see what effects the virtual elimination of *L. truncatula* has on the diet of seabirds and other species. Snails also eat algae but whether adjustments are made in the ecosystem by other herbivores to compensate for this loss is simply not known.

Effects of management techniques on relict wetland sites

Just as drainage poses the greatest threat to a 'natural' or unmodified wetland so adverse mechanical methods and most aquatic herbicides pose the greatest threat to the survival of any relict flora existing in the drainage channels.

Over three-quarters of our waterways, many of which contain a relict wetland flora and fauna, are actively managed by Water Authorities and Internal Drainage Boards. Part of the management programme, to maintain water supplies or to prevent flooding, involves the control of weeds where their growth displaces water or obstructs the flow. In the past, aquatic weeds were cut by hand but cutting stimulates more growth and therefore the operation often had to be carried out twice a year.[25] The decline of cheap labour has meant that several machines have been developed to speed up weed cutting. Boats with rakes, V- and U-shaped cutting blades, and dredgers have all been used, but herbicides have replaced mechanical methods where access is difficult.

In 1972, £$3\frac{1}{2}$m were spent by River Authorities and Internal Drainage Boards on cutting weeds. A further £$2\frac{1}{2}$m were spent by farmers. In the same year £800,000 were spent by River Authorities and Internal Drainage Boards on chemical weed control, with almost £2m spent by farmers. Farmers, therefore, spent almost as much on the chemical control of aquatic weeds as they did on cutting methods. Herbicides offer certain advantages to the farmer over manual and mechanical methods. They usually save on labour costs although this can often be offset by the high initial cost of the chemicals. Some herbicides control weed growth for several seasons, and some are highly selective, leaving certain weeds unaffected. Little is known of the ecological effects of mechanical methods and herbicides upon wetland habitats, but recent research suggests that ecological change may take place on a scale paralleled only by the effects of drainage.[26]

Intensive and extensive use of mechanical methods of weed control on drainage channels affect the flora and hence the wildlife in two major ways. The *intensive* use of a dragline or excavator, particularly if the interval of clearance is three years or less, eventually causes a decline in the numbers and species of aquatic plants: only the most vigorous may survive. The *extensive* use of a dragline or excavator reduces the sites from which recolonization might occur. If the nature conservation interest of a site is to be maintained then clearance must be reduced to a five to seven year interval.[27] Indeed, accepting that correct management is essential for maximum nature conservation interest, then this time interval is of benefit as it limits the cycle of hydroseral development to the most biologically interesting and diverse stages. However, one further condition of management is essential: the drainage channels must be cleared on a 'chequerboard' pattern in time and space rather than clearing all dikes in the same year so that sites of recolonization are not lost.

Any drainage scheme relies on water being fed out to the sea, and rivers small and large form an essential part of the system. The flora and fauna of a river are just as adversely affected by management techniques which are too intensive or too extensive. A river improvement scheme instigated by a Water

Authority is often no more than the canalization of a once attractive and functional river. Pollarded willows were planted alongside small rivers for two main reasons: they shade the water, thus preventing excessive weed growth, and their roots stabilize the bank; both conditions are necessary for a continuous flow. In Lincolnshire, where many small rivers have been canalized and the willows have disappeared, weed growth and bank erosion now require costly maintenance and the landscape has changed beyond all recognition. Paradoxically, canalization does not eliminate occasional flooding; it merely reduces the frequency.

Herbicide effects

Herbicides can be divided into two groups: selective and total.[28] Both types can be divided further into contact herbicides and translocated herbicides according to the 'mode of action'. By the end of 1975, eleven herbicides had been cleared under the Pesticide Safety Precaution Scheme.[10] The chemicals commonly used for fringing bankside vegetation are 2,4-D (amine salt), maleic hydrazide, dalapon, and dalapon with paraquat. Those cleared for use in water are chlorthiamid, dichlobenil, diquat, dalapon, dalapon with paraquat, terbutryne, asulam, glyphosate, and cyanatryn.

Aquatic herbicides are almost a subject in themselves but two review papers adequately summarize the state of our knowledge on these chemicals.[26,29] The two main requirements for research are a need to understand both the short-term ecological effects caused by herbicides (Figure 9) as well as their long-term ecological effects. The short-term effects are well-documented for some but not all herbicides, but the long-term effects are less well-known for any herbicide. The main differences between mechanical methods and herbicide treatment stem from these possible long-term effects on the dike flora and from fundamental differences in the technique of weed clearance.

Herbicides can only be applied in the spring, otherwise an excessive depletion of oxygen occurs. However, springtime application destroys habitat, food and cover for the many aquatic animals at a period which is critical to the viability of species because this is the time when production is most active. Herbicides are easily applied, so an area can be covered in a matter of days which would take many weeks to clear with more traditional methods. Habitat destruction from large-scale applications of herbicides can produce enormous changes in the ecology of whole areas and sites from which recolonization might occur are consequently lost. Most herbicides restrict the regrowth of the original flora because of the length of the phytotoxic period. Non-susceptible or resistant species can colonize the vacant habitat, which means that the original aquatic flora has little chance of regrowing. Thus, many dike floras are becoming grossly simplified and algae seem to dominate after many treatments. Algae are a poor habitat for aquatic animals.

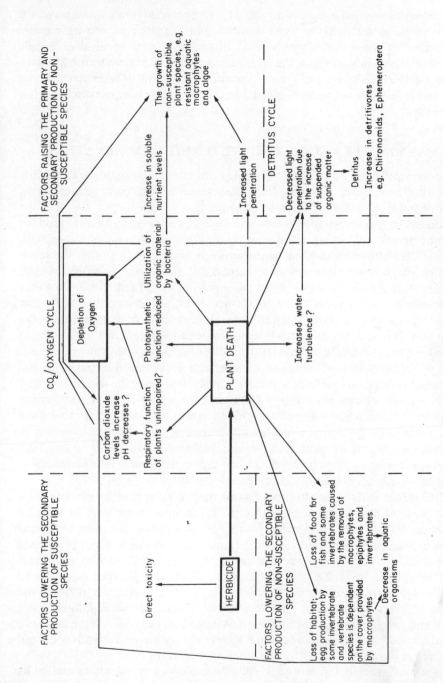

Figure 9. A schematic representation of possible ecological effects of herbicides

In conclusion, most aquatic sites could be safeguarded by a less intensive use of mechanical methods of weed control and a restricted use of aquatic herbicides in those areas which make them necessary because of access problems. Even in such areas, the code of practice as laid down by the Ministry of Agriculture Fisheries and Food[30] should be followed. It recommends that 400-metre lengths are treated, alternating with similar lengths which are left untreated.

FARMING PRACTICE AND WETLAND CONSERVATION

Conservation can be seen as the management of habitats towards specific aims with the intention of maintaining their scientific interest or rehabilitating their physical, chemical or biological quality.[31]

Conservation interests in wetlands are obviously affected by much in modern farming practice. Wetlands are one of the few groups of habitats where, with present agricultural methods, a compromise situation rarely exists. Wetlands require a high water table and waterlogged soil during one or more seasons; arable farming requires a low water table, and pasture land requires a water table at or below but never above the surface. For plant communities to remain unaltered, unpolluted water and nutrient stability (within acceptable limits) are necessary. It is not only farmers who cause water enrichment by their methods; areas such as the Norfolk Broads are probably affected more by sewage effluent than by fertilizer run-off. The ecological effects on wetlands of pesticide and herbicide residues are difficult to quantify, mainly because the industrial rivers of this country which carry levels of DDT, dieldrin, and γ-BHC high enough to exert an effect, are also polluted with many other chemicals. These rivers are simply not clean enough to allow the effects of one pollutant to be identified. Direct applications of molluscicides and herbicides will have varying, but generally damaging, ecological effects, but drainage, because of all its implications to a wetland, is the greatest threat.

If the larger wetlands are to survive at all, then farming practice in some areas must be modified to suit these habitats. Traditional crops may have to be forsaken, though cattle and sheep grazing could be tolerated in certain areas provided that the water table remained high and occasional flooding was not prevented; there are many breeds of cattle and sheep well adapted to producing high yields from the roughest sedges. The Ouse Washes Reserves in Cambridgeshire, owned by the Royal Society for the Protection of Birds, the Cambridgeshire and Isle of Ely Naturalists' Trust and the Wildfowl Trust, allow and even encourage such a policy. Wildfowl on the non-reserve areas are killed for sport but there is no reason why other much larger wetlands could not produce controlled yields of timber, reed and even fur.

On a smaller scale, farmers could help to conserve any relict flora and fauna of the modified and marginal wetlands remaining on agricultural land. Most dikes, ponds, ditches and even the persistent marsh probably contain some interesting plants and animals worth conserving. Preventing pollutants entering these habitats, keeping within the code of practice as set down by the Ministry of Agriculture for pesticides, and using mechanical methods wherever possible for dike management but with a sufficient time interval between clearance, will all aid the survival of species in these artificial but nevertheless important habitats. Farmers could also play a more active part in recreating those small wetland habitats, such as dikes and ponds, which have dried up, and retaining, rather than filling in, those which have fallen into disuse. These areas should be managed, by cutting their vegetation and leaving areas of open water, to maintain their interest as examples of previously common wetland types.

Conservation bodies cannot hope to purchase all the remaining wetlands before they disappear for ever. The retention of those which are more extensive, as well as the microwetland habitats of agricultural land, depends fundamentally upon the attitudes of Internal Drainage Boards and farmers. One solution which has been applied in Denmark is to devise an integrated policy, serving the needs of both the conservationist and of the farmer, whereby the farmer modifies his methods in areas of high scientific interest, but conservationists tolerate some commercial exploitation. Only by compromises such as this can there be any future for our remaining wetlands.

NOTES AND REFERENCES

1. Hoffman, L. (1968). *Project Mar.* Proceedings of Technical Meeting of the International Union for the Conservation of Nature and Natural Resources No. 12, pp. 36–50.
2. Bretherton, R. F. (1951). Our Lost Butterflies and Moths. *Entomologist's Gazette*, **2**, 211–240.
   The five species are: the Many Lined (*Euphyia polygrammata*), the Gypsy Moth (*Lymantria dispar*), the Orache Moth (*Trachea atriplicis*), the Grisette (*Apatele strigosa*) and the Reed Tussock (*Laelia caenosa*).
3. Green, F. H. W. (1973). Aspects of the Changing Environment: Some Factors Affecting the Aquatic Environment in Recent Years. *Journal of Environmental Management*, **1**, 377–391.
4. The person seeking election to an Internal Drainage Board is registered and the ratepayers of that district are the electorate. The tenure is for three years and a representative, after that period, must seek re-election. The minimum landholding required to qualify as a candidate varies according to the drainage act in force for that area. Most Boards also elect non-landowning representatives from the ratepayers.
5. Perring, F. H. (1970). The Last Seventy Years. In Perring, F. H. (ed.), *The Flora of a Changing Britain*, Report of the Botanical Society of the British Isles, No. 11.
6. Tomlinson, T. E. (1970). Trends in Nitrate Concentrations in English Rivers in Relation to Fertilizer Use. *Water Treatment and Examination*, **19**, 277–293.
7. Owens, M., Garland, J. H. N., Hart, I. C. and Wood, G. (1972). *Nutrient Budgets in Rivers.* Symposium of the Zoological Society of London, No. 29, pp. 21–40.

8. Vollenwieder, R. A. (1968). *Scientific Fundamentals of the Eutrophication of Lakes and Flowing Waters with particular reference to Nitrogen and Phosphorus as factors in Eutrophication.* Organization for Economic Co-operation and Development, Water Management Research Group, Report No. 159.

9. During the period 1962–64, an average of 249 tons of DDT/ha were used in agriculture and horticulture. The quantity of aldrin and dieldrin used for field treatments and transplanting dips for the same period was 148 tons. Only one-tenth of this amount was used on fruit crops. Source: Strickland, A. H. (1965). Some Estimates of Insecticide and Fungicide Usage in Agriculture and Horticulture in England and Wales, 1960–1964. *Journal of Applied Ecology*, No. 3 (Supplement), 3–14.

10. A voluntary 'Pesticide Safety Precautions Scheme' was introduced in 1954 under which industry co-operates with government to ensure that any new chemical passes certain tests relating to: mutagenic and carcinogenic effects; toxicity effects on plants or animals; hazards to users, and to consumers if the plants are edible; and, particularly with aquatic herbicides, the effective life of the chemical in water. The Wilson Report reviewed the wildlife implications of pesticides first approved under the Pesticides Safety Precautions Scheme in the late 1950s and early 1960s before the potential danger of pesticides to wildlife was appreciated.
    Wilson, A. (1969). *Further Review of Certain Persistent Organochlorine Pesticides Used in Great Britain.* Department of Education and Science.

11. Jefferies and French (personal communication).

12. Edwards, C. A., Thompson, A. R., Benyon, K. I. and Edwards, M. J. (1970). Movement of Dieldrin through Soils: I. From Arable Soils into Ponds. *Pesticide Science*, **1**, 169–173.

13. ng/litre = 1×10^{-9} mg/litre.

14. γ-BHC = benzenehexachloride.

15. Owens, M. (1971). Chemical and Pesticide Pollution. In *Water Pollution as a World Problem*, Europa, London, pp. 1–10.

16. Croll, B. T. (1969). Organochlorine Insecticides in Water: Part I. *Water Treatment and Examination*, **18**, 225–274; and Lowden, G. F., Saunders, C. L. and Edwards, R. W. (1969). Organochlorine Insecticides in Water: Part II. *Water Treatment and Examination*, **18**, 275–287.

17. Wurster, C. F. (1968). DDT reduces Photosynthesis by Marine Phytoplankton. *Science New York*, **159**, 1474–1475.

18. Sodergren, A. (1968). Uptake and Accumulation of C^{14} DDT by *Chlorella*. *Oikos*, **19**, 126–138.

19. Moriarty, F. (1972). The Effects of Pesticides on Wildlife: Exposure and Residues. *Science of the Total Environment*, **1**, 267–288.

20. Prestt, I. (1969). *Organochlorine Pollution of Rivers and the Heron (Ardea cinerea L).* Report of the Technical Meeting of the International Union for the Conservation of Nature and Natural Resources, 1969, Section B, p. 95.

21. Bengf, W., Johnels, A., Sjostrand, B., and Westermark, T. (1966). Mercury Content in Feathers of Swedish Birds from the past 100 years. *Oikos*, **17**, 71.

22. Parslow, J. L. F. (1973). Mercury in Waders from the Wash. *Environmental Pollution*, **5**, 295–304.

23. Shiff, C. J. and Garnet, B. (1961). The Short-term Effects of Three Molluscicides on the Microflora and Microfauna of Small Biologically Stable Ponds in Southern Rhodesia. *Bulletin of the World Health Organization*, **25**, 543–547.

24. The 48-hour LC_{50} (lethal concentration killing 50 per cent of the population) on rainbow trout for the active cupric ion is $0 \cdot 14$ ppm at a pH of $6 \cdot 5$ and $7 \cdot 5$. Other species of fish are not so sensitive but they are equally susceptible when the acceptable dose rate as a molluscicide is 30 ppm.

25. Bailey, T. A. (1965). *Commercial Possibilities of Dehydrated Aquatic Plants.* Proceedings of the 18th Weed Control Conference, pp. 543–551.
26. Newbold, C. (1975). Herbicides in Aquatic Systems. *Biological Conservation*, No. 7, 97–118.
27. George, M. (1975). *Mechanical Methods of Weed Control in Watercourses; An Ecologist's View.* British Crop Protection Council Seminar on Aquatic Weeds (in press).
28. Robson, T. O. (1973). *The Control of Aquatic Weeds.* Ministry of Agriculture Bulletin, 194, 2nd Edition, HMSO, London.
29. Brooker, M. P., Edwards, R. W. (1975). Review Paper on Aquatic Herbicides and the control of Water Weeds. *Water Research*, **9**, 1–15.
30. Ministry of Agriculture, Fisheries and Food (1975). *Code of practice for the use of herbicides on weeds in watercourses and lakes.*
31. Morgan, N. C. (1972). *Problems of the Conservations of Freshwater Ecosystems.* 29th Symposium of the Zoological Society of London, pp. 135–154.

Chapter 5

Lowland grasslands

D. I. Brotherton

One of the characteristic features of the British scene is a predominantly pastoral character, brought about largely by sheep rearing that has taken place in Britain since Neolithic times some 4000 years ago. The creation of grassland for sheep pasture was achieved by felling and clearing the forest which once covered almost the whole of the southern lowlands. Initially, the purpose may have been to obtain timber for construction, fires and tools but later, in response to the developing export trade in wool and cloth, land was cleared specifically to make room for more sheep and cattle. Sheep, and to a lesser extent, cattle rearing were pursued side-by-side with corn-growing. When corn prices were high grassland was ploughed and when the wool and cloth industries prospered land was returned to grass.

The First World War provided only a temporary check to a trend in which permanent grassland was becoming increasingly dominant in the agricultural scene. But with the Second World War and an acute demand for homegrown food a great deal of permanent pasture was converted to arable land. Since then the maintenance of a prosperous and efficient home agriculture has been a major item of government policy and the wartime increase in arable land has been largely maintained and increased in the east and the midlands, although pasture still dominates in the west. The emphasis on permanent pasture and rough grazing in western counties and in Wales is determined largely by rainfall. In the dryer areas of eastern England, where there are few hills and no land is over 1000 feet, the percentage of agricultural land occupied by permanent grasslands is low, in some areas as little as 5 per cent. Taking the whole of the United Kingdom, however, 61 per cent of the total agricultural area is currently classified as permanent grass or rough grazing.[1,2]

Despite market fluctuations and technical innovations since the war, much of lowland England still retains a predominantly pastoral character. This comprises extensive areas of enclosed fields (the permanent grasslands that are frequently manured and maintained for pasture or hay), unenclosed commons, downs and dunes, lowland heaths and rough marsh pastures. This character is determined by two factors.[3] Firstly, the oceanic climate of the British Isles with its normally cool summers, well-distributed rainfall and almost constant supply of moist air, is well-suited to the growth of grass. Secondly, most grasses

81

increase vegetatively from the base so that pasturing or mowing encourages their dominance at the expense of many of the herbs. Typically, the growth buds of grasses remain close to the ground and so escape destruction when herbage is cropped by grazing animals or cut with the scythe or by machine. Grasses can, therefore, withstand repeated grazing and treading by stock, whilst these same factors prevent the successful establishment of taller-growing, broadleaved plants. In this way, a succession through scrub to woodland is arrested. Except where soil depth, extreme exposure or some other environmental factor prevents the growth of taller plants, grassland is maintained because of grazing. Without grazing, there would be very little grassland in Britain, only scrub and forest. Sheep and cattle have been the main grazing agents, although horses and other domestic animals may have had a significant effect locally. Certain wild herbivores have also influenced the semi-natural vegetation to a marked degree, particularly on marginal land, and of these by far the most important is the rabbit.[4]

In addition to market requirements and climatic conditions, soil factors are also of importance in determining the most appropriate form of agriculture in a particular situation. The nature of the soil and its water regime, both of which may be subject to 'improvement' by the farmer, affect the structure and composition of the grassland and its associated fauna. The effect of seed mixture may also be evident, particularly during the early life of sown grass-lands, but as time progresses the vegetation will increasingly reflect, and be determined by, the prevailing edaphic and climatic conditions and by the use to which the area is put and its management. Evidence shows that a change in manuring to affect nutrient availabilities, or a change in grazing regime (altering, for example, the stocking density, the timing of grazing or the kind of animal) can cause dramatic changes in the presence and abundance of the species in grassland.[5] In considering the characteristics of the major lowland grassland types, soil, climate and the history of use are all relevant.

THE CHARACTER AND DISTRIBUTION OF MAJOR LOWLAND GRASSLANDS

The detailed species composition of an area of grassland is affected by many physical, chemical and biotic factors[6] but grasslands in Britain may be divided conveniently into three main groups—calcareous, neutral and acidic—depending on the pH of the soil.[7] Further subdivisions within these three major groups are achieved by considering other soil factors (particularly soil moisture content) and the history of use.

Calcareous grasslands are formed on soils derived from rocks largely composed of calcium carbonate. These soils are constantly saturated with an alkaline solution of lime since calcium carbonate is soluble in rainwater bearing CO_2 in solution. The presence of calcium in adequate quantity and appropriate form neutralizes the acids which are constantly liberated by decomposing plant material and in consequence calcareous soils have a high pH (greater than 7). The insoluble mineral particles of the parent rock are present in corresponding amounts in the derived soil, which tends to be thin, and because of this and the permeability of the underlying rock—also dry. In the main, the calcareous grasslands overlie the Cretaceous chalk and form the rolling downlands of southern England. Other important areas of calcareous grassland occur on the oolitic limestones stretching from Dorset to Lincolnshire.

Calcareous grassland forms the largest area of rough grazing in the south of England with around 100,000 acres on the chalk.[8] Traditionally this is sheep pasture, although in the present century sheep flocks have been very much reduced and partly replaced by cattle. The attractiveness of calcareous grassland lies in the springiness of the well-cropped and much interwoven turf that is a delight to the walker, and in the great variety of herbs. The plant communities of the shallow soils are amongst the richest in the country with as many as 40 species of flowering plants to the square metre. Although many species occur indifferently in grasslands, the distinctiveness of calcareous grassland arises partly from the considerable number of very constant species (examples include wild thyme, salad burnet and stemless thistle) and partly from the few strict calcicoles which occur very rarely elsewhere (for example, squinancy wort, rampion and horseshoe vetch).

Acidic grasslands are found on soils at the lower end of the pH scale and in lowland England this group is mainly represented by grass heath on sandy soils. These soils contrast markedly with the shallow calcareous soils in terms of acidity but show similarities in other respects. Sandy soils consist of relatively large particles, usually of silica, with pockets of air between, so that the soil's capacity to retain water is low. Dry sandy soils are often also relatively shallow and their generally low nutrient status provides another similarity with the soils of the chalk.[9] Over considerable areas, these dry, acid, sandy soils have been ploughed and improved for arable cropping, although the semi-natural vegetation cover is still found, for example, on the commons of Surrey, Berkshire and Dorset and in the Breckland of Suffolk and Norfolk. The vegetation comprises either a species-poor open grassland community of sheep's fescue, common bent and wavy hair grass interspersed with calcifuge (acid-loving) herbs; or a heathland community, dominated by ling.[7] The floristic poverty of these habitats contrasts markedly with the richness of calcareous grassland.[10]

The distribution of these two vegetation types of acid soils is typically moderated by grazing, which converts heath into grassland, this in turn being invaded by dwarf shrubs in the absence of grazing.[11] The sandy commons have a poor pasture value and a low stock-carrying capacity, limiting their use to the more or less casual grazing of commoners' animals. Many of these commons escaped enclosure when better-quality pastures and the arable common fields were fenced in the late eighteenth and early nineteenth centuries.[12] In some areas both calcicole and calcifuge species grow together in intimate association and this is of particular interest to ecologists.[13]

Neutral grasslands, as their name implies, develop on soils which are neither markedly alkaline, nor very acid.' The majority occur in southern and eastern England on either glacial or alluvial deposits. The physical and chemical characteristics of these soils depend on the nature of the transported material and on the process of deposition. Water regime is also of critical importance in determining the agricultural use and floristics of meadow grasslands and this factor has been used by Wells to distinguish between different types of neutral grassland.[14,15,16] For example, the *washlands* of East Anglia are subject to prolonged winter flooding, so that their agricultural use is restricted to summer grazing by cattle and cutting for hay. They are botanically poor but valuable for wintering duck. *Flood meadows* of permanent grass alongside rivers lie under water for short periods only in the winter. They are generally cut for hay, a use which may have been practised over long periods of time, and this constancy and continuity of management has probably contributed to their general floristic richness. Some flood meadows were transformed into *water meadows* which have systems controlling irrigation and drainage to provide an early grass growth in the spring for sheep grazing, although few examples survive today. Another type of grassland described in Wells's classification has developed on *ridge and furrow* giving evidence of past arable farming. This group is characteristic of heavy clay soils with impeded drainage and usually low fertility; many are grazed at low stocking densities throughout the year, whilst others are cut for hay, with aftermath grazing. The floristic richness of some of these pastures may again suggest that the form of management has been more or less constant for a long time.

Attempts to improve the productivity of these and related types of neutral grassland have been commonplace and the best pastures are now largely dominated by perennial rye-grass and white clover. The most widespread type, however, has a greater variety of species, having developed either as 'tumbledown' grassland following arable farming; as weed-infested sown pasture; or as semi-natural vegetation, improved by drainage, fertilizer and herbicide treatments. These formations are characterized by species such as crested dog's tail, cocksfoot, perennial rye-grass, white clover, bents, daisy, knapweed, creeping thistle and common meadow buttercup.[16]

Wetland communities of mire, marsh, fen or bog develop with increases in soil moisture. The two major factors affecting soil moisture are rainfall and the physical nature of the soil. Calcareous mire may form on areas where glacial drift, derived from limestone rock, is combined with impeded drainage; other wet areas, on the edges of lakes and ponds and the undrained flood plains of rivers, for example, may form marsh. These wetland communities arise on mineral soils and it is this distinction that separates them from the fens and bogs which are associated with organic soils. Where vegetation is waterlogged for most, if not all, the year, decay of plant remains is arrested and peat formation results, increasing the level of the soil with the accumulation of humus. In the development of marsh there is an increase in soil levels due to silting, the trapping of mineral particles. Fen peat is formed where the ground is saturated with water rich in lime and therefore alkaline. Bog peat develops on ground saturated by the water of acidic rocks; or on top of fen peat which has grown up above the influence of a neutralizing ground water, so that the surface is dominated by the acidity of the rain. The occurrence of bog in lowland England is more or less restricted to local depressions in areas of heathland where the water is held up by impermeable soil below. Bogs are dominated by carpets of moss and by grasses, rushes and sedges such as purple moor grass and black bog-rush. The conservation interest of these wetlands, whether marsh, mire, fen or bog, is often high, although their agricultural value is low and limited to rough grazing. As such they are particularly attractive targets for agricultural improvement involving drainage and conversion, through seeding and fertilizing, to more productive grassland.

THE CONSERVATION VALUE OF GRASSLANDS

The conservation or non-agricultural values of grassland are as many and varied as the interests of the people who hold them. At one extreme, a grassland may be valued for a variety of recreational purposes and function as a public open space; at the other extreme, the scientific or nature conservation interest may predominate; and in between, a whole host of values and activities associated to a greater or lesser extent with the broad outlines of the distant landscape or the details of the immediate scene may assume differing degrees of importance. Seldom is there only one interest in a particular area; more often, many divergent interests are focused on any particular site and competing, not only with an agricultural use, but also with one another. Just as there are many kinds of recreation activities, not all of which are compatible, so too there are competing nature conservation interests. This means that it may be difficult to group all the non-agricultural values of grassland together and treat them as a single factor with simple requirements, a point that can be illustrated by considering some of the different aspects of nature conservation interest.

The conservationist will wish to see the perpetuation of those areas of grassland which provide particularly good examples of their type; and of those which harbour populations of species which by virtue of their rarity, attractiveness or value for scientific purposes provide some particular interest. But any grassland community can be maintained in a variety of states by varying, for example, the intensity and frequency of defoliation. A high stocking density may be used to maintain a close-cropped and herb-rich turf, such as a botanist would probably favour.[17] An entomologist, however, might well favour a lower grazing pressure which would allow the development of a taller and better-structured grassland, containing a greater variety of aerial plant parts and more cover for a richer invertebrate fauna;[18] whilst an ornithologist would probably wish to limit the grazing to an even lower level, so as to allow scrub encroachment and the development of scattered bushes, which would enhance the bird life.[19] It is clearly of vital importance to decide the especial value of any area, in relation to the distribution and abundance of similar and contrasting habitats, before formulating and implementing the management policies and practices for a particular site.

The difficulties of generalizing about conservation interest are seen to be great. It is possible, however, to discuss, if only in very general terms, the conditions which favour floristic richness and the persistence of a wide variety of plant species including, typically, attractive and interesting ones, and this enables illustration of the kind of conditions that management for conservation purposes may need to perpetuate or encourage. Some of the more important factors which maintain, or are associated with, a high grassland plant-species density, are considered below within three groupings.

General factors

Age

Plant-species density generally increases with time, along with the probability that any given species will invade a site suitable for establishment within the habitat. Older grasslands are therefore richer in species than younger ones and it is for this reason that the ancient pastures, particularly those that have a high constancy in their history of management, are of great conservation interest. The composition of temporary (ley) grass which is sown as part of an arable rotation, normally reflects a grass–clover seed mixture, since the three to five years which pass before ploughing and the return to arable allow little opportunity for invasion and diversification by other species. As a consequence, the plant-species density and conservation interest of leys are generally low.

Habitat size

Larger habitats are found to support a greater number of species than smaller ones. Any species requires a certain area which must be exceeded if it is to maintain a viable population and clearly a larger habitat will satisfy the minimal area requirement of a greater number of species. Larger areas are also likely to be more heterogeneous (see below) and a greater variety of microhabitats will favour a greater number of species.[20]

Isolation

Remoteness from similar habitats has the effect of reducing the density of species present. The probability of random extinction is a reality for all populations, although it may well be small if the number of individuals is large. The invasion of new propagules to combat the local extinction of relatively small populations will be precluded if the distance for recolonization is too great, so that isolated habitats tend to have a lower equilibrium species density.[21]

Heterogeneities

Spatial heterogeneities within the habitat may include, for example, relatively minor differences in topography, aspect, soil depth, moisture, nutrient status or the occurrence of hoofmarks and molehills. A greater range of environmental variation is likely to cover the particular requirements of a greater number of species, so that environmental heterogeneity tends to promote higher species densities.

Physico-chemical factors

Nutrient status

Adequate availabilities of certain inorganic elements (nutrients) are essential for the growth and reproduction of all plants. High levels, particularly of nitrogen, however, promote the dominance of a few of the grasses, so that many of the smaller herbs tend to be excluded and a species-poor community is produced. Provided that minimum levels of nutrient are available, poorer soils support higher species densities, since limited nutrients prevent the vigorous growth of potential dominants.

Soil pH

All soils contain enough calcium for the nutritive needs of plants themselves but, as noted above, some soils are impregnated with calcium carbonate so that they are constantly saturated with an alkaline solution of lime. Alkaline (or basic) soils (those with a pH greater than 7) often have a higher species density than acidic soils (with a pH less than 7).

Soil depth

As a generalization, shallow soils tend to carry higher species densities than deep ones. This is similar to the effect of nutrient availability and it seems likely that the shallow soil places a limitation on the vigour and competitiveness of those species which would be dominant on deeper soil to the exclusion of many others.[22]

Soil moisture

Very dry and very wet situations impose similar stresses on plant growth and it may be that conditions more favourable to growth produce more vigorous dominants. Within limits, therefore, high plant species density may be associated with the environmental extremes of dry and wet soils.

Light

A high light intensity permits the illumination and therefore the development of a greater number of layers of leaf and there are indications that this may permit a high species diversity. Thus, it seems possible that high plant-species densities are promoted by adversity in the soil environment but favourability in the aerial conditions.

Biotic factors

Grazing

Grazing is a complex activity and its effects on species density defy simple analysis.[16,23] The sward is defoliated; enriched locally by dung and urine; and trampled. The structure and composition of the grassland will be influenced by the timing, intensity and frequency of grazing, as well as by the type of animal: sheep, cattle and horses showing different degrees of selectivity and grazing behaviour. The pattern of dunging and urination in a pasture may have an important effect on the redistribution of nutrients within a grassland and may also affect future grazing behaviour; both factors affect botanical composition. Treading causes physical damage to the plant shoots, as well as soil compaction, which reduces aeration, water penetration and regrowth, so that species adapted to withstand these stresses are favoured. Winter grazing, in particular, helps to break up the layer of litter (dead plant material) and to reduce the competitive ability of the grasses during a period when many of the dicotyledons are dormant with little growth above ground. Winter grazing, therefore, may increase floristic diversity although it may be precluded on some grasslands because of flooding and on heavy clay soils because of poaching. Promotion of floristic richness may also be achieved by controlling the growth of the dominant grasses by grazing (or cutting) during their major growth period, usually from late spring to early summer.[24]

It is clear that many factors affect plant species density and that this characteristic is not *invariably* associated with conservation interest. Nevertheless, if any general conclusion can be drawn, it is that conservation interest (based on plant species density) is often greatest in conditions which impose stresses on plant growth, for example, when the soil depth and its nutrient status are low, or when the soil is very dry or very wet. The agriculturalist, however, favours deep, fertile, well-drained soils and moderate rainfall evenly distributed throughout the year, since these factors maximize productivity. There is direct conflict here between agricultural and conservation interests.

CHANGES IN GRASSLAND MANAGEMENT

Traditional agricultural methods generally favour the development and persistence of species-rich grassland. As a result of technical innovation and present-day economic conditions, however, the conservation interest of many such grasslands is threatened. It is perhaps paradoxical that adverse effects on the conservation interest may be brought about both by the intensification and by the withdrawal of farming.

Intensification of agriculture

For many years, successive governments have encouraged moves towards a greater self-sufficiency in homegrown foods, using a wide variety of legislative, advisory and fiscal measures.[25] The area of land under cultivation and the proportion of arable to pastoral land has been extended through the ploughing of areas of old-established grassland and the reclamation of semi-natural 'waste', such as heath and downland. As a result, the surviving areas of old grassland in lowland England are small and fragmented. This is shown, for example, by Duffey[15] who has compared the present-day number of grass heaths in the Breckland area of Norfolk and Suffolk (37 sites, averaging 88 acres) with the 59 sites, averaging 941 acres, identified on the early Ordnance Survey map. Similarly, 931 of the 1225 fragments of chalk grassland identified in a comprehensive survey by Blackwood and Tubbs[8] had an area in the 5–50 acre range. The great majority of these remaining areas were confined to steep slopes on which cultivation is almost impossible.

In addition to the agricultural benefits which have been achieved by increasing the total acreage of land under cultivation, much research, advice and money has been directed towards improving the productivity of the land under pasture. The average output of hay from an acre of permanent grassland, as estimated annually by the Ministry of Agriculture, Fisheries and Food, has increased by almost 50 per cent over the last 20 years and corresponds to an increased application of fertilizers and herbicides and to greater attention to under-drainage. There has been a fourfold increase in application of nitrogen fertilizer to agricultural land in England and Wales over the last 20 years[16] and a sixfold increase in the area of land drained each year.[26] The technology of land drainage developed rapidly during the 1939–1945 war and Trist[27] considers that under-drainage has been the most important improvement to occur in British agriculture over the last 30 years. Herbicides enable much greater control to be exercised over the floristic composition of grassland and allow farmers to favour productive and nutritious grasses at the expense of 'weed' species. The grass breeder aids this process by developing varieties of grass with these and other favourable characteristics. All of these activities are likely to have a marked effect on the remaining areas of semi-natural grassland and all tend to reduce floristic diversity and exclude rare and attractive species.

Increasingly, this uniformity of grassland composition and structure is being reinforced by stricter control over the pattern of grazing, achieved by fixed or movable fencing; and by the trend to 'zero grazing', in which the grass is cropped and the animals fed indoors.

Withdrawal of agriculture

Not all marginal grasslands have suffered the fate of reclamation and intensification of agriculture. The management of some has not changed significantly whilst others have been subject to withdrawal of agriculture. Chalk downland and certain areas of lowland grass heath fall into this last category. The free-range system of grazing, especially by sheep, which for centuries helped to maintain the short, springy and herb-rich downland sward has almost completely disappeared and whilst these grasslands may have escaped the plough and afforestation, the structure and composition of many of them has been completely changed by the withdrawal of grazing.

Several social and economic factors have encouraged this withdrawal of grazing—notably, Government support for cereal production and the dairy industry, competition from cheap imports, labour costs, the housewife's increasing preference for smaller joints produced more conveniently from hill sheep and, on the urban fringe, trespass and vandalism. The effect of under-grazing on the composition of the grassland did not become wholly evident until the arrival of myxomatosis in 1954. This drastically reduced the rabbit population which previously had had a significant grazing effect and marked changes in the structure and composition of many lowland grasslands date from that time. The removal of a more or less intensive grazing regime of stock and rabbits has had various effects. Selectively grazed species have tended to increase at the expense of those species requiring bare ground or short, open vegetation, such as the smaller, short-lived herbs. The sward becomes dominated by ranker and more aggressive grasses, so that plant-species density is reduced. The accumulated litter and greater number of flower and seed heads may support a greater diversity of insect life, however. The absence of grazing also means that succession is no longer arrested and woody species are able to invade and establish successfully. Provided that the supply of seed is adequate, the soil is sufficiently deep and the climate favourable, the development of scrub and eventually forest may be expected.

RECONCILING FARMING AND CONSERVATION INTERESTS

It is abundantly clear that most agricultural improvements will conflict with the many non-agricultural values of grasslands. Reclamation of old pasture, drainage improvement, reseeding, fertilizer application and herbicide treatment are the farmers' means of securing a sward dominated by a few particularly productive and nutritious grasses and clovers. The best agricultural return is achieved from a green uniformity, whilst typically amenity and nature conservation value depend on a diversity of colour and form, such as is found in herb-rich pastures and meadows.

In general, conservation and agricultural interests cannot be maximized on the same piece of land. Although this was no doubt realized in the 1940s, relatively little importance was attached to it. For example, Tansley[28] concluded that it was scarcely probable that the extension of agriculture would go much further, as he considered that the limits of profitable agriculture must have been reached in most places and this view typified the majority of informed opinion at that time. It was generally thought that areas proposed as nature reserves would not be profitable for cultivation and the ploughing up of pastures which had occurred during the 1939–1945 war would be only a temporary phenomenon.[29] This opinion, coupled with the overriding need to produce food, influenced the content of much of the immediate post-war legislation dealing with agriculture and conservation and little attempt was made to regulate further reclamation of valued habitats or to encourage harmonious resolution where conflicts between agriculture and conservation did occur. Only now is widespread consideration being given to the means of reconciling conservation and agricultural interests, notably in the National Parks.[30]

It is important to appreciate that the proper management of some nature reserves and public open spaces for conservation and amenity purposes requires an understanding of how the traditional agricultural systems that have produced the special attractions of these areas can be maintained or reintroduced. Perpetuating an agricultural system, or its substitute, to maintain the character of an area to satisfy nature conservation, landscape or recreation functions will almost invariably involve a cost. Indeed, at the present time, the use of non-intensive agricultural systems to maintain characteristic and valued landscapes may be grossly uneconomic and yet be the only alternative to a change in landscape character.

A wide variety of factors may need to be assessed if the use of farming methods for conservation purposes is being considered and this is particularly true of areas such as country parks where the numbers of visitors may at times be very high. The main requirement of the management system will be that it is efficient in maintaining the desired grassland character. A more or less detailed knowledge of the suitability of different grazing regimes and their effects on vegetation will be needed (including the requirements and effects of different animals and stocking densities at different times) along with the characteristics of alternative methods such as burning or mowing at different heights and times, and the role that fertilizers and herbicides may have in achieving conservation purposes. The viability of any management system must also be viewed in terms of its costs and the associated problems and opportunities which it offers. Fencing and labour costs may be high, yet these may be offset to some extent through the disposal of marketable by-products. The preferred system must also be compatible with the other uses to which the area is put and the interaction between grazing animals and visitors may be particularly critical. Management methods such as grazing may affect the distribution, behaviour and enjoyment of visitors to an area. Bulls, for example, are obviously restrictive, yet animals can help to perpetuate the rural character of an area and rarer breeds may provide an additional attraction. Visitors themselves may affect the distribution and productivity of grazing animals and campaigns to counter litter and the uncontrolled activity of dogs may need to be pursued. It is clear that the choice of an appropriate management system for any given situation depends on many factors and the ways in which opportunities can be exploited and conflicts minimized need further investigation. Perhaps the most encouraging sign, however, is an increasing acceptance of the need for positive management to maintain valued environments backed by an increasing willingness to pay the cost.

NOTES AND REFERENCES

1. Ministry of Agriculture, Fisheries and Food (1972). *Agricultural Statistics: England and Wales*, 1970/71. HMSO, London.
2. Department of Agriculture and Fisheries for Scotland (1972). *Agricultural Statistics: Scotland*, 1971. HMSO, Edinburgh.
3. Tansley, A. G. (1968). *Britain's Green Mantle: Past, Present and Future*, second edition (revised by Proctor, M. C. F.), George Allen and Unwin, London.
4. Sheail, J. (1971). *Rabbits and their History*, David and Charles, Newton Abbot.
5. See for example Jones, M. G. (1933). Grassland Management and its Influence on the Sward. *Empirical Journal of Experimental Agriculture*, **1**, 43–57, 122–128, 223–234, 360–366 and 366–367; and Brenchley, W. E. (1958), *The Park Grass Plots at Rothamstead 1856–1949*, Rothamstead Experimental Station, Harpendon, Herts.
6. The action and relative importance of the many factors which affect the presence and abundance of species in grassland are often poorly understood. The strength of these controlling factors often changes in a more or less regular way from one place to another; marked discontinuities are relatively rare and, as a result, the composition of the vegetation which they determine also shows regular rather than abrupt change. For this reason, the classification of plant communities can be difficult and the boundary of groupings delineated from continuously varying vegetation may be more imagined than real. At a gross level, however, marked differences clearly do exist and enable the separation of one community from another in a way which achieves widespread acceptance.
7. Tansley, A. G. (1953). *The British Isles and their Vegetation*, Vols I and II, Cambridge University Press, Cambridge.
8. Blackwood, J. and Tubbs, C. R. (1970). A quantitative Survey of Chalk Grassland in England. *Biological Conservation*, **3**, 1–5.
9. The productivity of both calcareous and acidic grassland is generally limited by the availability of nutrients and also perhaps to a lesser extent by a lack of soil moisture. See Bunting, A. H. and Elston, J. (1966). Water Relations of Crops and Grasses on Chalk Soil. *Scientific Horticulture*, **18**, 116–120.
10. The difference in species richness and the restriction of some species to soils of high pH, others to soils of low pH, have yet to be fully explained.

11. Farrow, E. P. (1915). On the Ecology of the Vegetation of Breckland. *Journal of Ecology*, **3**, 211–222.

12. Chambers, J. D. and Mingay, G. E. (1966). *The Agricultural Revolution*, Batsford, London.

13. See for example Grubb, P. J., Green, H. E. and Merrifield, R. C. J. (1969). The Ecology of Chalk Heath, *Journal of Ecology*, **57**, 175–212.

14. Wells, T. C. E. and Morris, M. G. (1970). *Conservation Research and Management of Calcareous Grassland*. Symposium of the British Ecological Society, Tour Guide No. 5, July 1970. Natural Environment Research Council.

15. Duffey, E. A. G. (1974). Lowland Grassland and Scrub; Management for Wildlife. In Goldsmith, B. and Warren, A. (eds), *Conservation in Practice*, Wiley, London.

16. Duffey, E. A. G., Morris, M. G., Sheail, J., Ward, Lena K., Wells, D. A. and Wells, T. C. E. (1974). *Grassland Ecology and Wildlife Management*, Chapman and Hall, London.

17. Wells, T. C. E. (1971). A Comparison of the Effects of Sheep Grazing and Mechanical Cutting on the Structure and Botanical Composition of Chalk Grassland. *Symposium of the British Ecological Society*, No. 11, pp. 497–515.

18. Morris, M. G. (1971). The Management of Grassland for the Conservation of Invertebrate Animals. *Symposium of the British Ecological Society*, No. 11, pp. 527–552.

19. Williamson, K. (1967). Some Aspects of the Scientific Interest and Management of Scrub and Nature Reserves. In Duffey, E. (ed.), *The Biotic Effects of Public Pressures on the Environment*, pp. 94–100. Monks Wood Experimental Station Symposium No. 3. The Nature Conservancy.

20. Moore, N. W. (1962). The Heaths of Dorset and their Conservation. *Journal of Ecology*, **50**, 369–391.

21. MacArthur, R. H. and Wilson, E. O. (1967). *The General Theory of Island Biogeography*, Princeton University Press, Princeton, New Jersey.

22. Green, B. H. (1972). The Relevance of Seral Eutrophication and Plant Competition to the Management of Successional Communities. *Biological Conservation*, **4**(5), 378–384.

23. Arnold, G. W. (1964). Factors within Plant Associations Affecting the Behaviour and Performance of Grazing Animals. *Symposium of the British Ecological Society*, No. 4, pp. 133–154.

24. Cutting or mowing differs from grazing in being non-selective, and the effects of dung, urine and treading are removed.

25. See Chapter 1.

26. Carter, C. (1973). An article on Drainage in *Power Farming*, **51**(2), August 1973.

27. Trist, P. J. O. (1970). The Changing Pattern of Agriculture. In Perring F. B. (ed.), *The Flora of a Changing Britain*, Report of the Botanical Society of the British Isles, No. 11.

28. Tansley, A. G. (1945). *Our Heritage of Wild Nature*, Cambridge University Press, Cambridge.

29. Sheail, J. (1974). The Legacy of Historical Times. In Goldsmith, B. and Warren, A. (eds.), *Conservation in Practice*. Wiley, London.

30. Department of the Environment (1974). *Report of the National Park Policies Review Committee* (Sandford Report), HMSO, London.

Chapter 6

Hill and upland pasture

J. KING

The vegetation of the British hills and uplands is best defined in relation to the boundary formed by the upper limit of cultivation. Above this line unenclosed natural pasture predominates; below it the land is mostly enclosed, some under cultivation, the rest in permanent pasture. The boundary of cultivation also marks a change in the character of the farming system. Unenclosed hill land is ranched, predominantly by sheep; grazing is uncontrolled and man-made inputs to the system are low or absent. The farming system is based on the utilization of natural pastures: a true hill farm has only a very small area of enclosed land, usually less than 10 per cent of the total area, and only a part of this is cropped. Upland farms, on the other hand, generally have a substantial proportion of their area enclosed and subject to fertilizer and other inputs, cattle are more important, and the farming system is based on lowland agricultural practice, although at the same time making use of unenclosed natural pastures.

The lower boundary of unenclosed hill pasture is commonly about 500 feet (150 metres) but in western Scotland it may sometimes approach sea level. The upper limit is around 2000–2600 feet (600–800 metres), above which montane dwarf shrub-heaths predominate. Grazing may extend into the montane zone but this boundary normally defines the upper limit of pastoral use. Unenclosed pasture is characteristic of all upland areas in Britain, from Exmoor and Dartmoor in the southwest to the Pennines in the north of England and throughout much of Wales and Scotland. Geologically most of these are regions in which the predominant rocks are either acid or of intermediate acidity and this, combined with a normally high rainfall, gives soils that are mainly leached and podsolic. Except in the Pennines, large areas of calcareous rocks do not occur.

Most hill and upland pastures below 2000 feet (600 metres) have been formed by grazing and burning from forest or scrub.[1] Archaeological evidence indicates that the influence of man on the forest cover was small until Bronze Age times when pressure increased progressively until, by the fifteenth century, much of the accessible forest had been destroyed. Associated with this was an increase in pastoral agriculture and in the numbers of both sheep and cattle. In the seventeenth and eighteenth centuries, however, sheep numbers

95

increased more rapidly than cattle, creating sheep farming in a form and on a scale very similar to that which prevails to-day.[2] Many hill areas, therefore, have been grazed for as much as 600 years, although in the Scottish Highlands the history of grazing is somewhat shorter, with large-scale sheep farming first being introduced not more than 200 years ago.

VEGETATION TYPES AND THEIR VARIATION

The variation shown by the present vegetation of the hills and uplands is related to three main environmental gradients; those of soil nutrient level, soil drainage and biotic pressure (Figure 10) which are themselves a function of

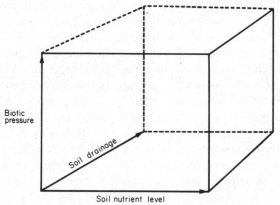

Figure 10.   Main environmental gradients
influencing vegetation composition

climate, soil parent material, topography and the available fauna and flora.[3] Each axis in Figure 10 represents a complex of interrelated factors, of which one can be used as an index. Biotic pressure, for example, represents both grazing pressure and the influence of burning, although on many vegetation types only grazing is involved. A suitable index of nutrient level on upland soils is provided by their pH as this is correlated with the rate of organic matter decomposition and the supply of available nitrogen, phosphorus and other nutrients. The soil drainage axis reflects soil aeration and moisture level which are inversely related. The range extends from, at one extreme, poorly drained mineral soils and peats waterlogged and anaerobic throughout the year, to freely drained aerobic soils which may be subject to drought in summer. There are intermediate soils which remain moist throughout the summer but are only moderately anaerobic even in winter.

Upland soil types

The range of soil types most commonly found in hill and upland areas is summarized in Figure 11 and the associated vegetation types in Figure 12. The

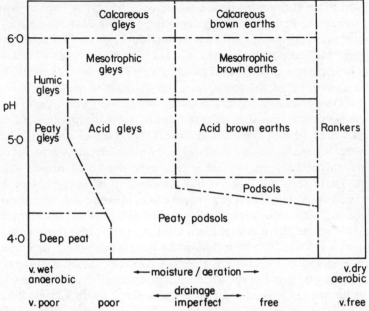

Figure 11. Soil profile types in relation to environmental gradients of soil pH and drainage

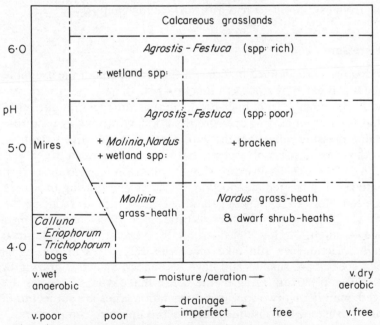

Figure 12. Major hill vegetation types in relation to environmental gradients of soil pH and drainage

axes of soil pH and drainage define an array of soil types each of which can support a range of vegetation types depending on the biotic pressure.

The most poorly drained soils are peat and humic gleys. Characteristic of the former is the blanket peat found typically in western Scotland and Ireland at all altitudes or in eastern districts at altitudes greater than 2000 feet (600 metres). On lower slopes, below the spring line, poorly drained mesotrophic and acid gleyed soils are common.[4] Peaty podsols with 15–30 cm of peat, and iron-humus podsols with thin surface raw humus, are widespread on freely and imperfectly drained parent materials, especially on upper slopes where leaching is severe. Where the parent materials are only moderately acid, for example in eastern districts where rainfall is not excessive, acid brown earths are common. These soils are leached but no downward movement of iron has occurred and the profile is that of a brown earth. Mesotrophic brown earths are mainly characteristic of the lower valley slopes on base-rich parent materials or alternatively where there is slight irrigation by base-rich spring water. Their distribution is co-extensive with that of the harder limestones in Scotland and northern England but elsewhere they are confined to soils subject to the requisite irrigation conditions. Such soils are found in all hill districts but, except on limestones, do not cover large areas. On the softer limestone rocks in the relatively low rainfall of the Pennines the equivalent soil is a calcareous brown earth. The most freely drained soils, the skeletals and rankers, are widespread on steep slopes and hill tops. They vary widely in base status ranging from calcareous to acid with surface raw humus.

Biotic pressure

Grazing pressure, defined in terms of the proportion of the available edible herbage that is eaten by stock, is a function both of herbage growth rate and of the intake by animals. Thus, high-producing pasture types require higher stock densities for a given grazing pressure than do low-producing pastures.

Grazing pressure influences the extent to which selective grazing can take place between the parts of a plant, between species or between vegetation types. In each case this is an expression of animal preference and is particularly associated with intermediate stocking densities and grazing pressures where animals can afford to reject less palatable species without reducing their food intake. At high stock densities there is little scope for selection and most of the herbage is eaten. At low densities all the vegetation is undergrazed and although selection can still take place the differences in grazing pressure between species are smaller and have less effect. Selective grazing does not necessarily imply overgrazing in the sense that favoured species are being damaged, merely that two species or vegetation types are subject to different grazing pressures with consequential effects on pasture composition.

Low grazing pressures on grassland lead to the accumulation of uneaten residues, and in shrub-heath allow the growth-form to become tall and woody.

Burning is the traditional cure for this. However, the effects of burning are varied, especially on shrub-heaths, depending on the frequency of fires, their temperature, the stage of growth when burned and the grazing pressure on vegetation regenerating after a fire.[5] The general result of grazing combined with burning is to favour unpreferred and fire-tolerant species such as *Molinia*, *Nardus* or *Eriophorum* and to eliminate dwarf shrubs such as heather.

Historically, animals on unenclosed hill pastures have always had free choice of pasture: thus grazing pressures have varied widely on different vegetation types, modifying the vegetation in characteristic ways. In areas of low biotic pressure dwarf shrubs and erect grass and fern species can survive and so the dominant communities are those in which shrub-heath species, bracken or tall grasses are abundant, for example *Calluna-Vaccinium*, *Myrica*, bracken, *Brachipodium pinnatum* and *Arrhenatherum elatius*. Areas of moderate biotic pressure are characterized by grassy undergrazed plant communities in which unpreferred fire-tolerant species predominate, for example *Molinia*, *Nardus*, *Deschampsia cespitosa* or bracken, and moorland sedge communities from which dwarf shrub species have been eliminated. Closely grazed grassland in which unpreferred species scarcely occur is characteristic of areas of high biotic pressure.

Vegetation types

Each soil type is associated with a characteristic range of vegetation types depending on the current biotic pressure and on the previous biotic history. Six major categories of natural and semi-natural hill vegetation are considered in the following section.[6–13]

Dwarf shrub-heaths. These are heather moors of various kinds. The principal shrub is heather (*Calluna vulgaris*) associated with other dwarf shrubs such as *Vaccinium* spp, *Erica* spp, and *Empetrum* together with many of the same species found in grass-heaths, notably the grasses *Molinia* and *Nardus*. The soils are podsolic, nearly always with surface peat and of pH 3·7–4·7.

Bog vegetation. This is found on deep blanket peat (pH 3·5–4·6) in high rainfall areas. There are two major types, *Calluna-Eriophorum* bog commonly found at 1000–2500 feet (300–700 metres), and blanket bog which occurs at lower altitudes in western Scotland and Ireland. In both, *Sphagnum* is normally abundant along with *Calluna*, *Eriophorum*, *Trichophorum* and *Molinia*, but the composition can be greatly altered in favour of one or other of these species by fire and grazing. The *Eriophorum* moors of the Pennines are an example of this.

Grass-heaths. These are grasslands, poor in species, characterized by an abundance of *Festuca ovina* and *Deschampsia flexuosa* which can give a short, close-grazed sward. Usually, however, *Nardus* or *Molinia* are also abundant giving the vegetation the characteristic undergrazed appearance of *Nardus* and *Molinia* heaths. They are found on acid, podsolic soils (pH 3·8–4·8).

Agrostis-Festuca grassland. This is a variable category of grassland found on soils ranging from dry brown earths to poorly drained gleys and from pH 4·7–6·0. There are two major types on hill land: *Agrostis-Festuca* (species-poor) where *Agrostis tenuis* and *Festuca ovina* predominate in a floristically poor sward, and *Nardus, Molinia* or *Deschampsia cespitosa* are common on wetter sites (soil pH 4·7–5·2); and *Agrostis-Festuca* (species-rich) where *Agrostis tenuis, Festuca ovina* and *Festuca rubra* predominate with many other grasses and herbs including white clover, and with *Holcus lanatus* and *Carex* species abundant on wetter sites (soil pH 5·0–6·0).

Calcareous grassland. In the uplands, this is developed on soils derived from the softer limestones, as on the Pennines. *Festuca ovina* is the characteristic species with a profusion of grassland herbs. Other floristically rich upland calcareous grasslands occur on Cambrian limestone and calcareous mica-schist soils in the Scottish Highlands. Much of this is essentially a type of herb-rich *Agrostis-Festuca* grassland with variants characterized by particular herbs such as *Alchemilla alpina* or *Saxifraga aizoides.*

Mires. These are distinguished from bogs by their relatively nutrient-rich water supply. The soils are humic or peaty gleys, pH 4·5–6·0. The commonest community types are dominated by *Juncus* or *Carex* species with an abundance of mosses.

Ecological status

It is generally accepted that the soil and vegetation of hill land has deteriorated since the removal of the original forest cover and the introduction of grazing. The changes that have taken place are of several kinds. Firstly, there has been a loss of nutrients, probably mainly as a result of leaching following the removal of the trees and the breakdown of the forest nutrient cycle. Where this has occurred the resultant lower nutrient level can be presumed to have given rise to a more impoverished vegetation some of which, like heather, would increase the tendency to podsolization. Secondly, the removal of the tree canopy has probably affected directly the competitive balance between species in the ground vegetation; bracken, for example, might be expected to thrive in the increased light. Thirdly, the presence of grazing animals at different stocking densities, combined with periodic burning of some vegetation types, has affected the competitive balance of many species and has led to changes in the composition of the vegetation.

It has also been suggested that removal of nutrients in the carcases of animals, and losses associated with heather-burning, have contributed to soil deterioration. However, investigation has shown that both the mean annual loss through burning and the loss in animal carcases is small, usually smaller than the input of nutrients dissolved in rainwater.[14,15,16] On a few sites considerable inputs of nutrients occur as a result of weathering or of natural irrigation by spring water and on these probably little deterioration has occurred. On sites, such as blanket bog, already nutrient-deficient before sheep were introduced, deterioration, if any, will have resulted from the effects of grazing and burning on the composition of the vegetation. Vegetation change implies a lack of stability, but with only circumstantial evidence available this is a subject for conjecture. The composition of the present vegetation appears to be closely related to the existing rather stable soil conditions and may therefore, itself, be rather stable. Such changes that are taking place are perhaps more likely to be in response to biotic factors. Dominance by *Nardus, Molinia* and bracken, for example, is thought to result in this way. However, it is quite possible that in many areas these species have already reached the limits of suitable soils and where this is so such communities will also be relatively stable. Dwarf shrub-heaths and bog vegetation are probably the types most susceptible to biotic changes. Their growth-form renders them more sensitive than grasslands and even where stability exists at the present time, grazing and burning pressures can quickly and easily change.

Value of vegetation types for pastoral use

Agricultural value is related both to the quantity and the quality of dry matter produced. Since pasture regrowth is affected by the way in which defoliation has taken place, it is not easy to obtain yield data from continuously grazed pastures and as a result most of the information available has been obtained by cutting plots that have been protected from grazing. On this basis a rough comparison can be made of the relative yields of the main hill vegetation types (Table 12). The greatest yields are obtained from *Agrostis-Festuca* pastures, and the smallest from grass-heath and bog vegetation. The production of edible material from heather is similar to that of the poorer grassland types.

Table 12. Comparative values for herbage yield of hill vegetation types subject to cutting

Vegetation	Dry matter yield (kg/ha)	Basis	Data source[a]
Molinia grass-heath	1000	4-weekly cuts	17
Nardus grass-heath	2000	4-weekly cuts	18
Agrostis-Festuca	2100–2400	4-weekly cuts	17
grassland	3300	4-weekly cuts	19
Heather moor	1000–2000	Season's growth	20
	2200–2800	Season's growth	21
Heather in bog vegetation	1300	Season's growth	22

[a] Numbers refer to notes and references at end of chapter.

Although these data are of interest, it is abundantly clear from recent work[23,24] that, under the management systems currently in use, the main limitations to animal production are qualitative rather than quantitative. The value of a hill pasture is a function of its ability to provide *digestible* nutrients to grazing animals when subject to appropriate management. The digestibility of the diet is important, both for its own sake and because it influences the amount of dry matter ingested. Animals will eat larger quantities of grass when digestibility is high than when it is low so that improved digestibility has a considerable effect on the total amount of nutrients ingested and on the level of animal production. Digestibility is to some extent a function of plant species and of pasture composition, but it is also greatly affected by stage of growth and by the frequency and closeness of defoliation.

On grassland, high grazing pressures lead to short leafy swards in which the herbage is eaten while still highly digestible before it has had time to mature. In contrast, low grazing pressures lead to a situation where uneaten herbage matures and digestibility falls. Under these conditions selection of the younger and more digestible leaves by the animal can provide a diet that is better than the average of what is available. However, the most selective animal is unable to avoid taking a proportion of the indigestible material so that the diet is nearly always in some degree poorer than it might otherwise be. This process commonly occurs on many grassland communities, such as species-poor *Agrostis-Festuca* and grass-heath, wherever grazing pressure is low, and as a result the full potential of these pastures is not realized. The digestibility of the diet obtained from such undergrazed pastures varies seasonally from about 45–50 per cent in winter to a peak of 70–75 per cent in summer (Figure 13). If grazing pressure is increased the opportunity for selection is reduced. As a result more material of low digestibility is eaten and as the quality of the diet falls, so does the quantity which is ingested. This is well illustrated by the data in Table 13 which relate to a pasture containing a typically high content of dead herbage. As the stocking rate is increased and the animals are obliged to eat more of the sward, utilization per hectare increases but intake per animal falls.

Table 13.   Effect of accumulated dead herbage in a sward on the quality and quantity of intake by sheep of digestible organic matter (DOM)

Dead herbage in the sward (kg/ha)	Stocking rate/ha	Total DOM utilized (kg/ha)	DOM intake/animal (gm/head/day)
High: 2220	7·4	642	1135
	12·3	915	930
	18·5	1285	815
Low: 605	14·8	1295	1155

Source: Eadie, J. (1967). The Nutrition of Grazing Hill Sheep: Utilization of Hill Pastures, *Hill Farming Research Organization, 4th Report 1964–1967*

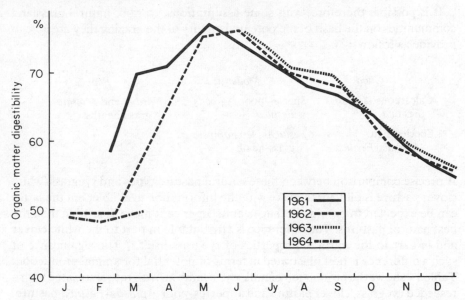

Figure 13. Seasonal changes in digestibility of pastures consumed by sheep set-stocked on a Scottish hill grassland. (Source: Eadie, J. (1967). The Nutrition of Grazing Hill Sheep: Utilization of Hill Pastures, *Hill Farming Research Organization, 4th Report, 1964–1967*)

When the amount of indigestible dead herbage in the sward is reduced, high utilization rates are maintained without depressing intake per animal.

Although low grazing pressures allow animals to select the more digestible material from low-quality swards, such grazing permits unpreferred species to increase, thus leading to the predominance of both *Nardus* and *Molinia* and further increasing the indigestible component of the pasture. In contrast, some pasture types, such as species-rich *Agrostis-Festuca*, attract high grazing pressures[25] and as a result, the accumulation of uneaten dead herbage is small, digestibility is not depressed and the animal's initial preference is reinforced. Bracken is often assumed to diminish the grazing value of pastures even where it is unable to develop a frond density sufficient to kill the vegetation beneath. However, it is not known to what extent herbage yield or utilization is in fact reduced by a bracken canopy and although differences in seasonal distribution of grazing due to bracken have been shown to exist[25] this need not be a disadvantage. So while dense bracken involves a production loss and is wholly undesirable, it is less certain that open stands of bracken cause a serious loss of grazing, particularly when grazing pressure and utilization rates are low. Nor can it be assumed that all open stands will become dense; in many areas bracken density appears to be static, in equilibrium with soil and climatic factors.

It is possible therefore, with some assumptions, to rank natural grassland communities on the basis of the potential quality of the grazing they are able to provide as follows:

Good	Moderate	Poor
Calcareous *Agrostis-Festuca*	Species-poor *Agrostis-Festuca*	*Nardus* and *Molinia* grass-heaths
Species-rich *Agrostis-Festuca*	*Festuca-Deschampsia* grass-heath	

A precise comparison between these natural pasture types and ryegrass/white clover pasture is difficult to make with the information available, but the latter can be expected to provide herbage about 5 per cent more digestible than the best natural pastures. The difference is attributable in part to the white clover and in part to the intrinsic properties of ryegrass itself.[26] The significance of such a difference is best illustrated in terms of potential for animal production. Table 14 shows the production of milk and a lamb growth rate associated with a reseeded ryegrass/clover pasture and a species-poor *Agrostis-Festuca* pasture.

Table 14. Milk yield and lamb growth rate of single and twin lambs on natural hill pasture and on a reseeded ryegrass/white clover sward

		Nine week means, gm/day	
		Hill pasture	Reseeded pasture
Single lambs	Milk yield	930	1110
	Lamb growth rate (mean)	213	258
	Lamb growth rate (range)	186–268	204–326
Twin lambs	Milk yield	1010	1775
	Lamb growth rate (mean)	154	218
	Lamb growth rate (range)	114–172	204–245

Source: Eadie, J. (1967). The Nutrition of Grazing Hill Sheep: Utilization of Hill Pastures. *Hill Farming Research Organization, 4th Report 1964–1967.*

It is apparent that the latter cannot provide for adequate growth rates of twin lambs although for single lambs it is satisfactory. In contrast the ryegrass/clover pasture can adequately feed ewes with twin lambs and indeed its full potential is not realized if only ewes with single lambs are grazed.

While the digestibility and intake of upland grassland has been the subject of much investigation, shrub-heaths and moorland community types have received much less attention. Heather has been the most studied, but, because of technical difficulties, reliable estimates of the digestibility of the current season's shoots—the portion eaten by sheep—have only been obtained recently. Estimations made *in vivo* by Milne[27] give a range of values varying within the season from 56·8 per cent in July to 42·7 per cent in March (Table 15). These values are low and the intakes associated with them are also low, lower even than would be the case with grass of comparable digestibility. As a result only the sheep eating the July material were in a state of positive energy balance. In general, the difference in nutritive value between underutilized natural grasslands and heather is greatest in summer and least in winter when both can be very poor.

Table 15. Seasonal changes in the nutritive value of heather to sheep[a]

Time of harvest	Intake of organic matter (gm/kg $W^{0.75}$/day)	Digestibility of organic matter (%)
July	37·0	56·8
September	32·8	47·5
November	34·6	47·2
March	28·0	42·7
Standard error	±2·77	±1·67

[a] *In vivo* measurements of digestibility and intake of digestible organic matter of material containing 85 per cent current season's shoots.
Source: Milne, J. A. (1974). The Effects of Season and Age of Stand on the Nutritive value of Heather (*Calluna vulgaris* L. Hull) to Sheep. *Journal of Agricultural Science*, **83**, 281–289.

Analyses of young shoots of heather on plants of different ages have shown that the concentration of nutrients such as nitrogen and phosphorus declines with age over the first six years.[21,28] But for sheep, at least, digestibility measurements[27] show no significant difference between material from heather stands in the pioneer, building and mature stages. The generally low digestibility and intake values obtained for heather suggest that it is a less valuable feed than was once thought and it may be that the satisfactory performance of sheep on heather moorland owes much to the grassland communities associated with the heather.

The nutritive value of blanket bog vegetation cannot be assessed as yet. Heather is of course a major component but there is insufficient data for *Eriophorum* spp and *Trichophorum*. If in terms of nutritional quality heather moorland is ranked below the natural grassland types, it is unlikely that bog vegetation will prove to be any better.

Wildlife conservation and landscape importance of hill and upland pastures

Value for wildlife is determined by both the abundance and the diversity of native plants and animals. Although in the lowlands the majority of habitats on agricultural land have been greatly modified and often impoverished as a result of man's activities, large areas of natural and semi-natural vegetation still remain in the uplands. The extensive nature of these habitats makes them important for wildlife conservation as does the presence of less frequent vegetation types such as upland calcareous grassland and mire. Several rare plants are found only, or mainly, in upland pastures, for example mountain avens (*Dryas octopetela*), shrubby cinquefoil (*Potentilla fruticosa*), dwarf cornel (*Cornus suecicum*) and bog rosemary (*Andromeda polifolia*), and their protection and appropriate management is of the highest importance if these species are to survive.

Hill and upland vegetation, particularly in the national parks, is also highly valued for its contribution to the landscape, as Chapter 7 discusses in detail. The conservation of wildlife and the present landscape character depends upon the traditional systems of upland land management and these are now being replaced by new pastoral systems posing a threat to wildlife and landscape conservation values.

The remainder of this chapter describes the traditional systems of hill and upland farming and the new systems being introduced, their effects on agricultural production and on the existing vegetation, and the implications for conservation and land use.

TRADITIONAL HILL FARMING

The pastoral systems by which natural hill vegetation is utilized today have developed over the last 250 years following the enclosure of the lower and more fertile lands. These systems vary between Scotland, northern England and Wales but essentially they are all ranching systems based upon sheep, though usually with some cattle. The sheep may be kept on natural pastures throughout the year. Alternatively, they may spend the winter period (December to April) on enclosed land. Sometimes, especially in Wales, there may be an intermediate area of enclosed natural pasture, the *fridd*, which is used at various times in the year. A normal characteristic of these ranching systems is that the natural pastures are set-stocked, that is, the stocking rate of breeding ewes is constant irrespective of seasonal variations in pasture growth. Cattle wintered on enclosed land or indoors can be used in summer to increase the grazing pressure but they are hardly ever present in sufficient numbers to control herbage growth. To accommodate seasonal variations in vegetation growth rate sheep numbers are adjusted to a level which allows a certain minimum level of nutrition during the winter. The resultant stocking rate may range from about 1 sheep/acre (2·5/ha) where the overall quality of the pasture is relatively high, to 0·1 sheep/acre (0·25/ha) on the poorer vegetation. These low stock densities inevitably lead in summer to severe undergrazing and to poor herbage utilization rates which may be less than 30 per cent on grasslands and as little as 10 per cent on shrub-heaths and bogs. Animal production is equally low being in the range 3–30 kg/ha of weaned lamb liveweight per year. The effect of undergrazing on the nutritive value of the sward has already been discussed. It gives rise to a year-round cycle of ingested pasture quality that is characteristically poor.

Eadie[23] has recorded the annual cycle of digestibility of ingested herbage on a Scottish hill grazing consisting for the most part of *Agrostis-Festuca* grass-land, half of it with bracken, and *Nardus* and *Molinia* grass-heaths. The area was stocked with breeding ewes at about 0·7 sheep/acre (1·7/ha). The results (Figure 13) show that maximum digestibility of ingested herbage ranged from 70–75 per cent during lactation, falling steadily post-weaning when ewes recovered their body condition, reaching about 55 per cent at the time of mating in December. The lowest values, about 48 per cent, occurred in January and February.

The maximum values for digestibility might be expected to lead to intakes of about 1550 gm of digestible organic matter (DOM)/day. From the peak the decline is relatively slow but from November to March values could be as low as 350–450 gm DOM/day, which is below the level necessary for the mainte-nance of bodyweight. These intake levels are very poor by lowland standards and are quite inadequate to exploit the potential fecundity of the ewe.[24] This level of nutrition during lactation is insufficient to provide acceptable early growth rates of twin lambs and even those of single lambs may be inadequate. After weaning, the bodyweight recovery by the ewe is limited by declining pasture quality in the period from August to October. Low body condition at mating results in low ovulation rates and an increased risk of barrenness, while the low nutritional level during pregnancy leads to reduced lamb-survival rates.

The conclusion overall must be that while there are variations in the degree to which various phases of the sheep's production cycle are limited by the poor nutritional environment, these phases are so interdependent that if significant increases in sheep production are to take place the level of the whole annual cycle must be raised.[24] Indeed, the present level of individual animal perfor-mance is so low that it is excessively dependent on year-to-year variations in winter weather conditions and on the rate of herbage growth in spring. The animal is insufficiently buffered against these variations so that a bad year can lead to disastrous losses both of production and of ewe stock. This conclusion is based on a study of the Scottish traditional system but there is every reason to suppose that it is also true of other local systems that are characterized by low stocking rates, low output per hectare and low levels of individual sheep production.

The limitations to cattle production of natural hill pastures have not been explored so far to the same extent as for sheep. It is recognized however that acceptable suckled-calf growth rates are not obtained from shrub-heath and blanket bog vegetation, but cattle on grassy vegetation are useful not only as a source of income in themselves but also as a means of improving the nutritional quality of the pastures as a result of the higher grazing pressure and the less selective nature of cattle grazing. Recent investigations of cows with single suckled calves[29] have shown that while bodyweight losses may well occur during the grazing season as a result of low pasture quality, this need not be inconsistent with generally satisfactory levels of nutrition taking the year as a whole.

The major limitation on cattle numbers is usually the amount of winter feed that can be conserved. In contrast, sheep can survive with very little conserved fodder and for this reason replacement of sheep by cattle is not possible without either importation of fodder from the lowlands or a large increase in the area of enclosed land suitable for fodder production.

NEW SHEEP PRODUCTION SYSTEMS

The principal shortcomings of the traditional upland ranching systems arise from the lack of grazing control and poor pasture quality. In consequence, an essential feature of new pastoral systems is enclosure, which permits grazing control and which allows pasture to be improved.[30,31]

Enclosed and improved pastures can be integrated with a much larger area of unenclosed hill vegetation in a year-round grazing system for sheep (Figure 14) and the essential features are as follows. Paddocks are used to provide a relatively high nutritional level for lactation and lamb growth and to maintain body condition in late autumn before mating. Both mating and lambing take place in a paddock. Since the number of ova produced by the ewe at any one oestrus is influenced by body condition, the use of paddocks increases the number of twins born and, by also influencing lactation, provides an adequate growth rate for these twins. The unenclosed hill land is grazed by the whole ewe

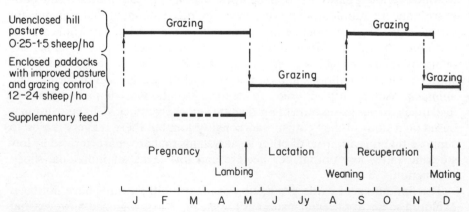

Figure 14.   Integration of unfenced natural vegetation and enclosed improved pastures in an annual cycle of grazing management. (Based on: Eadie, J., Armstrong, R. H. and Maxwell, T. J. (1973). Hill Sheep Production Systems: Development on the Cheviots, *Proceedings of the 3rd Colloquium of the Potassium Institute*, Potassium Institute, Edinburgh, pp. 139–144)

stock during the winter and again in the recuperative phase after weaning. At other times it is either rested or grazed lightly by non-breeding stock and by cattle so that herbage tends to accumulate for later use. In August and September selective grazing of the summer growth allows considerable improvement in sheep body condition which is then maintained from September onwards by the paddock grazing. Since the animals are in good body condition at mating they can be allowed to live, at least partly, at the expense of their body reserves over winter when food is scarce. With existing hill breeds of sheep which have been selected to survive in this way, it is possible, in the absence of snow cover, for sheep to come through the winter in declining body condition with no supplementary food without harm to the unborn lambs. However, towards the end of pregnancy, supplementary food must be given since at this time the nutritional requirements of the foetus increase rapidly until in the last few weeks it equals or exceeds that of the ewe.[24] In the event of deep snow all food, usually hay, must be supplied.

Although this is essentially a sheep production system, cattle are also assumed to be present wherever conditions are suitable. Their number will depend on the availability of conserved fodder, and it is safe to assume that their individual performance will be at least as good as that achieved by cattle associated with traditional sheep production systems, relying only upon unenclosed hill grazings.

Table 16 summarizes some of the improvements in production brought about by the introduction of paddock grazing systems of various levels of sophistication. In the first example the management aim is to increase stock numbers considerably, and to achieve a modest increase in individual animal performance. To this end costs and inputs have been kept low and full use is made of existing vegetation. The paddocks are formed by enclosing *Agrostis-Festuca* grassland which is then subject to increased grazing pressure to improve diet quality but is otherwise unimproved. The results show that over the first four years weight of lamb produced per hectare was doubled and wool production increased by 75 per cent. In this particular system, pasture quality in the enclosed paddocks is the limiting factor and further increases in production could only be obtained by upgrading the composition of the vegetation. The second paddock system, in a blanket bog/heather environment, uses relatively high-quality pasture dependent on fertilizer application.

This high-input approach is essential wherever there is insufficient natural vegetation of adequate quality. Over four years lamb production per sheep increased by 21 per cent but this is far short of the potential maximum for good-quality pasture and ultimately the limiting factor will be either the area of improved paddocks that can be formed or the capacity of the residual unimproved hill land to carry sheep without vegetation damage. Financially, sheep systems such as these can be expected, over 10 years, to produce a return of 20 per cent on the extra capital employed and to increase gross margins by 75 per cent.[32] Further development of these systems is possible by removing stock

Table 16. Improvement in sheep production brought about by introducing new pastoral systems in two areas with contrasting vegetation

System A	Objective:	To increase both stocking rate and production per animal
	Location:	South Scotland
	Vegetation:	On unenclosed land: *Agrostis-Festuca* and grass-heath 223ha
		In paddocks: *Agrostis-Festuca* 60ha
	Input:	Fencing and grazing control in paddocks. No pasture improvement and no fertilizer
	Breed:	Cheviot
	Data:	Eadie, Armstrong and Maxwell, 1973 (reference 30)

			Year		
		1969	1970	1971	1972
Sheep numbers		398	451	518	529
Stocking rate/ha		1·41	1·59	1·83	1·87
Weaning (%)		84·7	86·5	103·3	105·1
Total weight of lamb	kg/ha	26·0	32·4	51·9	49·8
weaned	kg/ewe	18·5	20·4	28·4	26·7
Total weight of wool	kg/ha	2·8	3·6	4·5	4·8
	kg/ewe	2·0	2·2	2·5	2·6

System B	Objective:	To increase production/animal with a slight increase in stocking rate. Stocking rate originally 0·52/ha raised to 0·94/ha in 1968 without increase in individual animal production
	Location	Argyll
	Vegetation:	On unenclosed land: Blanket bog and heather 340ha
		In paddocks: Blanket bog and heather 75% with improved grassland patches 25% 69 ha
		Ryegrass/clover 22 ha
	Input:	Fencing, fertilizers and reseeding in paddocks
	Breed:	Blackface
	Data:	Eadie, Maxwell, Kerr and Currie, 1973 (reference 31)

			Year		
		1969	1970	1971	1972
Sheep numbers		339	361	373	384
Stocking rate/ha		0·79	0·84	0·87	0·89
Weaning (%)		85·0	92·5	103·5	103·0
Total weight of lamb	kg/ha	16·7	19·7	23·8	22·9
weaned	kg/ewe	21·3	23·6	27·5	25·7
Total weight of wool	kg/ha	1·5	1·8	1·8	1·9
	kg/ewe	1·9	2·1	2·1	2·1

from the hills from January to April and feeding them in sheltered enclosures. The winter carrying capacity of the unimproved hill land is then not a limiting factor and both sheep numbers and individual animal performance could be further increased.

Red deer and grouse

At present, sheep-based systems associated with some cattle offer the only practical means of animal production on hill land. A third form of production that may become viable in future is the domestication and farming of red deer (*Cervus elaphus*). By raising their nutritional levels, growth rates of red deer can be greatly increased and food conversion rates at least as good as that obtainable from sheep are possible. Red deer farming is at present being tried experimentally in northeast Scotland[33] and while it is too early to conclude that such an enterprise is either technically or economically viable, the results so far are promising. Even so, deer farming is unlikely to compete with or supplant the exploitation of wild red deer as a game animal in Scotland: it may simply prove to be an alternative use of land presently devoted to sheep production.

Wild red deer have long been hunted as game animals in the higher and more inaccessible hills where they are often the principal grazing animal. Their range overlaps that of sheep but there is little information available on possible interactions between the two, although experience on the island of Rhum indicates that there is some benefit to the deer when both species graze together, possibly as a result of the higher combined stocking rate.[34]

Red grouse (*Lagopus scoticus*) is the only other species of sufficient economic importance to rival sheep. Grouse shooting is a valuable source of income on Highland estates and in some areas is the primary land use. Grouse are dependent on heather for food and the quality of the diet obtained, especially in spring, exerts a major influence on population density and breeding success.[35] Young heather is preferred for food but older heather is needed for cover, so that an appropriate mixture of the two is required within each grouse territory. This calls for a small-scale patchwork of young and older stands whereas for sheep, larger stands are suitable. Grouse utilize no more than 5 per cent of the annual growth of young shoots of heather[36] and it is unlikely, therefore, that they compete with sheep seriously for food, at least at normal sheep stocking rates.

Enclosures

Enclosure serves two major functions. Firstly, it allows control of grazing pressure and hence the quality of the animal's diet. For this purpose the vegetation enclosed should be more or less homogeneous so that the opportunity for selective grazing is minimized. Secondly, it permits high utilization rates and efficient cycling of nutrients through the animal. The importance of this is seen from the data of Floate[37] (Table 17). Acid grasslands are associated with nutrient cycles in which the total amount of nutrients present is quite large but very little is present in a form available to plants. The supply of nitrogen and phosphorus available from the decomposition of ungrazed herbage is very small, but when all the herbage is grazed and the dung and urine returned to the sward the quantity of nutrients available increases greatly. Nevertheless, although the effect of grazing is dramatic, the quantity of nutrients is still low and a further input is required. Applications of lime and phosphatic fertilizer enable white clover to be introduced and if such a pasture is grazed, thus recycling the nitrogen fixed by the clover, the situation is transformed[38] (Table 18). This combination of nutrient input, efficient grazing and nutrient recycling is essential for high-producing pastures. Without fenced enclosures the full

Table 17. Effect of grazing and the cycling of nutrients through the animal on the potential availability of nitrogen and phosphorus to the sward

		Potentially available nutrients from:	
Nutrients in herbage (kg/ha)		(a) decomposition of herbage in complete absence of grazing (kg/ha)	(b) excreta derived from grazed herbage assuming 100% utilization (kg/ha)
Nitrogen	52·70	0·02–2·89	32·90–34·10
Phosphorus	5·44	0·43–1·76	4·19–5·60

Source: Floate, M. J. S. (1970). Plant Nutrient Cycling in Hill Land. *Hill Farming Research Organization, 5th Report 1967–1970.*

Table 18. Effects of controlled grazing, alone and combined with fertilizer inputs and reseeding with ryegrass and clover, on the amount of nitrogen and phosphorus recycled through the animal

	Utilized dry matter (kg/ha)	Excreta Nitrogen		Faecal Phosphorus	
		kg/ha	% Soil pool	kg/ha	% Soil pool
Uncontrolled grazing low grazing pressure	895	16	0·48	2·4	0·39
Grazing control	2070	38	1·08	5·8	0·90
Grazing control +Ca, P, K, N +reseeding grass and clover	6430	179	5·21	21·5	2·45

Source: Floate, M. J. S., Eadie, J., Black, J. S. and Nicholson, I. A. (1973). Improvement of *Nardus* Dominant Hill Pasture by Grazing Control and Fertilizer Treatment and its Economic Assessment. *Proceedings of the 3rd Colloquium of the Potassium Institute*, pp. 33–39. Potassium Institute, Edinburgh.

benefit of the nutrient input is not obtained, partly because herbage utilization cannot be controlled and partly because nutrients are dispersed over a wide area where their influence is imperceptible.

Herbicides and pasture improvement

Control of plant succession is the essence of pasture improvement. The principal improvement successions are shown in Figure 15 which differentiates between those dependent on biotic and edaphic factors. In theory, it should be possible to set in motion the biotic successions leading to the elimination of bracken, *Molinia* or *Nardus* simply by applying high grazing pressures in fenced enclosures, where necessary after burning. In practice only *Molinia* can be dealt with in this way because it is relatively susceptible and because there are limits below which animal intake cannot be reduced by applying high

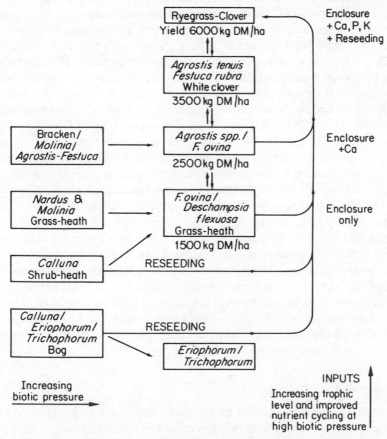

Figure 15. Vegetation successions associated with various input levels for pasture improvement

grazing pressures to poor-quality herbage. Alternatively, herbicides can be used, provided that the change is maintained thereafter by grazing pressure, and by this means all three species can be selectively eliminated from grass-heath or grassland.[39,40] However, the low quality of the resultant pasture makes it doubtful if the cost is justified, especially on unenclosed land without grazing control. The proper use of herbicides at the present time is as part of a comprehensive scheme of pasture up-grading involving enclosure, fertilizers and reseeding.

Pasture upgrading and reseeding

The *Agrostis-Festuca* grasslands and grass-heaths on acid podsolic soils are relatively species-poor. With increasing soil pH, *Agrostis tenuis*, *Festuca rubra* and white clover become abundant along with many other species and species diversity reaches a maximum.[41] With further increase in nutrient level, especially of phosphorus and nitrogen, accompanied by enclosure and controlled grazing a very productive pasture can be supported containing *Poa pratensis* or ryegrass amongst the dominant species, although with reduced species diversity. The pasture types throughout this succession are stable in their composition so long as they are in equilibrium with the appropriate soil nutrient level.

Although it is theoretically possible to upgrade a pasture in this way, or to introduce new species by oversowing existing vegetation, it is normal practice to destroy, or partially destroy by cultivation and herbicide, a low-grade vegetation and then to sow a ryegrass/white clover sward. This sward will change progressively, the ryegrass component diminishing until the composition equilibrates with whatever soil nutrient level and grazing regime can be maintained. Stability of composition is also a function of physical soil conditions and where drainage is poor the final equilibrium state will reflect this, an important factor when reseeding methods are extended to poorly drained sites. For example, it is possible to reseed blanket bog sites with grass and clover after suitable fertilizer applications. The resultant swards are spectacular but owing to the waterlogged conditions their long-term stability must be in doubt. Invasion by *Juncus* spp is a likely outcome and may be difficult to prevent at an acceptable cost. The normal form of drainage on hill land is open ditches which are used on poorly drained gley soils and peats. Both are difficult to drain and in a high rainfall climate open drains probably do little more than remove the surface run-off more rapidly.

Moor-burning

Molinia grass-heath, heather and bog vegetation are all subject to periodic burning in the interests of improving grazing quality. In the case of *Molinia*, the process is rather ineffective and succeeds principally in increasing the dominance of the species. For heather, burning is essential to renew the stand before it reaches a mature state. Gimingham[5] has reviewed this subject in detail and here reference will be made only to certain aspects. If heather regrowth is grazed heavily after burning, a branched, prostrate growth form results which maintains a fairly steady level of production of edible shoots for many years, about 2000–2500 kg/ha (1800–2200 lb/acre) per year being normal. Regeneration of a stand after burning is most rapid if the stand is not older than 12–15 years and the fire temperature does not exceed 500°C; both requirements are met by a 10-year burning cycle. Regeneration is then mainly from stem bases, whereas in older stands or stands partially killed by higher fire temperatures, re-establishment from seed is necessary, which may be slow. If re-establishment is very slow there may be a risk of surface erosion or of invasion by grasses and bracken, and this is further encouraged by heavy grazing. It is likely that, in the past, large areas of grass-heath, especially *Molinia* and *Nardus* grass-heaths on peaty podsol soils, have developed in this way from mixed communities in which heather was dominant.

Burning of *Calluna*-rich blanket bog is also practised. The various species such as *Molinia, Trichophorum, Eriophorum* and Sphagnum associated with *Calluna* react differently to the fire and, combined with the differential effects of selective grazing, marked changes in the vegetation can result. *Eriophorum, Trichophorum* and *Molinia*-dominant bogs may result from this process and it is thought that peat erosion may also be caused when the ground cover is severely damaged.[42]

CONSERVATION AND LAND USE

A major conservation objective must be to arrest and if possible reverse the deterioration in soil and vegetation that has taken place on many hill sites. This can be achieved within the context of a grazing ecosystem by an adequate input of soil nutrients along with improved grazing control. Such management is appropriate for land devoted to agricultural production but it does not imply that the indigenous vegetation is preserved, only that the vegetation be suitable for its productive function, is stable and is in equilibrium with the environment.

It is relatively easy to achieve this objective in the production paddocks of the new pastoral systems. Indeed, it is likely that for brown earth and other freely drained soils nutrient inputs from fertilizer and from clover combined with efficient nutrient cycling will result in much higher production levels and a stable vegetation. However, if this process of enclosure, fertilization and reseeding is extended to sites where soil physical conditions are poor and cannot economically be improved, on blanket bog sites for example, the long-term stability of the resultant sward must be in doubt.

Where the costs of fertilizers and pasture upgrading cannot be justified, as is the case on unenclosed hill land, resource conservation is restricted to what is possible by manipulation of the biotic factor alone. Since it is possible for stock numbers to be doubled and in time increased still further, the unenclosed hill land is potentially open to increased grazing pressures. This could be undesirable for some vegetation types but advantageous for others. The fact that grazing control exists on part of a farm implies that a degree of control can be exercised on the remainder, at least to the extent that season of use can be determined; if a boundary fence exists, overall stocking rate can also be controlled. If the farm boundary is fenced, high stocking rates can be used if desired, but if not, increasing stock numbers will cause the animals to extend their range either on to neighbouring farms or upwards onto the dwarf shrub-heaths above 2300 feet (700 metres) which will then be subject to increased risk of damage. This is ecologically undesirable anywhere but is specially so in the case of the rarer ecosystems such as the *Dryas* heaths in Scotland.[7]

The ability to control season of use and overall stock density is an advance on what is possible with traditional sheep farming in which no control is possible. However, within an area of hill land selective grazing will still operate and this must be taken into account. For example, if stocking rate is increased, little increased pressure will fall on the unpreferred species *Molinia* and *Nardus*. Bracken will also be unaffected but, on the other hand, *Agrostis-Festuca* grassland will be more heavily grazed. Mire and blanket bog communities are possibly most endangered when grazing pressures are high. Present-day stocking rates in regions where blanket bog is common range from 0·25–0·6 sheep/ha, the stock density on the bog itself probably being rather less. Increased stock densities in the range 1–2 sheep/ha might give utilization rates as high as 25–40 per cent for preferred species compared with present values in the range 5–20 per cent.[16] The long-term effect on the vegetation is so far unknown and will depend partly on the seasonal distribution of grazing pressure but some rare species may be at risk. Burning might become less necessary and since this is thought to be a major cause of damage to bog vegetation[8] benefits from this would have to be set against possible damage from high grazing pressure. Heather moors also are susceptible to high grazing pressures if burning is mismanaged; and on extreme podsols, especially on steep slopes, a stable grass cover may be slow to establish with consequent risks of erosion. However, since control of stocking rate and season of use is possible in these pastoral systems, there is no reason in principle why this cannot be used to prevent excessive grazing pressures on sensitive vegetation. For this to be successful, it is essential to know what is the optimum composition and structure of various community types, the tolerable limits of variation and the effects of grazing pressure. Without this information no positive conservation goal can be set and unless a goal is set it cannot be taken into account by management.

Conservation of the production potential of soils and vegetation will become a much more important goal in the agricultural management of the hills and uplands. But, as has been shown, this may not always be compatible with wildlife conservation and the achievement of other amenity objectives. The degree to which the output of pastoral farming can be improved depends upon the amount of capital invested in enclosure, fertilization and drainage, and in the level of biotic control that is possible. Conservation of plant species, natural vegetation, wildlife and visual amenity is also dependent on farming in the uplands but in its more traditional forms, and it is becoming increasingly clear that the greater intensity of production that is characteristic of the new pastoral systems makes it difficult to maintain wildlife conservation and amenity values on improved land. As Mutch[43] has pointed out, increasing intensification leads to a lesser degree of tolerance being shown by the primary user and to greater competition between alternative uses. A consequence of this will be that only a limited range of conservation objectives will be possible on the more intensively grazed land. However, not all land is equally suitable for the new pastoral systems, and some land may pass out of agricultural use altogether, giving new opportunities and problems for wildlife conservation. Elsewhere the more important wildlife features should be identified and managed to protect and enhance their wildlife values.

NOTES AND REFERENCES

1. In southwest England, in Wales and in areas of acid soil in the Pennines this was oak–birch forest which extended northwards as far as the Highland boundary fault, beyond this giving way to pine associated with birch and oak while in the far north birch forest was predominant.
2. Hughes, R. E., Dales, J., Williams, I. E. and Rees, D. I. (1973). Studies in Sheep Production and Environment in N.W. Wales: I. The Status of the Sheep in the Mountains of N. Wales since Mediaeval times. *Journal of Applied Ecology*, **10**, 113–132.
3. Jenny, H. (1941). *Factors of Soil Formation*, McGraw-Hill, New York and London.
4. The pH of these soils varies widely according to the base content of the parent material or of the spring water which percolates down the slope. The soils are commonly surface-water gleys in which an impermeable layer causes water to percolate laterally so that the upper part of the soil profile is more severely waterlogged than the lower part.
5. Gimingham, C. H. (1972). *Ecology of Heathlands*, Chapman and Hall, London.
6. Detailed accounts of individual vegetation types may be found in The Vegetation of Scotland (note 7); Plant Communities of the Scottish Highlands (note 8); and in many individual publications and papers including those by Gimingham (note 5); King (note 9); Edgell (note 10); Ratcliffe (note 11); Lloyd, Grime and Rorison (note 12); and Lloyd (note 13).
7. Burnett, J. H. (ed.) (1964). *The Vegetation of Scotland*, Oliver & Boyd, Edinburgh.
8. McVean, D. N. and Ratcliffe, D. A. (1962). *Plant Communities of the Scottish Highlands*; HMSO, London.
9. King, J. (1962). The *Festuca-Agrostis* Grassland Complex in S.E. Scotland. *Journal of Ecology*, **50**, 321–355.
10. Edgell, M. C. R. (1969). Vegetation of an Upland Ecosystem: Cader Idris, Merionethshire. *Journal of Ecology*, **57**, 335–359.
11. Ratcliffe, D. A. (1959). The Vegetation of the Carneddau N. Wales: I. Grasslands, Heaths and Bogs. *Journal of Ecology*, **47**, 371–413.

12. Lloyd, P. S., Grime, J. P. and Rorison, I. H. (1971). The Grassland Vegetation of the Sheffield Region: I. General Features. *Journal of Ecology*, **59**, 863–886.
13. Lloyd, P. S. (1972). The Grassland Vegetation of the Sheffield region: II Classification of Grassland types. *Journal of Ecology*, **60**, 739–776.
14. Allen, S. E., Evans, C. C. and Grimshaw, H. M. (1969). The Distribution of Mineral Nutrients in Soil after Heather Burning. *Oikos*, **20**, 6–25.
15. Allen, S. E., Carlisle, A., White, E. J. and Evans, C. C. (1968). The Plant Nutrient Content of Rainwater. *Journal of Ecology*, **56**, 497–504.
16. Grant, S. A. (1974). Personal communication.
17. Milton, W. E. J. (1949). Effect of Manuring, Grazing and Cutting on the Yield, Botanical and Chemical Composition of Natural Hill Pastures: I. *Journal of Ecology*, **28**, 326–356.
18. Nicholson, I. A. (1969). Personal communication.
19. Eadie, J. (1970). Personal communication.
20. Grant, S. A. (1971). Interactions of Grazing and Burning on Heather Moors. *Journal of the British Grassland Society*, **26**, 173–181.
21. Miller, G. R. and Miles, A. M. (1969). Productivity and Management of Heather. In: *Grouse research in Scotland, 13th Progress Report*, Nature Conservancy, Edinburgh.
22. Forrest, G. I. (1971). Structure and Production of N. Pennine Blanket Bog Vegetation. *Journal of Ecology*, **59**, 453–480.
23. Eadie, J. (1967). The Nutrition of Grazing Hill Sheep: Utilization of Hill Pastures. *Hill Farming Research Organization, 4th Report 1964–1967*.
24. Russel, A. J. F. (1971). Relationships between Energy Intake and Productivity in Hill Sheep. *Proceedings of the Nutrition Society*, **30**, 197–204.
25. Hunter, R. F. (1962). Hill Sheep and their Pasture: A Study of Sheep Grazing in S.E. Scotland. *Journal of Ecology*, **50**, 651–680.
26. Armstrong, R. H. and Eadie, J. (1973). Some Aspects of the Growth of Hill Lambs. *Hill Farming Research Organization 6th Report, 1971–1973*.
27. Milne, J. A. (1974). The Effects of Season and Age of Stand on the Nutritive Value of Heather (*Calluna vulgaris* L. Hull) to Sheep. *Journal of Agricultural Science*, **83**, 281–9.
28. Grant, S. A. and Hunter, R. F. (1968). Interactions of Grazing and Burning on Heather Moors and their Implications in Heather Management. *Journal of the British Grassland Society*, **23**, 285–293.
29. Russel, A. J. F., Foot, J. Z. and Maxwell, T. J. (1973). Personal communication.
30. Eadie, J., Armstrong, R. H. and Maxwell, T. J. (1973). Hill Sheep Production Systems: Development on the Cheviots. *Proceedings of the 3rd Colloquium of the Potassium Institute*, pp. 139–144. Potassium Institute, Edinburgh.
31. Eadie, J., Maxwell, T. J., Kerr, C. D. and Currie, D. C. (1973). Hill Sheep Production Systems: Development on Blanket Peat. *Proceedings of the 3rd Colloquium of the Potassium Inst.*, pp. 145–154, Potassium Institute, Edinburgh.
32. Maxwell, T. J., Eadie, J. and Sibbald, A. R. (1973). Economic Appraisal of Hill Sheep Production. *Hill Farming Research Organization 6th Report 1971–1973*.
33. Blaxter, K. L., Kay, R. N. B., Sharman, G. A. M., Cunningham, J. M. M. and Hamilton, W. J. (1974). *Farming the Red Deer*, HMSO, London.
34. Lowe, V. P. W. (1970). Some Effects of a Change in Estate Management on a Deer Population. In *The Scientific Management of Animal and Plant Communities for Conservation*, 11th Symposium of the British Ecological Society, pp. 437–456.
35. Jenkins, D., Watson, A. and Miller, G. R. (1967). Population Fluctuations in the Red Grouse (*Lagopus scoticus*). *Journal of Animal Ecology*, **36**, 97–122.

36. Miller, G. R., Jenkins, D. and Watson, A. (1966). Heather Performance and Red Grouse Populations: I. Visual Estimates of Heather Performance. *Journal of Applied Ecology*, **3**, 313–326.
37. Floate, M. J. S. (1970). Plant Nutrient Cycling in Hill Land. *Hill Farming Research Organization 5th Report 1967–1970*.
38. Floate, M. J. S., Eadie, J., Black, J. S. and Nicholson, I. A. (1973). Improvement of *Nardus* Dominant Hill Pasture by Grazing Control and Fertilizer Treatment and its Economic Assessment. *Proceedings of the 3rd Colloquium of the Potassium Institute*, pp. 33–39. Potassium Institute, Edinburgh.
39. Allen, G. P. (1968). The Potential Role of Herbicides in Grassland Improvement. *Proceedings of the 9th British Weed Control Conference*, pp. 1231–1237.
40. Scragg, E. B., McKelvie, A. D. and Kilgour, D. W. (1972). Control of Bracken with Asulam in the North of Scotland. *Proceedings of the 11th British Weed Control Conference*, pp. 335–341.
41. Such community types (species-rich *Agrostis-Festuca*) occur naturally on limestone and other base-rich soils.
42. Tallis, J. H. (1973). Studies in S. Pennine Peats: V. Direct Observations on Peat Erosion and Peat Hydrology at Featherbed Moss, Derbyshire. *Journal of Ecology*, **51**, 1–23.
43. Mutch, W. (1972). Land Resource Use. *Minutes of Evidence of Select Committee on Scottish Affairs*, pp. 495–500, HMSO, London.

1. Harvesting 220 acres of barley in Gloucestershire (photo: *Farmers' Weekly*, K. Huggett)

In 30 years British agriculture has been transformed by more capital and by more skilled men to become one of the most productive industries in Europe. Its capacity to change the environment has grown along with the technical developments.

2. Ploughing after the barley crop in Hampshire (photo: *Farmers' Weekly*, P. Adams)

3. The Bedfordshire landscape in 1968 (photo: Aerofilms)

The environmental consequences of postwar developments in agriculture are most clearly visible on the arable lands of the east and south where the loss of cover, particularly in hedges and hedgerow trees, is now substantially complete. By 1970, nearly all the land shown here had been ploughed with large fields of about 80 acres in size. Little now remains of the former Enclosure landscape (Chapters 1, 2 and 7).

4. Traditional Enclosure landscape near Bath, Avon (photo: Countryside Commission)

Even in areas of mixed and pastoral farming, the maintenance of cover is no longer vital. These areas will increasingly reflect developments in grass and stock farming (Chapters 1, 5 and 7).

5. Chalk grassland at Wye and Crundale Down National Nature Reserve, Kent (photo: Nature Conservancy Council, P. Wakely)

Much of this once widespread habitat has been destroyed; it remains only on scattered sites. Even if these are not ploughed, their scientific interest may be threatened by lack of management or by 'agricultural improvement' to increase the output of grass at the expense of flowering plants.

6. Ridge and furrow pasture at Upwood, Cambridgeshire (photo: T. Wells)

Arable strips in the open fields of Saxon and medieval England were grassed over to form extensive sheep and cattle pastures between the fifteenth and seventeenth centuries. Like flood meadows, ridge and furrow pastures often had a consistent pattern of management over many centuries which allowed a rich flora to develop. Most of these pastures have now been 'improved' or ploughed.

7. Flood meadow at North Meadow, Cricklade National Nature Reserve, Wiltshire (photo: Nature Conservancy Council, P. Wakely)

Meadows which are regularly flooded in winter are often cut for hay. Those which have been managed in the same way over long periods have a rich flora which may include the Fritillary (Plate 13). Their conservation interest is threatened by grazing improvement with herbicides and fertilizers.

8. One of the few remaining working water meadows at Great Durnford, Wiltshire (photo: Nature Conservancy Council, P. Wakely)

These areas are not especially rich biologically but they are of great interest to the social historian.

9. Rich dyke flora at Coleman's Drain, Woodwalton Fen, Cambridge-shire (photo: Nature Conservancy Council, P. Wakely)

Because of more frequent dyke management and the use of herbicides, many dykes have lost most of their biological interest. It is usually possible to modify management practices to accommodate both drainage and conservation requirements (Chapter 4).

10. Trees in the modern farm landscape are often taken for granted: they suffer from lack of any positive management. With just a little attention such as rotational pollarding or coppicing, the life of some species, like the willows on this farm in Oxfordshire, can be significantly prolonged (photo: R. Cobham)

Local or rare plants threatened by the destruction of their habitat (photos: Nature Conservancy Council, P. Wakely).

11. Round-leaved Fluellen (*Linaria spuria*), a cornfield weed

12. Pasque Flower (*Anemone pulsatilla*), a plant of chalk and limestone grassland

13. Fritillary (*Fritillaria meleagris*), a characteristic plant of flood meadows cut for hay; now largely confined to the Thames Valley

14. Early Spider Orchid (*Ophrys sphegodes*), a plant of chalk and limestone grassland; now largely confined to Dorset

15. A severely cropped hedge near Dullingham, Cambridgeshire (photo: Countryside Commission)

The landscape and wildlife value of hedgerows is reduced if not extinguished by bad management such as cropping too close to the ground which removes shelter and prevents saplings from growing up (Chapter 3).

16. The ideal hedge shape for wildlife seems to be an 'A' form with maximum cover at the base, like this one in Cambridgeshire on the Stetchworth Estate (photo: Countryside Commission)

Chapter 7

Landscape and agricultural change

P. L. LEONARD AND C. STOAKES

The British landscape is like a very old building: it still bears unmistakable marks of the original construction but reveals the numerous alterations of later occupants.

The rural landscape was much changed by the Industrial Revolution. The growth of industry, and the cities it supported, resulted in a loss of farmland and had a marked impact on the land that remained in rural uses. In recent times energy, water and transport developments have also changed the face of the countryside. Motorways and power lines have had a particular impact on remote areas, changing the scale of landscapes. Similar effects have followed from forestry and water catchment activities in the uplands. Many of these changes have been superimposed on the landscape from outside; they have taken place as part of national policies largely unrelated to the rural economy. But in the last two decades the countryside has begun to change dramatically from within: farming, the creator of most of our rural landscapes, has undergone a revolution. This chapter deals with the effects of this revolution on the landscape.

THE RURAL LANDSCAPE TODAY

The rural landscape of the British Isles can be broadly subdivided according to the use to which the land is put. Some 80 per cent of our land is in productive agriculture, about 7 per cent is forest or woodland, 8–9 per cent serves urban, industrial or transport needs, and the remainder performs water catchment, military, recreation or nature conservation functions. Precise land use statistics do not exist but information is available from two land use surveys undertaken in the last 40 years, and also from sources such as the Ministry of Agriculture's annual returns. Although the proportion of land in the various use categories varies from region to region, there can be no doubt that productive uses for food and fibre dominate the countryside (Table 19). The prominence of agriculture in land use terms means that farmers and landowners are largely responsible for shaping the rural landscape; they also carry the burden of maintaining it.

121

Table 19.   Land use in the UK

Use	England and Wales millions of acres	%	Scotland and Northern Ireland millions of acres	%	UK millions of acres	%
Agriculture:	29·5	80	17·8	79	47·3	79
improved	24·5	66	5·8	26	30·3	51
rough grazing	5·0	13	12·0	53	17·0	28
Woodland	2·5	7	2·0	9	4·5	8
Urban/industrial/ communications	4·0	11	0·7	3	4·7	8
Other	1·0	3	2·0	9	3·0	5
Total	37·0	100	22·5	100	59·5	100

Source: Estimated from Ministry of Agriculture, Fisheries and Food Annual Returns, 1970.

The varied geology of Britain, combined with different histories of development, had produced landscapes noted for their local and regional diversity.
Improved technology, communications and the move to specialist agricultural
systems have reduced this variety and agricultural landscapes are today much
simpler and more uniform. For convenience, they can be divided into two
major groups of farmed landscapes: the *uplands* which include those areas
above the 800-feet contour (although officially they are defined on the basis of
the hill cow line[1]) and the *lowlands* which include all the areas of intensive
arable and livestock farming. The basis of this separation rests upon differing
topography, soils and climate, and the contrasting farming systems which have
evolved.

UPLAND LANDSCAPES

While the uplands may be defined by the geographer as land above a certain
contour, in agricultural terms they are considered to be those areas where the
hill sheep and hill cow subsidy applies.[1] Certain other areas, such as parts of
Exmoor and South Wales, although they lie just outside the hill cow subsidy
line, share many common features with upland farms and for landscape
purposes may be included in the same category. Of a total agricultural area of
47 million acres, 14 million, or nearly one-third, are situated in the hills. Of this
land, only about 16 per cent is enclosed and cultivated for crops and grass; the
remaining 84 per cent is rough grazing. One-quarter of our total land area
produces only 4 per cent of our agricultural output.[2] In terms of farm
economics upland enterprises are marginal, and since 1946 this fact has been
recognized by successive governments who have made special forms of assistance available.

Physical constraints have never allowed farming in the uplands to develop and intensify in the way that it has in the lowlands. Rather, a relatively stable system operates, based upon the rearing of hill cattle and sheep for sale for fattening on lowland farms: this system has changed remarkably little over the centuries. There are two major types of farm: true hill farms which occupy the wildest, most remote and inhospitable country and adopt an extensive system of farming; and upland farms at slightly lower altitudes where the general environment is less severe. While stock rearing is the basic enterprise for both, the lower farms with better soils, less steep slopes and some sheltered land are more likely to rear cattle and also to sell some fat rather than store stock.

The distinctive landscape pattern in upland areas reflects both the distribution of settlements and the zonation of land use intensity. The villages, hamlets and farmsteads are located in valley bottoms and on the foothills of mountains. Traditionally all the buildings are fashioned of local stone and roughly faced; they are surrounded by a few trees of varied species, either isolated or in small clumps. Farmsteads are normally strategically sited in small hollows, nestled into hillsides or elsewhere where some degree of protection and shelter is afforded. With many of the older farmhouses, barns for in-wintering stock are part of the main building so that the farmstead is compact in appearance.

Around the farmsteads and on the lower hill slopes is enclosed land (in-bye, in-tak, allotments or ffridd). Centuries ago, the in-bye consisted of a single large field around the farm buildings which had to serve multi-purpose uses— growing crops such as potatoes, oats and rye, and also pasturing stock in winter and spring. The productivity of the field was considerably improved by the application of manure, by the removal of stones and by cultivation. As time passed more and more of the rough grazing near at hand was taken in and added to the in-bye. Enclosure in the uplands has traditionally been by the erection of dry stone walls, partly for durability and partly to clear the land of stones. Except around hamlets and farmsteads, the walls follow straight, rectangular patterns reflecting the fact that they were built during the enclosure movement in the late eighteenth and early nineteenth centuries.[3] There are, however, some hedged enclosures on pockets of lower ground in certain regions. Apart from enclosing the fields (at a cost in 1800 no greater than the cost of planting a hedge, and much less taking long-term maintenance costs into consideration), stone walls are also valuable in the uplands as shelter for stock. The walls, like the buildings, closely reflect local geology.

The enclosed in-bye land varies in quality, the best usually lying near the farmstead. Enclosed fields or allotments, however, are often amenable to improvement. In the past this consisted of ploughing, cultivating and applying fertilizer in the form of manure and rock phosphate on the flatter land, and fertilizing alone on the steeper fields. Further improvement resulted from the use of basic slag, which began in the mid-nineteenth century. More advanced machinery in this century enabled many of the allotments to be ploughed up and reseeded with more productive grass swards for the first time. These allotments are now mainly used for grazing livestock from about October–April and, of course, for lambing. On the better land it is possible to grow some arable crops (roots, barley) in rotation with leys; on the poorer land only permanent pasture is possible.

Many of the allotments contain small stone huts (field houses or hog houses) which were originally used both for the storage of hay and also sometimes to house stock in winter. They are usually sited near the edge of a field close to a gateway, and in some areas clumps of trees grow around them. Most of these field houses have for long been redundant and are falling into decay.

The fell wall traditionally marks the limit of enclosure, and separates the rectangular allotment fields from the open rough grazings above. The position of the wall on the hill slope has shifted continually in the past, reflecting the economic vagaries of hill sheep and cow production. In most upland areas it reached its highest position on the fellside in the mid-nineteenth century. Since this date, especially during the agricultural depression of the 1930s, much of the upper enclosed land has been abandoned by hill farmers, as it became no longer economic to manage it to a sufficient degree of intensity. This trend is reflected in the landscape by the encroachment below the old fell wall of bracken, and in places of scrub such as hawthorn or gorse. In the past, bracken was controlled by annual cutting in autumn, and the dead vegetation of the previous summer's growth was often used for bedding livestock in winter.

Above the fell wall lie the open 'rough grazings' which it has always been considered uneconomic to improve. They are used mainly for extensive sheep grazing at very low densities (usually less than 1 sheep/acre) but also for grouse shooting, and increasingly in this century for forestry or defence training. The moors are characterized by particular semi-natural vegetation communities which vary according to topography, slope, soil type, local climate, and other factors. The most common community is heather moor, but on gritstone edges, bilberry moor is typical. Likewise on poorly drained, peaty plateaus, bog vegetation is found which often consists of a mixture of sphagnum, deer sedge, cotton grass and purple moor grass. Above altitudes of about 2000 feet mountain vegetation types occur, sometimes with rare and interesting 'relict plants' which, while common in early post-glacial times, have now retreated to the most inaccessible sites. These habitats are described in some detail in Chapter 6.

The visual effect along open hillsides is one of horizontal bands of vegetation merging into one another as the altitude increases. First is the green, productive grasslands on the lowermost slopes of the in-bye (their colour probably intensified by the application of fertilizers); this is followed by a zone of rust-coloured bracken; a band of whitish, bleached mat-grass (*Nardus*) indicating more heavily leached soils further up the slope; and finally come the purple hues of heather moor or the dark tones of bog. This horizontal zonation of vegetation with the contours, although it varies in detail from place to place, is typical of the uplands. But the zonation is changing with the selective spraying of bracken on both allotment and moorland, and the improvement of pasture, particularly on enclosed land.

The general absence of trees and woods is striking, considering that woodland is the natural vegetation type over most of the land below about 1700 feet. Although all the upland grassland and much of the moorland was once under tree cover, centuries of interference by man have so altered the nature of the soil that native trees can no longer become established in many areas. Elsewhere, grazing or burning effectively prevent the growth of any tree seedlings. Only fragments of woodlands now remain in the uplands and it is doubtful whether any of these are truly 'natural'. They occupy distinctive habitats such as narrow valleys and gorges, small cliffs and rocky outcrops, and steep slopes. The most common type is mixed deciduous woodland but ash dominates in limestone gills, with oak on the more acid soils, alder in wet places, and birch and rowan at higher altitudes. In parts of Scotland there are remnants of the old Caledonian pine forest. Although the condition of all these woodland patches is variable, those which are accessible to grazing animals are frequently overmature or derelict and are not regenerating.

To summarize, the existing landscape of the farmed uplands is one which, because of physical constraints, has altered little over the last few centuries. Most of the notable landscape features are natural or semi-natural, such as the zones of vegetation of different texture and colour on the fell sides and summits; rock outcrops, screes and cliffs; mountain streams and becks with fringing vegetation; and patches of woodland on steep slopes and in ravines. Man's artifacts are limited to buildings usually of local materials, field boundaries which are typically stone walls, and groups of trees planted around buildings or as shelter belts. While the positive process of changing agricultural practices is affecting the face of the uplands, as Chapter 6 shows, the decline and neglect of existing features, such as woods and groups of trees, stone walls and vernacular buildings, is likely to have most impact on the landscape.

LOWLAND FARMED LANDSCAPES

Below about 800 feet, where soils are more fertile, the climate less extreme and relief more subdued, farmers are able to take full advantage of developments in agricultural science and technology. In addition, the availability of rapid bulk transit for produce and raw materials permits much greater flexibility in the type of enterprise which can be undertaken. It is in the lowlands that the full impact of the post-war agricultural revolution has been felt.

The traditional landscape, typically depicted in tourist brochures and perhaps in the eyes of most town dwellers, is one of a patchwork of small fields enclosed by hedgerows, with abundant hedgerow trees and small woodlands. In parts of the country, particularly the southeast and southwest, hedges, banks and ditches have for many centuries divided the land into small fields. In the midlands and elsewhere, however, enclosure was carried out in an orderly, planned fashion in the eighteenth and early nineteenth centuries at the request of landlords seeking increased agricultural efficiency. Open fields, farmed communally by villagers, were divided up by straight hedges into regularly sized units in which soil and sward improvement and controlled stocking could take place. The hedgerows of the enclosure movement were commonly planted of thorn with regularly spaced standard trees of oak, ash or elm. They were cut and laid at intervals and thus provided effective stockproof boundaries with sticks and firewood as a bonus. Hedgerow trees contributed timber to estate sawmills.

Changes in agricultural practices in the last 20 years, particularly those of increasing specialization and mechanization, have radically altered the appearance of the lowlands. The trend has been for the eastern counties to adopt arable systems, displacing the traditional mixed husbandry, and for livestock enterprises to dominate in the western half of the country. The replacement of the horse by the tractor, the substitution of ever more sophisticated machinery for hand labour, the adoption of chemical methods of weed control and other improvements have enabled agricultural efficiency to more than double in the post-war period, and this has been encouraged by government policies and economic support, as Chapter 1 describes.

Changes in farm management and practice have had four major impacts on the lowland landscape:[4]

1. Large-scale industrialized buildings have been erected. Modern mechanized farming requires new farm buildings to store machinery, fertilizers and grain and to house livestock. Most of the pre-war buildings are far too small to accommodate the larger modern machines or to house stock on an economic scale. Furthermore, they are usually located at the farmstead rather than at the optimal point for timely distribution or collection from all parts of the holding. Buildings are by far the most expensive item of capital expenditure on the farm and they must be flexible enough to avoid early obsolescence. Flexibility is largely dependent on eaves height and the design of new farm buildings is often constrained by this factor. Standardized, factory-made farm buildings and components are the cheapest, but they are of necessity fairly uniform in design, colour and shape. Their adoption has contributed to the decline in regional character as local building materials have ceased to be commonly used.

2. Fields have been enlarged. Field sizes have increased from an average of about 15–20 acres in 1945 to at least double this acreage today. The major landscape effect has been the loss of hedges and hedgerow trees as internal field boundaries on farms have been removed in the interests of agricultural efficiency. Not only do hedges obstruct machines and restrict the flexibility of operations, they also impose a considerable maintenance burden on the farmer, often impede drainage improvements, and harbour pests and weeds. They now perform no useful agricultural function.

3. Trees have been lost without replacement. The loss of hedgerows and hedgerow trees has been most apparent in the arable east. In parts of Hunting-

donshire, for example, an average of 140 feet of hedge/acre has been removed since 1945 and the number of hedgerow trees has declined by 80 per cent. However, the loss of trees is likely to be a more serious problem than the loss of hedgerows in the future. The Merthyr Committee[5] concluded in 1952 that a ratio of six saplings to every mature tree had to be maintained for full replacement of the tree population. Surveys by the Forestry Commission revealed that this ratio was two saplings to each mature tree in 1951[6] and one sapling to each mature tree in 1965.[7] The New Agricultural Landscapes Study area surveys[8] show that the ratio of saplings to mature trees in arable areas is only about 1:5 although on an average for the whole country it is 1:2·6. This suggests that the decline in the number of trees in the countryside will accelerate even if no positive action is taken to remove trees in the future. The spread of Dutch elm disease and the recent dry summers have clearly compounded an already acute problem.

4. Chemical control has improved crop yields, reduced weeds and eliminated other species which make no direct contribution to food production; this has altered the microlandscape of tilled land.

The combination of all these changes in lowland arable regions has resulted in farmed landscapes characterized by large, even-sized fields of about 50 acres in size, though often reaching over 100 acres, separated usually by poor-quality hedges, with prominent large-scale new farm buildings. The old 'patchwork' pattern of fields has largely disappeared as traditional mixed farming systems have made way for increasing specialization in roots or cereals. Cover is sparse and large new buildings prominent. Farming systems are now so uniform that the same crop may be seen over hundreds of acres at any one time. The increased simplicity of the arable landscape extends to the small scale as well as the large since 'microfeatures' such as stooks and colourful cornfield weeds have also disappeared.

In some arable areas of eastern England these changes have already come about, and little remains to remind us of the enclosure landscape. Elsewhere they are either taking place at the moment or have hardly begun. Evidence from the New Agricultural Landscapes report[8] suggests that these changes will revolutionize the appearance of the countryside throughout the lowlands within the next 10 or 20 years. Although the post-war changes have been less dramatic on livestock farms, partly because government subsidies have been focused on encouraging more intensive cereal production, animal husbandry is itself undergoing a revolution. It is possible to walk through the fields of a stock farm today and see no evidence of the animals themselves, except perhaps for the effluent lagoon by large new animal-housing sheds, often occupying a site away from the traditional courtyard farmstead. These are the farms of zero grazing where grass is cropped and brought to the animals. When the stock are permanently housed, the rest of the farm is managed in exactly the same precise, mechanized way as a well-run arable farm, and hedges, trees and odd patches of unproductive land face a similar fate.

LANDSCAPE VALUES

There are many different views about the values of various features in the landscape. Whereas most wildlife conservationists might agree on the general values that they would subscribe to, and indeed on the order of priorities that might be set out in any programme of nature conservation, those interested in the landscape often have diverging and sometimes opposing views. There seem to be seven main ways in which landscape may be valued: as a record of the past; as an expression of local or regional character; as a contrast to the urban scene; as an artform which confers status; as a reflection of pride in work; as a backcloth for informal recreation; and for its wildlife interest—a value which is fully considered in other chapters.

As a record of the past

Until the Industrial Revolution, the society of Britain was agrarian. The landscape contains a historical record of that society; for Professor Hoskins, it is the oldest and richest record we possess.[9] Certain elements of the record, such as the remains of Roman settlements or early English villages, field patterns and ancient roads, are often protected as ancient monuments.[10] But there are many other historical features which are also worthy of conservation, including, for example, strip cultivations and many hedgerows, some of which as Hooper shows have existed since Saxon times.[11] Like the work of eighteenth-century landscape gardeners and examples of early canal and rail systems, these are important features of the rural landscape and worth protecting.

As an expression of local or regional character

The large metropolitan city, the new town and the suburb often seem characterless. Airport buildings, modern office blocks and residential estates in many countries show the same uniformity of design. This is not yet true of the British countryside, where distinctive regional landscapes have evolved. The diversity of the British scene has remained surprisingly intact under the influence of local differences not only in physical conditions but also in the habits of man. It is the record of human use, for example, that distinguishes the Somerset Levels from the Fens or the Lancashire Mosses.

As a contrast to the urban scene

It is ironic that despite continuing demands for the facilities of the city, despite worldwide drifts of population to urban centres, despite the efforts of planners and architects to improve the urban environment, many people who live in the cities seem to be discontented with them. It may be as a contrast to this deteriorating urban environment that most townsfolk place a high value on the countryside. Those who have moved to towns in the recent past may have a more specific reason for valuing the countryside—as reminders of a rural background which they sometimes idealize.

As an artform which confers status

Veblen[12] has suggested that we value that most universal and useless of possessions, the garden lawn, because it consumes labour without producing anything. The owner acquires status by virtue of such possessions; certainly in Victorian times it was the non-functional elements of buildings which often gave status. So it may be with landscape parks, with great estates, and with other smaller areas. Whatever the merits of Veblen's theory of conspicuous consumption, the assigning of values to the non-functional is an important element within society. This poses serious problems for landscape conservation, because people seek to preserve agricultural landscapes which are now largely redundant. A practical extension of this philosophy can be seen in the attitudes of many people who have recently chosen to live in rural areas. They feel protective about the landscape in their immediate surroundings as this is seen to add to the value of their property. This attitude is most apparent in designated areas such as Green Belts and National Parks.

As a reflection of pride in work

There has been a recent revival of interest in a whole range of rural and semi-rural crafts which can be seen in part as a reaction to the impersonal products of mass-production. This movement echoes the suggestion of William Morris[13] that art is a matter of pride and understanding applied to work. In the rural context, many people value well-laid hedges, dry stone walls, thatched roofs, and other features which show fine workmanship.[14] Advocates of an alternative society founded upon 'intermediate technologies', subsistence production and the work of craftsmen, reject a machine-moulded landscape as much as the products of modern agriculture. The movement appears to be a growing one but so far has had no significant impact on the landscape.

As a backcloth for outdoor recreation

In much the same way that we value the landscape attributes of an urban park, so we value the rural area used for recreation. People derive pleasure from pleasant and varied surroundings whether these are found in places set aside for recreation (such as country parks) or more generally in the countryside. For most people, a visit to the countryside is particularly a visual pleasure. Although this may be derived from a consciously designed recreation landscape, the rapid growth of countryside trips increases the significance of agricultural landscapes as a backcloth for recreation.

Society and landscape values

For a sizeable group of the population interest in landscape is concerned only with the contrast it provides with urban environments and the arena it offers for certain outdoor activities. But three other groups are also worthy of attention: the farming community, amenity pressure groups, and other special interest groups, each of which appear to value the landscape in a quite specific way.

It is sometimes alleged that farmers and landowners are insensitive to the appearance of their land. What is seldom appreciated is that many farmers have a different concept of landscape to that held by the rest of society. Farmers probably do value landscape highly, but the scene they want to see is one created by an efficient and prosperous farming industry. The new asbestos-clad Dutch barns of the lowlands and barbed-wire enclosures in the uplands may give considerable pleasure to farmers, as symbols of progress and higher productivity. Likewise they favour a tidy landscape with neatly trimmed hedges and fields free of weeds, reflecting the needs of food production.[8]

Some members of amenity pressure groups, particularly those which are urban-based, may long for the idealized countryside of Thomas Hardy (although they seem unaware of the heavy human price that was paid for such a landscape). For these it is the features of human and biological history in the landscape rather than its expression of modern functions which are to be valued. Historical and archaeological societies have for long played an active role in the conservation of certain elements of the landscape. A new and expanding group are the natural history societies and county conservation trusts, who particularly value the biological interest of landscape. For these specialist groups, the objectives are explicit and most often well-publicized.[15] For others, notions of how the landscape should evolve, what should be protected and what forgone, are vague and indeterminate. Both pose problems for conservation: with such diversity of view and such a range of values at stake, the objectives of action are difficult to define. Meanwhile the landscape changes at an accelerating rate.

PROBLEMS IN LANDSCAPE CONSERVATION

Until recently, farmers produced a landscape which was acceptable because the main materials of agriculture (land and vegetation) were those of the natural environment. Agriculture as a biological science was strongly governed by the natural factors of soil, relief and climate and it conflicted little with other demands on the countryside.[16] Modern agriculture, however, has all the modern industrial characteristics of uniform layout, mechanization of routine and a reduced labour force, which have enabled higher productivity per unit to be achieved.

The extent to which the modern farmed landscape serves the various functions which other groups in society expect from the countryside is increasingly being questioned. As farming intensifies its activities, agricultural land is less able to accommodate the demands of the other interests. Many farmers see their task only in terms of producing food as efficiently as possible. If they acknowledge other values in their land, they often do not have the resources, or sufficient interest, to contribute to their conservation in any practical way.[17]

Cheap food imports have gone forever and Britain will need to encourage as high a degree of self-sufficiency as possible, continuing the achievements of the agricultural industry since the war, with more than a doubling of total output. But it can be argued that this increase in the efficiency of food production has turned much of the countryside into a single-purpose food factory. Farmers have been conditioned to believe that their only job is to stock the nation's larder. As Chapter 8 shows, universities and agricultural colleges and the advisory services of the Ministry of Agriculture have all encouraged this philosophy: the other responsibilities which farmers might reasonably bear as rural managers seem to have been forgotten. These include the provision and maintenance of public rights of way for access, the care and protection of valuable wildlife habitats and features of historic and scenic interest, and a practical concern for the conservation of landscape quality in general.

In towns, society accepts that privilege in the ownership of property carries with it certain responsibilities. Where conflicting interests require to be reconciled, as is the case with the development of land, elaborate planning procedures have been evolved to bring about a compromise between the individual and the social interest. In rural Britain this has not in the past been necessary; the strongly established mediaeval custom which gave a landowner many rights and privileges also imposed on him many duties. But the demands on and expectations of farmers and landowners have changed; the safeguarding of wider values in land, which seemed so assured three decades ago, has been threatened by the pressures to increase production, in the absence of adequate legal means of landscape protection.

What measures of landscape conservation should now be pursued? In theory the choice is wide: ranging from a continuation of faith in the ability of landowners to care for landscape values, to greater government intervention in landscape protection. But there are fallacies in a number of the present arguments; we examine, as examples, the following:

1. All is well, the farmer knows best;
2. If farmers could earn a decent living from the land, a healthy landscape would result;
3. Protective designations will ensure a good landscape;
4. The problem will be solved by voluntary action.

The farmer knows best

Farmers have always created a working landscape. An outcry accompanied enclosure and this was in part based upon contemporary aesthetic arguments;

but with the passage of time most people have grown to accept the enclosure landscape as one which is pleasing. Farmers would argue that the current objections are to the process of change rather than to the end result. The greatest strength to this argument is that man is adaptable and will probably accept and even like a poorer environment if he is given no choice. But choices do exist, for example between the production of food more economically and the better conservation of landscape quality. The problem is that the consumer can express a demand for cheaper food through the market mechanism more readily than he can argue a case for good landscapes.

If farmers could earn a decent living

There is a widely held belief among farmers and many countrymen that the depression of the 1930s, which led to widespread neglect of inessential jobs such as hedging and ditching, caused a rapid and noticeable decline in landscape quality. Many believe that the best landscapes are now being created by farmers who enjoy high incomes and can afford to devote resources to new planting. The fear is that Capital Transfer Tax and the proposed Wealth Tax will add to the rising cost burdens farmers face, reducing their ability to maintain and improve the appearance of their land, and forcing some to augment their income from such activities as felling trees. However, the scant evidence available suggests that it is the farmers with increasing incomes who are removing landscape features without replacement. Hedge removal and reclaiming marginal land for agriculture costs money and many poorer farmers can ill afford to spend money on such activities. Thus, even if some farmers were exempted from extra taxation on amenity grounds, there is no guarantee that the money saved would be used for amenity and conservation measures. What is more likely is that any additional investment would be designed to improve farm efficiency in an industry which has been short of capital. Moreover, apart from a few eighteenth-century landlords, farmers are not, nor have ever been, adept at planting or maintaining vegetation for aesthetic or ecological reasons.

Protective designations will ensure good landscape

The main protective designations (National Parks, Areas of Outstanding Natural Beauty and Green Belts) have not been accompanied by specific powers to encourage the creation or maintenance of a high-quality agricultural landscape. The designated areas may have been protected from the worst effects of building, mining, transport and other developments, but agricultural improvement remains outside the scope of development control, as Chapter 10 discusses. As the National Park Policies Review Committee have emphasized (and the government have accepted), it is farming, and particularly grazing, which is mainly responsible for the open landscapes of the national parks which are so highly valued, yet the National Park Authorities still have few powers with which to influence agricultural activity.[18] Without the means of intervention in land uses which profoundly affect landscape values, protective *designation* alone can have little or no positive conservation effect.

The problem will be solved by voluntary action

There are two distinct parts to this argument. The first concerns the education of farmers and suggests that by persuasion, often through the medium of conferences, farmers will begin to appreciate the wildlife and landscape values of their land and will then maintain and enhance them. The limited evidence available suggests that most of these conferences preach only to the 'converted' and that where landscapes have been changed to the point where new features are needed, farmers are unprepared to establish enough new cover, even if it were made worth their while financially.[19] The second thread to the argument suggests the use of voluntary labour to bring about the better maintenance of existing landscape features. This may help to bring townsmen and countrymen together but many of the jobs required (such as hedging and stone-walling) need skills only learnt over some years. The number of farmers and farm labourers who have such skills to pass on are declining so that voluntary action of this type, although it should be encouraged, will not provide any general panacea.

In all, the *laissez faire* situation under which farmers and landowners in the past created the traditional landscapes now so highly valued is unlikely to produce equally pleasant vistas for future generations. The landscape of the past was a functional one; and its detail and components related to a whole series of crafts and skills which have now largely passed away. The agricultural landscape of the future must also be functional, and landscape features will need to be compatible with modern mechanized farming. But a place must be found for shrubs and trees, for wetland and for odd pockets of wilderness to maintain the diversity which is so important to visual and wildlife quality.

STRATEGIES FOR LANDSCAPE CONSERVATION

It is clear that there are numerous and diverse interest groups to be satisfied in any landscape conservation policy. But this should not preclude the development of national objectives which can provide the basis for regional and local landscape policies. An appendix to this chapter describes how other European countries have approached the conservation of their agricultural landscapes.

The Countryside Commission, drawing upon their consultants' findings, have already put forward a number of objectives which might make up a national policy;[20] these could be modified in the light of recent discussions, as follows.

1. Existing landscape features of particular historic, wildlife or architectural importance should be identified, and those responsible for their management made aware of their importance.

2. Existing features which contribute to the landscape and do not unduly interfere with food production should be managed in such a way that their landscape significance does not decline.

3. New landscape features should be introduced where appropriate. They should be established on land of least agricultural potential within the unit concerned, where they do not conflict with existing valuable features and where they contribute to an interconnecting network.

4. Trees and shrubs planted either for replacement or as new features should be of indigenous species and selected to tolerate modern farming conditions and to provide colour, texture and form.

5. Retained or newly established features should serve as many purposes as possible. Shelter, wildlife conservation, the production of timber, visual amenity, game-rearing, recreation and historical and education uses have all been suggested.

6. Past dereliction, unsightly buildings and other structures should be removed or improved.

7. New structures, and in particular farm buildings, should be so sited that they positively enhance the landscape.

8. Local and regional character in the landscape should be conserved by ensuring that the features introduced are appropriate to the area, and that the management reflects traditional practices insofar as this is possible.

Implementation

Several means of achieving these objectives have been suggested which involve both national and local action.

At a national level there is conflict between the policies of the Ministry of Agriculture, Fisheries and Food, which is required by the Agriculture Act of 1947[21] to encourage an efficient food production industry, and those of the Countryside Commission, Nature Conservancy Council, and others concerned with safeguarding the natural environment and beauty of the countryside. These conflicts of interest could be resolved and policies co-ordinated in a number of ways. Section 11 of the Countryside Act, which requires all departments of government to have due regard to landscape and nature conservation, could be strengthened and made to be effective.[22] A new Ministry of Rural Development could be established to embrace all the interests and to develop a more balanced programme of rural development and protection. The Town and Country Planning system could be extended to bring some agricultural activities within the ambit of planning control, involving the Department of the Environment and local planning authorities in farming activities. Amongst the measures which might be appropriate to a broader planning system is the introduction of compulsory notification of intended change to landscape features[15] and the transfer of felling-licence controls to local authorities.[23]

Various other approaches at national level have been suggested. Fiscal incentives could be introduced, including exemptions from Capital Transfer and Wealth taxation for those who covenant to implement a management plan which accords with locally agreed landscape conservation objectives. Such an approach would encourage the co-ordination of policy at a local level while demanding only modest action by government. There could be a programme of public acquisition of important landscape features. A professional advisory service on landscape conservation for farmers and landowners might be developed. A new National Landscape Agency might also be considered, with powers to acquire the more valuable tracts, enter into management agreements with landowners elsewhere, and give advice.

All these measures, however, are likely to be of little avail if the farming and landowning community are not party to the proposed objectives. It is at the local level that action will be particularly important. It is not possible to list all the measures for landscape conservation that could be taken, but those interested in the conservation of landscape and wildlife must come together with the farming community to identify and conserve the best of the inherited landscape and to seek out opportunities for the creation of new features. This will require recognition on the part of many organizations and individuals of the important role the farmers play. District and County Councils must also be involved, as well as other public and private organizations. There can be no set recipe for achieving action, but the appointment of a local 'activist' whose job it would be to initiate action would seem sensible. The catalytic effect of employing a person of this kind may greatly outweigh the direct achievements.

The opportunity for action exists. Failure to take advantage of this opportunity will inevitably lead towards a landscape which becomes the less desirable by-product of modern agriculture, increasingly uniform and decreasingly satisfying. The remainder of this book examines in detail how action might be achieved.

Appendix

LANDSCAPE CONSERVATION IN EUROPE

Technological, economic and social changes since the war have had as great an impact on the appearance of the countryside abroad as they have in Britain. In particular, the densely populated states of Western Europe, which have equally long and intricate land use histories as this country, share many of the same problems. Public intervention in landscape planning has already begun in these countries, but it has been prompted not by a concern for aesthetic or wildlife values but by a need to replan agricultural holdings. The old tradition of dividing holdings between sons has led to such fragmentation of land in some regions that farming has become hopelessly inefficient; for economic reasons a policy of land consolidation or 'remembrement' is therefore being pursued. In the Netherlands, where land has been reclaimed from the sea, there is an obvious need to plan efficient new farm units. In this case, landscape planners can 'create' an entirely new landscape. In all other situations, the task is one of balancing the interests of efficient farming with those of the quality and wildlife values of existing landscapes, and the interests of those who live in the area, whose families may have worked the same farm for generations.

The examples which follow show the approaches adopted by various countries and are based on each country's own concept of land ownership and management. The systems are based on legislation which takes account of different national attitudes and social climates: it must be emphasized that what is a fitting system for one country does not necessarily work in another.

West Germany

Legal recognition of the need for conservation has a lengthy history in the Federal Republic of Germany.[24] Article 14 of the German Federal Republic's constitution requires that, while the rights of ownership by individuals are guaranteed, ownership brings social obligations. Owners of land are vested with the responsibility to act in the interests of the community in the enjoyment of the property. If the general interest is clearly not being considered, then the state can intervene and then expropriate the land. Landowners must, for example, allow the general public right of entry to their land for recreational purposes. The extent to which a farmer may change his existing land management is carefully regulated so that a balance is struck between the needs of economic agriculture, conservation and public access.

A Nature Conservation Act was passed in 1935 to protect particularly valuable areas of landscape features by designation as either 'nature monuments', 'nature reserves' or 'protected landscapes',[25] which preserve a particular form of land use. The 1935 Act is now inadequate because it provides no control over new land uses such as recreation, large-scale industrial farming or the restoration of derelict land. Many States have therefore introduced their own landscape conservation legislation.

In 1971 a Federal Land Conservation Bill was drafted to update and strengthen regulations on landscape and nature conservation, and to include measures to ensure the maintenance of visually attractive, ecologically varied and healthy agricultural landscapes. Certain management restrictions were written into the legislation; for example no plant cover may be burnt, and riparian vegetation such as reeds must not be destroyed by any means without a special licence. Furthermore, *de facto* access was granted to all woods, open lands, mountain meadows above the tree line, river banks and coastal zones. Footpaths and cycleways through private land were to be set out in landscape plans and maintained by highway authorities.

The Land Conservation Act, passed in June 1973, now empowers State Authorities to declare as Landscape Conservation Zones those areas:

(a) in which serious landscape damage (including that caused by agricultural improvement) has taken place or is threatened;
(b) which are largely left unused by owners or occupiers with the result that their appearance is adversely affected; or
(c) which are required for recreational use.

In these areas, land use and management are strictly controlled. Characteristic or historically valuable 'traditional' landscapes may also be safeguarded in this way. Further protection can be given to individual landscape features which are seen to be valuable (such as trees, groups of trees and shrubs, hedges, reed beds, water meadows) by issuing legal orders or decrees. Following the Federal lead, many States in Germany have now enacted their own legislation. In North Rhine Westphalia, for example, landscape planning measures impose legal restrictions on landowners which prevent the development of existing open land; restrict afforestation; create rights of access to some forest and agricultural land and to all river banks. Similar laws have also been passed in Bavaria, Schleswig Holstein, Rheinland-Pfalz and Hesse. In some states the drainage of marshes, bogs and wetland and the erection of enclosures or fencing are items which fall within landscape planning control.

The mechanism for landscape planning in Germany is relatively complex. In each 'state' or province, nominated land conservation authorities (either the Ministry of Agriculture or local authorities or both) have been established to take responsibility for landscape planning at a local or subregional level. An independent Advisory Council of up to 15 people is established in each area, with representatives of the various government specialist agencies involved in land use management, local unions and associations and also members of the public who live and work in the area. The Council reports to an interministerial council set up by the provincial government, and this council advises the Land Conservation Authorities.

The landscape planning system is still in its development period in Germany and, although moderately successful in terms of identifying important landscapes and landscape features, difficulties have been encountered in landscape management, particularly in areas where agriculture is in decline and farmers are being encouraged to maintain traditional enterprises for reasons of landscape maintenance or to encourage recreation. Farmers appear to be reluctant to continue with outdated techniques even if financial incentives are given for using them.

Sweden

Sweden,[26] like her Scandinavian neighbours, has for centuries accepted the principle of common responsibility for the countryside, and today environmental protection is accepted as a public obligation. The jealously guarded right of free access to the countryside and the very small proportion of Sweden's countryside that is intensively farmed have given rise to conservation measures which differ from those of continental Europe.

Swedish law has for centuries recognized a general right of common access, regardless of land ownership, to all 'natural' areas such as forests, water courses, beaches and meadows. This customary right effectively limits the rights of private property owners in the public interest, and implies that anyone can move where they like in the countryside, stay on someone else's land, pick wildflowers or fruits and use any lake or stream for swimming or boating provided they do not cause damage or interfere with the owner's privacy. Swedish citizens traditionally respect this right and the responsibility for trusteeship, a responsibility which has been reinforced by educational programmes in recent years. Despite this, the growth of second homes on the coast, on river banks and lake shores has increasingly limited *de facto* access and recent legislation reflects a growing feeling amongst many Swedes that the time has come to control this type of development.

The 'Nature Conservancy Act' of 1964 introduced measures to protect the interests of nature conservation, outdoor recreation and landscape conservation in the countryside. Areas of value from cultural or scientific points of view were afforded statutory protection. Tracts of land valuable for recreation, along rivers, beaches and around lakes, extending up to 300 metres from the water's edge, were designated and no development permitted within them. Control by licence was introduced for economic activities affecting the landscape such as stone-quarrying, and landowners whose rights were restricted became eligible for compensation. In Sweden, unlike Britain, the Nature Conservancy is attached to the Ministry of Agriculture, and is the body responsible for wildlife conservation, water and air pollution control, outdoor recreation and hunting. Landscape control in Sweden rests with the Nature Conservancy rather than with planning authorities. This agency deals with a wide range of interests in the rural environment, and its connection with the Ministry of Agriculture ensures that policy is co-ordinated as far as possible.

France

The concern for landscape conservation is growing in France as elsewhere in Europe. Two of the reasons for this are the decline in farming (in some areas farmers on marginal land are being encouraged to leave agriculture) and the consolidation of holdings, which is proceeding rapidly in various parts of the country. Some 6 million hectares have already been consolidated and a further half a million are under active consolidation.[27] The consolidation of holdings involves fundamental changes in holding and field size, and many hedgerows and other boundaries are lost. Efforts are made during consolidation to identify the critical landscape elements which should be retained and to encourage the planting of new areas, particularly shelter belts. The effect of consolidation is as fundamental for farming and landscape as were the technological changes in arable farming which took place in East Anglia in the 1950–60s. Whether the outcome for the landscape will be more acceptable remains to be seen. Advice on landscape issues, and particularly on the place of buildings in the landscape, is available and is surprisingly similar to that in Britain. In a study published by the Ministère de l'Agriculture of the area to the southwest of Troyes[28] the main recommendations were:

(a) to maintain the quality of horizons;
(b) to retain the simplicity of the landscape;
(c) to protect mixed and deciduous forests;
(d) to manage woodlands; and
(e) to plant and manage village edges.

Although the emphasis on networks of cover and on natural and artificial boundaries is absent, the message is similar to that of the New Agricultural Landscapes Study in England. Methods of achieving these objectives are not suggested.

The Netherlands

The policy for landscape conservation in the Netherlands is a direct outcome of land reclamation from the sea. Areas of new polderland have been set aside for nature conservation, recreation and forestry, and tree planting has been carried out on farms, roads and canal banks. In the polders there are two organizations concerned with reclamation,[29] the Zuiderzee Works Service (ZZW) which is responsible for the reclamation work, dikes, pumping sluices, roads and bridges; and the Ysselmeerpolders Services (RYP) which is responsible for soil reclamation, farms, villages and houses and the creation of a good environment.

In the early polders, a harsh rectangular block system of planting was adopted. Planting took place only along roads and around farm buildings and consisted mainly of fast-growing poplars. The more recent polders of East and South Flevoland show a changed approach. The proportion of reclaimed land devoted to farming has declined, with greater importance given to forestry, nature conservation and recreation. Recreation in particular has influenced landscape design, and many of the coastal sites are now landscaped. The rectangular planting of earlier polders has given way to groupings of mixed woodland, with more emphasis upon scrub and semi-natural vegetation. A situation in which most of the planting, development and management of the non-farm lands lies in the hands of one agency is unusual. It has allowed for the development of expertise in landscape planning and management that would not otherwise have been possible.

Over half a million acres of land in the Netherlands have been reclaimed from the sea, and the work may have useful lessons for Britain. So also may the landscape work in the rest of the country. Over 90 per cent of Dutch landscapes relate directly to farming: the so-called 'outland landscapes'. Subdivision of land through the laws of succession has posed a serious threat to the efficiency of Dutch agriculture, and is the primary reason for land consolidation which began in 1924 when the first Land Consolidation Act was introduced. Subsequent legislation introduced modifications allowing for greater consultation and consideration of non-agricultural matters.

Before the start of a consolidation scheme, 5–10 per cent of the land in the area under consideration will be in public ownership. A landscape plan is prepared by the State Forest Service on behalf of the provincial landscape authority. Recreation and nature conservation plans are also prepared and a period of extensive consultation follows. The essence of the procedure is to balance all the demands made on land in an orderly way. The resultant plan never requires more land for non-agricultural purposes than is already in public ownership and thus no net loss of land is suffered by farmers and landowners. The plan is then presented to landowners and tenants who must accept it by a majority vote. Government grants are available towards the carrying out of agreed works (normally at a rate of 65 per cent of the cost). Some of the landscaping works involve new planting in much the same way as on the polders. More frequently, however, the case is one of identifying landscape features of importance and suggesting a management plan for these. Increasingly, the forest service is playing a direct role in the management of such features although agreements with landowners, and between landowners and voluntary organizations, also play a part.[30]

There is little doubt that attempts at landscape conservation have progressed further in a number of European countries than they have in Britain. One common feature is the linking of landscape planning to agricultural development, whether this involves subsidies in marginal areas or land consolidation in the more productive areas. The Netherlands, in particular, has attempted to involve all the groups who value landscape in the planning process. But none of the countries examined has satisfactorily solved the problem of maintaining those landscape features that are dependent upon traditional agriculture.

NOTES AND REFERENCES

1. The 'hill cow line' is used by the Ministry of Agriculture to delimit the area within which hill cow subsidy payments are made under the Hill Farming Act 1946 and the Livestock Rearing Act 1951.
2. Davidson, B. R. and Wibberley, G. P. (1956). *The Agricultural Significance of the Hills*, Wye College, Studies in Rural Land Use, No. 3.
3. Raistrick, A. (1966). *The Pennine Walls*, The Dalesman Publishing Co., Clapham, Yorkshire.
4. Wibberley, G. P. (1974). *The Proper Use of Britain's Rural Land*, Paper delivered to RTPI Diamond Jubilee Conference, June 1974.
5. Forestry Commission (1955). *Report of the Committee on Hedgerow and Farm Timber* (The Merthyr Committee Report), HMSO, London.
6. Forestry Commission (1953). *Hedgerow and Park Timber and Woods under Five Acres 1951*, Forestry Commission Census Report No. 2, HMSO, London.
7. Forestry Commission (1970). *Census of Woodlands 1965–67*, HMSO, London.
8. Westmacott, R. and Worthington, T. (1974). *New Agricultural Landscapes*, Countryside Commission publication No. 76.
9. Hoskins, W. G. (1955). *The Making of the English Landscape*, Penguin, Harmondsworth; and Hoskins, W. G. (1973). *English Landscapes*, BBC Publications, London.
10. The various forms of protection are described in Chapter 10.
11. Pollard, E., Hooper, M. D. and Moore, N. W. (1974). *Hedges*, Collins, London. (See in particular Chapter 2).
12. Veblen, T. (1970). *The Theory of the Leisure Class*, Unwin Books, London.
13. Morris, W. (1962). Innate Socialism. In Briggs, Asa (1962), *Selected Writings and Designs*, Penguin, Harmondsworth.
14. Blythe, R. (1969). *Akenfield*, Penguin, Harmondsworth.
15. See, for example, Council for the Protection of Rural England (1975), *Landscape—the Need for a Public Voice*; and Chapter 10 of this volume.
16. Bonham Carter, V. (1971). *The Survival of the English Countryside*, Hodder and Stoughton, London.
17. See, for example, Chapter 8 for a discussion of a recent survey of farmers' attitudes to wildlife on their land.

18. Department of the Environment (1974). *Report of the National Park Policies Review Committee* (The Sandford Report), HMSO, London.
19. Westmacott, R. and Worthington, T. (1974). *New Agricultural Landscapes*, Chapter 7.
20. Countryside Commission (1974). *New Agricultural Landscapes—A Discussion Paper*, CCP 76a.
21. Agriculture Act (1947). Chapter 48, HMSO, London.
22. Countryside Act (1968). Chapter 41, HMSO, London.
23. See discussion on felling licences in Chapter 10.
24. Stein, E. (1971). Vorwort zu dem Entwurf eines Gesetzes über Landschaftspflege und Naturschutz (Landespflegegesetz). *Recht der Landespflege*, No. 17, December 1971.
25. Haber, W. (1973). Conservation and Landscape Maintenance in Germany; Past, Present and Future. *Biological Conservation*, **5**(4), October 1973.
26. Sand, P. H. (1972). Legal Systems for Environmental Protection: Japan, Sweden, United States. *Legislative Studies*, No. 4, F.A.O., Rome.
27. Fondation de France (1972). *Batiments Agricole et Paysage*, Paris.
28. Acat, F. (1973). *Etude de Paysage dans le Pays D'Othe*. Ministère de l'Agriture, Paris.
29. Ministry of Foreign Affairs (1972). *The Kingdom of the Netherlands—Facts and Figures, No. 23, Agriculture and Horticulture*, Government Printing Office, The Hague.
30. Those interested in a detailed account of land consolidation in the Netherlands should refer to publication B125 of the Foreign Information Service of the Netherland Ministry of Agriculture and Fisheries.

17. Hedge laying by volunteers (photo: British Trust for Conservation Volunteers)

Traditional methods of estate management like hedging or ditching by hand may be ecologically beneficial but they are time consuming and expensive to execute. Modern farms have neither the labour nor the financial resources to spend on manual methods.

18. Hand ditching near Tetbury, Gloucestershire (photo: Countryside Commission)

19. Burning wheat straw too wet to bale on a farm in Buckinghamshire (photo: *Farmers' Weekly*, K. Huggett)

Some farming operations such as straw burning, crop spraying or the application of fertilizers may indirectly damage habitats like hedgerows, ponds and watercourses that run alongside fields. Codes of practice, such as the *Straw Burning Code*, can help and more are probably needed (Chapter 8).

20. Aerial spraying with pesticide in Cambridgeshire (photo: *Farmers' Weekly*)

21. Elms near Soham, Cambridgeshire (photo: Countryside Commission)

Not all landscape changes in the lowlands are the result of agricultural developments. Elms are a major feature of the lowland scene but their numbers have been drastically reduced by Dutch Elm Disease. By the end of 1976 no less than nine million elms had been killed by the disease and more than half of the non-woodland elms were either dying or dead. The proportion for some counties is much higher.

22. The end of a landscape; near Gotherington, Gloucestershire (photo: R. Lloyd)

23. Farms at Mickleden in the Lake District (photo: Countryside Commission)

Much of the scenery of the uplands is dependent upon the regimes of hill farming, yet upland landscapes, habitats and access are being lost as more valley land is cultivated and hill pastures are enclosed and improved (Chapter 6).

24. Moorland at Dunkery Beacon. Reclamation of moorland to agricultural use is a particular problem in some parts of Exmoor (photo: Countryside Commission)

25. A wooded valley on an arable farm in Gloucestershire (photo: Countryside Commission)

Westmacott and Worthington suggest that unproductive land on farms, including slopes too steep to plough, can be planted up to create the framework for a new agricultural landscape (Chapters 7 and 8).

26. There are many small areas available for planting on farmland. It is often difficult to work efficiently into field corners with modern farm machinery and more farmers may be willing to see these areas planted up. The replacement of hedgerow trees poses greater problems, but this farmer in Gloucestershire is prepared to accept the inconvenience of young trees when cutting his hedges (photo: Gloucestershire County Council)

27. Many small woods are in urgent need of management: selective thinning and replanting could ensure the continuation of important landscape features, some of which could provide cover for a game enterprise associated with farming (photo: Gloucestershire County Council)

28. Roadside planting could do much to replace trees lost by agricultural improve — ments and Dutch Elm Disease (photo: Gloucestershire County Council)

29. A plantation of Rauli (*Nothofagus procera*) at Flaxley, Gloucestershire (photo: Forestry Commission)

This hardwood appears to have considerable commercial potential. Its rapid early growth (these trees were planted only twelve years previously) reduces weeding costs and this may be a particular advantage for plantations on farmland where labour for management is often difficult to supply.

30. Country Park on the Goodwood Estate, Sussex (Photo: Countryside Commission)

Some private owners have taken advantage of grants made under the Countryside Act to create recreation areas on their land. The diversification of agricultural enterprises to provide for other activities can yield economic, social and environmental benefits (Chapter 11).

31. Much advice on landscape and wildlife management already exists for farmers but it is often difficult for busy people to find and is not associated with the regular technical advice that farmers receive (Chapters 8 and 12) (photo: R. Lloyd)

32. There seems to be no substitute for personal contact in persuading farmers to take account of other interests in the management of their land. Here John Baily, project officer for the Lake District Upland Management Experiment, discusses a fencing job with local farmers (photo: Countryside Commission)

PART II

THE MEANS OF CONSERVATION

Chapter 8

Voluntary action in conservation

C. KEENLEYSIDE

Individual farmers make the day-to-day decisions which shape the landscape and wildlife habitats of 80 per cent of the land in Britain. If landscape and wildlife conservation is needed on this scale, much of the responsibility must rest with farmers. Whether or not they accept this responsibility depends upon their attitudes to landscape and wildlife and upon their ability to recognize and exploit opportunities for conservation. This chapter reviews the efforts made to influence farmers, the attitudes and actions of the farmers themselves, and the long-term prospects for the conservation of landscape and wildlife by their voluntary efforts.

Farmers are in the business of producing food to make a living for themselves and to provide a return on the capital invested in the farm. There is no basic reason for a farmer to conserve either landscape or wildlife in the course of his business. Conservation does not improve the efficiency of the farm, nor does it generate extra income. Although it may enhance the capital value of the holding, this is of no advantage to the farmer if it increases his rent or tax liability, but not his income. Farmers who do accept conservation as being among the objectives of management usually do so for one of three reasons: they have some personal interest; they acknowledge a social duty; or they are involved in game conservation.

Some farmers enjoy wild plants and animals for their own sake and will maintain wildlife habitats for this reason alone. A similar interest in the appearance of the farm may encourage landscape conservation, especially around the farmhouse. However, many farmers apply agricultural rather than aesthetic standards to the appearance of their land; tidiness, healthy weed-free crops and a 'well-farmed' look will probably be much more important to them than the visual pattern of the countryside. There is an important difference between the attitudes of a casual observer and of a farmer looking at the same landscape; one sees a pattern, the other looks critically at the land uses which create that pattern. Farmers may value modern agricultural landscapes as evidence of technical progress, whilst the public may see only the decay or destruction of a traditional landscape. A farmer may feel that he has a social responsibility to look after the balance of nature or to maintain the landscape resources of his holding in the same way that a good farmer is expected to

147

maintain its soil fertility. Some landowners, particularly those who have inherited family estates, may have a traditional approach to landscape conservation and wish to maintain the landscapes created by their forebears or to create new landscapes of similar quality. Some farmers accept the cost of maintaining game cover because they value the sport it offers.[1] The cover and feeding areas needed for game can also provide habitats for wildlife and create new landscape features if suitable sites, plants and management techniques are used, as discussed in Chapter 11.

Not all farmers who accept these reasons for conservation will necessarily put them into practice. A farmer may not be able to afford the additional costs, the time, or the loss of land which might otherwise be improved for agriculture. Also, he may lack the specialist knowledge which would enable him to identify opportunities for conservation and to justify his actions. Unlike most other industrialists, farmers operate in full view of neighbours, competitors and anyone else who cares to look over the fence. Understandably, farmers may be reluctant to manage their land in ways which might be considered 'bad' agricultural practice or just inefficient farming. Those who do conserve landscape and wildlife can do so only if this is compatible with maintaining a viable farming unit: the extent to which this is possible will vary from one farm to another, depending on its size and type, the methods of conservation, and the attitudes of the farmer.

An individual farmer can organize his business more or less as he wishes, but his attitudes and actions are influenced by the many organizations and individuals which support the farming industry (such as the Ministry of Agriculture, Fisheries and Food, the National Farmers' Union and the specialist press), by public and private conservation bodies outside the industry, and by the agricultural education system. The efforts of all these organizations to persuade farmers to accept an increasing responsibility for wildlife and landscape conservation are reviewed in this chapter.

WILDLIFE AND LANDSCAPE CONSERVATION ORGANIZATIONS

Ministry of Agriculture, Fisheries and Food

The Ministry of Agriculture (MAFF) is responsible for maintaining a stable and efficient farming industry which can produce as much of the nation's food as is thought desirable by the government of the day. MAFF had no formal responsibility for wildlife conservation until the 1968 Countryside Act required every government department to 'have regard to the desirability of conserving the natural beauty and amenity of the countryside'.[2] In January 1970 the then Minister of Agriculture announced that he intended to introduce more emphasis on the opportunities for conservation in the training of advisory staff. New courses would be designed to achieve a broader understanding of conservation management and its relationship with farming practices. Advisers would then be better able to suggest to farmers and others in what ways and at what cost conservation interests could be safeguarded.[3] Following this statement, a two-day training course was organized for advisory staff in each of MAFF's eight regions: these courses included the preparation of a hypothetical farm plan taking account of wildlife, landscape and recreation interests, and discussions with staff from the Nature Conservancy, the Countryside Commission and local County Conservation Trusts. Since then, MAFF has organized further, more detailed training courses on wildlife and landscape conservation at a national level. At first these were held twice a year for the Ministry's Agricultural Development and Advisory Service (ADAS) staff from all regions, but since 1974 only one course has been held annually. When these advisers return to their work on individual farms they have no specialist conservation staff to support them—within the 5265 staff of ADAS there are no landscape architects and no ecologists concerned with wildlife conservation.[4] In each ADAS division (covering one or more counties) one member of staff acts as a link with outside organizations such as the Nature Conservancy Council. Additional training at a regional level has been organized in some areas and the Ministry training manual now includes a section on conservation.

It is difficult to assess how much effect this conservation training has had on the detailed advice which is given to farmers. ADAS staff seldom, if ever, get requests for advice on wildlife management, so the implementation of a MAFF wildlife policy depends on advisers being able and willing to introduce the subject of conservation when they are giving agricultural advice, dealing with grant applications, or visiting farms on other Ministry business. ADAS staff do consult the Nature Conservancy Council on farm grant applications which affect Sites of Special Scientific Interest. Sometimes a farmer will modify his improvement scheme to avoid damaging the wildlife interest, but even if MAFF were to refuse grant aid for agricultural improvement of an SSSI, the farmer might choose to carry out the work without grant.

Farmers may also use some of the technical advisory publications produced and distributed by MAFF, many of them free of charge. None is specifically on wildlife management although some give instructions about avoiding damage to wildlife and beneficial insects.[5] The Ministry now take wildlife conservation into account when preparing new or revised leaflets and have already produced an advisory leaflet on the appearance of farm buildings. This is intended for the use of local planning authorities and landscape groups as well as farmers and landowners. A film on the same subject has been made for the use of ADAS staff.

The Ministry's most recent contribution has been the first national survey of farmers' attitudes to wildlife conservation which was undertaken in conjunction with the Nature Conservancy Council.

But MAFF still has no defined policy on landscape and wildlife conservation, despite the requirement of the 1968 Countryside Act that these interests should be considered. No specialist staff were appointed at that time or since to do this work; yet in response to an EEC directive on the socio-economic problems of marginal farming, eight specialists were appointed in ADAS to advise farmers on other sources of income such as recreation, tourism and rural industries.

In April 1975, the government decided to increase the proportion of home-produced food and to aim for a steady rise in agricultural production until the early 1980s. A white paper stated that: 'the projected increases in the output of British agriculture should not result in any undesirable changes in the environment; the continuing improvement of grazing land and of hill land can contribute to a better looking as well as to a more productive countryside'.[6] Some of this increased productivity will result from ADAS staff persuading farmers to improve their farming methods; it remains to be seen if advisers will have either the time or the skill to ensure that such improvements do not harm the wildlife and landscape of farmland. Any contribution to the *enhancement* of these resources seems unlikely, unless a more active conservation policy is adopted, supported by specialist staff.

National Farmers' Union

Apart from the Ministry, the National Farmers' Union is the most powerful farming organization, with 145,000 members, thought to represent about 80 per cent of the farmers of England and Wales. The Union has considerable political influence, not only through its consultation with the government on the Annual Price Review, but also on legislation affecting rural land and on land use policies at both national and local levels.

The importance of the NFU in wildlife and landscape conservation lies in the Union's own policies and actions and also in its support for conservation schemes promoted by others. It is almost essential to have NFU support for any conservation scheme which requires the active co-operation of farmers, and this is recognized by the Countryside Commission and by voluntary bodies.

The NFU code of practice for straw-burning is its most widely publicized contribution to wildlife and landscape conservation but not necessarily the most important. The Union was a founder member of the voluntary Farming and Wildlife Advisory Group to which it has more recently made a financial contribution. NFU branches are represented on most of the liaison groups involved in similar work at a local level. The Union has been consulted on the content of some conservation advisory leaflets; it has distributed one of these leaflets nationally and at least two more locally to its members. In the absence of any formal countryside policy statement from the NFU, the view of Michael Darke in 1970 is probably still a clear indication of priorities: that the primary responsibility of the agricultural industry is to produce food; the second is concerned with the welfare of rural people dependent upon the prosperity of agriculture for their livelihood; and the third is responsibility for the appearance of the landscape and the conservation of nature.[7] But the NFU remains defensive about the environmental effects of farming, and aggressive in its concern to protect the interests of farmers. For example, the Union has argued that the Countryside Commission New Agricultural Landscapes Study exaggerated the effects of agricultural operations on the landscape. The Union has opposed the use of management agreements and remains particularly concerned about the impact of landscape controls and informal recreation on the farming industry—not surprisingly, since these issues cause problems for individual members. But statements of political viewpoints and criticisms of individual proposals should not be interpreted as opposition to the conservation principle. It is far more significant that the Union is willing to be involved in conservation schemes and ready to give support to other organizations; the commitment of the Union to its members' interests may not make it the easiest of allies but certainly makes it one of the most valuable.

Country Landowners' Association

The Country Landowners' Association is smaller and less powerful than the NFU but nevertheless has considerable influence, particularly in the House of Lords. It covers a wider range of land interests, including game and forestry, and seems to accept the claims of non-agricultural uses of rural land more readily than does the NFU. In a report on small woods and tree planting on the farm, the CLA argues the case for new planting on farmland, preferably of native hardwoods, creating landscapes to replace those now being lost and improving wildlife and recreation resources.[8] The Association suggests that the Forestry Commission should be the sole agency of advice and grant aid on such tree-planting schemes. These proposals are similar to those of the New Agricultural Landscapes Study[9] although the suggested means of implementation and the scope of new planting schemes are rather different.

The CLA, like the NFU, is represented on the Farming and Wildlife Advisory Group, local liaison groups and the steering groups of a number of Countryside Commission projects concerned with landscape conservation.

Private advisory services

There are several firms of private consultants which offer management services including the preparation of farm and estate plans, day-to-day management on an agency basis, and advice on all the financial aspects of rural land management. A farmer is unlikely to seek (and pay for) advice on wildlife management from private consultants when he can get it free from the Nature Conservancy Council, so it is not surprising that none of the firms specializes in wildlife management.

But *game* management, the concern of the Game Conservancy,[10] does have a profound effect on both the wildlife and landscape of a farm and it comes closer than any other farm enterprise to 'pure' wildlife and landscape conservation, although not all game management techniques are of benefit to these interests (for example the use of cultivated shrubs and the strict control of predators).

Commercial advisers must always reflect the interests of their clients and they cannot afford to introduce management objectives which the landowner does not want. It is therefore unlikely that wildlife and landscape objectives will be integrated with advice given by any of the firms (even the game specialists) until these objectives are widely accepted and actively pursued by landowners.

National Agricultural Centre, Stoneleigh

This agricultural demonstration and conference centre near Coventry is the permanent home of the Royal Show and a shop-window for the latest developments in farming. Several thousand farmers and advisers visit the NAC each year to see the livestock demonstration units, the Farm Buildings Information Centre and the Farm Electric Centre, or to attend one of the 20–30 farming conferences held annually. The Centre has small demonstrations of commercial timber production and also a game covert. One member of the MAFF advisory team permanently stationed at Stoneleigh is responsible for advice on wildlife and landscape conservation; yet, in spite of this apparent interest in wildlife and the landscape, an attempt to establish a conservation advisory unit at Stoneleigh has failed.

Agriculture and the press, radio and television

There are two national weekly publications dealing with general agriculture (one of them controlled by the National Farmers' Union), a daily radio programme, and weekly television programmes for farmers. There are also many specialist publications, local NFU journals and farming papers, and local radio programmes. Advisory divisions of the Ministry of Agriculture distribute their own local journals, and make extensive use of press, radio and television to inform farmers of new developments, to give advice and to demonstrate management techniques. Even 'The Archers', with a reputation for meticulous attention to agricultural detail, is used to put across new ideas or to highlight current problems. In general, the coverage of wildlife and landscape conservation issues is infrequent and usually in response to the newsworthy activities of conservation organizations.

WILDLIFE AND LANDSCAPE CONSERVATION ORGANIZATIONS

Nature Conservancy Council

The government agency responsible for wildlife conservation was established in 1949 as the Nature Conservancy. Farmland was soon recognized as an important wildlife habitat and the Nature Conservancy began to investigate the harmful effects of some agricultural practices. In 1960 a Toxic Chemicals and Wildlife Section was established, and the Conservancy research programme has covered several other aspects of wildlife conservation on farmland, including detailed studies of hedgerows and old grassland and, more recently, work on the minimum area of different habitats required for the continued existence of wild species.

The results of research were publicized in scientific circles but the research staff concerned also recognized a need to communicate with those responsible for the management of agricultural land and with their colleagues in the Conservation Branch of the Nature Conservancy (who managed nature reserves and advised farmers and landowners). To provide this communication, the Agricultural Habitat Liaison Group was established in 1971 with members drawn from the Research and Conservation Branches of the Conservancy and a senior officer from the Ministry of Agriculture and, later, from the Department of Agriculture and Fisheries for Scotland. The Nature Conservancy appointed an Agricultural Liaison Officer to service the Group, which met at regular intervals over the next two years to review the need for action and advise its member organizations on research, advisory work and training programmes. Research included a national survey of farmers' attitudes to wildlife conservation (with the Ministry of Agriculture), and a contribution to the Countryside Commission study of New Agricultural Landscapes. The group initiated the publication of four advisory leaflets for farmers explaining how and why different habitats should be maintained on farms (see Appendix) while training courses in conservation were organized for staff in the Ministry of Agriculture and the Nature Conservancy. This agricultural liaison work with the Ministry of Agriculture had just become well-established when the Conservancy was reconstituted in 1973. The new Nature Conservancy Council (NCC) was given responsibility for nature reserves, advice and information, while most of the existing research projects (and staff) were transferred to the Institute of Terrestrial Ecology.

Advice is to be the most important function of the Nature Conservancy Council and among those having first priority for advice are the Ministry of Agriculture, and landowners and occupiers in their day-to-day operations and on schedules sites (especially nature reserves).[11] In their first report the Council state that:

> We believe that means should be found to ensure that wild flora and fauna and physical features of special interest are safeguarded throughout town and countryside—and not just in a few select places—so that all can benefit. . . . Our own main contribution must be informed advice, and we have devoted, and shall continue to devote, much effort to promoting an understanding of the importance of nature conservation and to giving advice to those responsible for making decisions affecting it, both nationally and locally, from Government Ministers to individual land-users.[12]

This amounts to a commitment to undertake a major information and education programme, and to provide advice to any adviser or any farmer who asks for it. However, as the Council themselves point out, their existing staff resources can only just cope with the present work load. If their efforts to persuade farmers and landowners to take account of wildlife conservation are successful, the Council may find that they cannot meet the demand for technical advice and thus will lose the co-operation and goodwill of the farming community.

At present a farmer is unlikely to be advised by NCC staff unless he farms land within a National Nature Reserve (where the Council control land use through ownership, lease or by agreement) or he has land which has been scheduled as a Site of Special Scientific Interest. In the case of an SSSI the farmer retains complete control of the land but he will have been given a map showing the site boundary and a brief note on its scientific interest; he will not necessarily have been visited by NCC staff to explain why the site is important and how it should be managed. If the farmer submits an application for planning permission or for an agricultural grant affecting the SSSI, the Nature Conservancy Council will be consulted by the planning authority or by the Ministry of Agriculture. This gives NCC staff an opportunity to advise the authority concerned (which may or may not take their advice) and also to visit the farmer. But he will already have definite plans for the land by the time he submits an application and it may then be too late to influence his decision. An added disadvantage is that the farmer may associate the NCC with the local planning authority and statutory controls, and treat their advice less favourably than he might otherwise have done. It is clear that the Council cannot provide more specialist advice to individual farmers until they have more staff. The detailed advisory leaflets were an imaginative attempt to fill this gap, and have been well received, but many farmers also need the advice of an expert on site.[13]

The Nature Conservancy Council have begun a complete review of their policies in relation to agriculture, because they believe that current pressures on wildlife require new initiatives. The implication is that the Council will become much more closely involved in agricultural developments at all levels from individual farm plans to Ministerial decisions, and will try to strengthen their relationship with central government agricultural departments and with the agricultural colleges.

Voluntary wildlife conservation organizations

Voluntary groups have been active in wildlife conservation since the early part of this century, long before any government action. These groups are still strong and active: they have political influence, own and manage their own nature reserves and provide advice, information and education. Voluntary organizations were the first to publicize the need for wildlife conservation on farmland and they led the attempts to influence farmers' attitudes with advice on wildlife management. The 1969 'Silsoe' Conference on farming and wild-life, arranged by voluntary organizations in conjunction with the Ministry of Agriculture and the (then) Nature Conservancy, marked the beginning of a general movement to conserve wildlife on farms.

After the Silsoe Conference the Farming and Wildlife Advisory Group (FWAG) was established with a full-time adviser financed by the three organizations which had promoted the conference: the Royal Society for the Protection of Birds, the Society for the Promotion of Nature Reserves (now the Society for the Promotion of Nature Conservation) and the British Trust for Ornithology. Other members of the Group are the NFU and the CLA, and staff from the Ministry of Agriculture and the Nature Conservancy Council, although these attend only in an advisory capacity. The objectives of FWAG are to identify the problems of reconciling the needs of modern farming with the conservation of nature; to explore the possibilities for compromise and to make the findings as widely known as possible. With only one full-time adviser FWAG have concentrated upon encouraging and helping others to take on practical projects and advisory work: their adviser has organized, in conjunction with the Ministry of Agriculture, national farming and wildlife conferences modelled on the Silsoe exercise, and a number of smaller local exercises. He has also helped to set up local liaison groups. 'Farming with Wildlife', a film made for FWAG, has been widely used by the Ministry of Agriculture, local conservation groups and commercial firms.[14] A general advisory leaflet for farmers and several detailed information sheets have also been published.[15]

FWAG is a national organization, but at the local level the county conservation trusts work towards similar objectives, often advised and assisted by FWAG (the trusts' parent organization is a member of FWAG). About one-third of the county conservation trusts are known to have established advisory services for farmers although mostly on a small scale.[16]

Some trusts adopt a different approach to wildlife conservation on farms; the Gloucestershire Trust has tried to persuade local farmers to join; and in West Wales the local trust has established a number of Farm Nature Reserves. Several trusts have made contact with local Ministry of Agriculture advisers and one has an NFU representative on its steering committee. Local trusts have the advantage of personal contact with individual farmers and possibly with ADAS advisers too; they are also free to pursue whatever method is most suitable for a particular situation. However, their influence is limited by shortage of manpower; some do not employ any staff and rely entirely on spare-time work by members; where there are administrative or conservation officers, they must normally deal with the whole range of a Trust's activities and can devote only a small proportion of their time to one specific project.

Practical help with the establishment and maintenance of wildlife habitats on farms may be given by local trusts or by the National Conservation Crops (the British Trust for Conservation Volunteers) which provides labour for conservation tasks. The BTCV have produced practical guidance on conservation management, including a detailed manual on hedging.[17]

Countryside Commission

Government responsibility for advice on landscape conservation rests with the Countryside Commission, but the organization has neither the staff nor the structure to provide a local advisory service for individual farmers and land-owners.[18]

In 1971, consultants were appointed to find out how agricultural improvement can be carried out efficiently but in such a way as to create 'new agricultural landscapes' no less interesting than those being destroyed.[19] The Countryside Commission have accepted their consultants' conclusions that farmed lowland landscapes will continue to decline in quality if no action is taken. They will recommend to the government what action they consider to be necessary, taking into account the response to ideas they have already put forward for discussion.[20] More recently, the Countryside Commission have initiated a project to establish demonstration farms showing how landscape and wildlife conservation can be combined with commercial farming.

In 1969 the Commission initiated experimental work on upland management in Snowdonia and the Lake District where a variety of landscape and recreation management tasks were carried out with the agreement of local farmers.[21] Experimental work of this kind was developed further in the Bollin Valley south of Manchester, and now continues on the fringe of London. In these experiments, the Commission's project officers have worked directly with farmers. Advice of a practical nature is likely to form part of any conservation strategy and the Commission did earlier put forward a proposal for an advisory unit, to be run jointly by the Ministry of Agriculture, Nature Conservancy Council and the Commission, based at the National Agricultural Centre, Stoneleigh, to provide farmers with co-ordinated advice on landscape, wildlife conservation and recreation provision. The proposal was not implemented but the Commission are still seeking the agreement of the other government departments to establish a similar advisory unit elsewhere.

In their recent research work, the Commission have involved both farming and conservation interests, with the Ministry of Agriculture, Nature Conservancy Council, NFU and CLA represented on project steering groups. In particular, the Commission have recognized the importance of the Ministry of Agriculture 'whose policies have a more profound impact upon the rural landscape than those of any other (government department)'.[22] The Commission have already suggested that the Ministry should employ a team of specialists to advise on the ecological and landscape implications of agricultural policies (especially grants), to prepare management plans for landscape and wildlife on the Ministry's own farms, to train ADAS staff and to publish advice for farmers. The Commission have also argued that much more attention should be paid to ecology and landscape issues in existing agricultural education courses.[23]

Voluntary landscape conservation organizations

The Council for the Protection of Rural England, the largest of the voluntary landscape groups, seeks to influence policymaking on the landscape at two levels: nationally through government bodies such as the Department of the Environment and the Countryside Commission, and locally by commenting on the decisions of local planning authorities. CPRE working parties have reported on problems of particular significance, such as tree and hedge cover in the landscape, and planning control of buildings.[24] The Council have criticized the New Agricultural Landscapes Study and the Countryside Commission's approach both to the problems of the lowland landscape and to possible solutions. The Council argue the need for greater protection of existing lowland landscapes, and not just the creation of new ones.[25] Although the CPRE, like the Countryside Commission, supports the notion of local liaison groups to prepare landscape conservation plans for a group of farmers, the Council have, as yet, little experience of working with the farming community: their proposals for landscape conservation would rely heavily on the increased involvement of local planning authorities.

Local planning authorities

In the past, few local planning authorities offered individual farmers advice on landscape conservation; their contact with farmers was limited to discussion about planning applications for farm buildings, or tree-preservation orders. But many authorities are now providing technical advice on tree-planting schemes and, with financial support from the Countryside Commission, they have introduced incentive schemes to encourage farmers to plant trees, often in an effort to repair the damage caused by Dutch elm disease. The schemes vary from county to county but the following example illustrates the possibilities. Early in 1972 Essex County Planning Department set up a scheme to restore tree cover in the Essex countryside; it was intended that the County Council would supply and plant trees on private farmland by agreement with the owners. The response of the farming community was so encouraging that after six months the scheme was extended to include planting by the farmers themselves; the County Council grant aided this planting and published an advisory leaflet which was sent to all NFU members in the county. In two years over 250,000 trees were planted in more than 200 separate schemes. Farmers and landowners have continued to support the scheme and some return each season for additions to their planting scheme.[26]

While many authorities now have the necessary skills available among their own staff, planning departments often have no precedent for advising farmers and they may be hampered by their image as a development control authority. The relationship between farmers and local authorities needs to be improved, and the agreement in the Dedham Vale Area of Outstanding Natural Beauty of voluntary consultation between farming organizations and the planning authority over permitted development is encouraging, as is the preparation of design guides for farm buildings by some counties.

RECENT DEVELOPMENTS TO INFLUENCE FARMERS

Codes of practice and advisory leaflets

Codes of practice were one of the first methods used to promote the protection of wildlife on farms. They usually give specific advice on carrying out a particular job, rather than advice on conservation as part of a farm plan. Codes of practice now exist for scrub clearance, straw-burning, chemical spraying and the use of pesticides: the more important codes are described in the Appendix to this chapter. The best known is probably the NFU straw-burning code, published annually since 1964 with minor alterations as new problems have been identified. The code is widely publicized by posters, leaflets, the agricultural press, radio, the Ministry of Agriculture, the Home Office (fire brigades), conservation organizations and agricultural shows. Yet in spite of these efforts it has been necessary, after 10 years' use of the code, to provide byelaws to control straw-burning in some counties. The straw-burning code was prepared in response to a problem which was easily seen and which affected the public living near farms or driving through cereal-growing areas; if such an obvious problem cannot satisfactorily be solved by voluntary means it seems unlikely that less visible problems (which may be more harmful to wildlife) can be controlled in this way. However, as a means of *advice* rather than *control*, codes of practice are of value. They provide specific information which can readily be referred to and they are one of the few conservation measures directed at farmworkers. For this reason alone, other codes could usefully be introduced, preferably by one of the major agricultural organizations through its own publicity network.

Advisory leaflets have been used to persuade farmers to include conservation in their farm plans and to manage and create areas for this purpose as well as taking account of conservation in normal farming operations. The list of advisory leaflets in the Appendix illustrates the range of subjects covered—from conservation principles to detailed advice on tree planting. But to be effective, published conservation advice must reach the majority of farmers, and be closely linked to agricultural advice and grant aid (for example on tree planting for shelterbelts). Almost all of the conservation leaflets have been published by non-farming organizations which lack direct contact with farmers; despite the help of the NFU and others, the publicity and distribution of existing conservation leaflets cannot match that of the Ministry's own advisory publications which number several hundred and are often free. The extent to which the landscape and wildlife leaflets link conservation advice with sources of agricultural advice varies, although some, like those published by the Nature Conservancy, do this carefully. The need for better distribution and co-ordination points to even closer links with the agricultural advisory services; one possibility might be for advisory material to be prepared by conservation organizations (in conjunction with the Ministry of Agriculture) but published and distributed as part of the Ministry's advisory services.

Farming and wildlife conferences

The first working conference at which groups of conservation experts and farmers prepared detailed farm plans embracing conservation objectives was the one at Silsoe in 1969.[27] Delegates were given background information on a 400-acre farm. Groups then prepared four agricultural plans (based on different farming systems) and a detailed wildlife evaluation of the farm. These five plans and a game plan were presented to the conference and criticized by conservation specialists, and finally a compromise plan was put forward for discussion. The costs of wildlife conservation (in outlay and lost income) and the profitability of different intensities of farming were demonstrated. However, the cost of intensive farming, in terms of wildlife lost, was less easily shown although it was partly measured by the loss in diversity of species when habitats were removed. This quantitative approach clearly demonstrated the conflicts between farming and wildlife conservation. The delegates became involved in the subject as they argued a specialist case and prepared plans which were criticized; they also had the opportunity to work with others and to hear their points of view. But a great deal of background information is needed for this kind of study; agricultural data is already available or can be obtained for most farms but detailed information on wildlife has to be collected by special surveys which may take a year or more to complete.

Since 1969 a number of farming and wildlife conferences have been held on the same pattern as at Silsoe but dealing with other farming systems and including topics such as timber production, landscape conservation and recreation.[28] The realism of exercises like these depends on the careful choice of farms with potential for the different land uses to be examined, but in trying to cover a wide range of problems there is a risk of losing realism and demonstrating compromise for its own sake. These conferences have shown that conservation must be part of the plan for the whole farm, or even for a group of farms in a large-scale landscape; that wildlife conservation experts must be prepared to specify exactly what they want; that wildlife conservation has a real cost (estimated at 50p–£1/acre in 1970); and that many farmers and conservationists simply do not understand each other's jargon. Often, conservationists do not know enough about farming to gain a farmer's confidence or to give him detailed workable advice.

Detailed reports have been prepared for most of the conferences and some had a wide press coverage. Nevertheless the costs have been high, in terms of time and effort spent on organization by voluntary conservation groups, the Ministry of Agriculture, the Nature Conservancy Council and others. The benefits are difficult to assess. Individual delegates must have gained, as did the Ministry of Agriculture officers who were involved. The direct benefits to other farmers have probably been small. Nevertheless, as introductory educational exercises they have worked well in publicizing the principles of conservation and in establishing contacts between farming and conservation groups. But these conferences can only be a base to build upon, not an end in themselves.

Demonstration farms

The logical development of the farming and wildlife conferences is that farming and conservation advisers should prepare conservation plans to be implemented on commercial farms. In 1975 the Countryside Commission appointed a consultant to arrange the demonstration of voluntary conservation measures on 10 working farms representative of the main farming types in England and Wales. With the help of local conservationists, landscape architects and ADAS staff, the Commission's consultant and the farmer will prepare a plan for each farm, to provide an adequate return on agricultural investment and to create (or maintain) an aesthetically pleasing landscape of value to wildlife. In addition to the main objective of demonstrating the principles and techniques of conservation to farmers and advisory staff, several long-term benefits should stem from this exercise. Staff from both farming and conservation organizations will gain practical experience in planning and managing conservation on farms while the local organizations formed could be used for other projects or to discuss local conservation problems.

Local liaison groups

When the Minister of Agriculture announced a conservation training scheme for his staff in 1970, he also suggested that a liaison group of farming and conservation representatives should be established in each county to consider how best to promote an understanding of wildlife conservation problems on farmland. At first few groups were established but the number has grown recently, probably from contacts made at farming and wildlife conferences or as a result of pressure from the Farming and Wildlife Advisory Group. A typical liaison group has representatives from the Ministry of Agriculture, National Farmers' Union, Country Landowners' Association, Nature Conservancy Council, the local County Conservation Trust, the county planning authority, and the local agricultural college, with the Forestry Commission and other interests sometimes represented. All groups provide an opportunity to discuss conservation problems; several have organized visits and talks, and some have prepared conservation plans for individual farms, although only one so far is being implemented. One liaison group has introduced a scheme for tree planting on farms, in which the planting and maintenance is carried out by local members of the Royal Society for the Protection of Birds who will also monitor the sites for 10 years.[29] These liaison groups already provide a useful point of contact for several different organizations who would not otherwise work together, but their real value will only be demonstrated if the links are used to achieve practical conservation schemes and to provide co-ordinated advice for farmers.

AGRICULTURAL EDUCATION AND TRAINING

Only a minority of the agricultural workforce have formal qualifications, but they are likely to hold influential positions in the industry and the proportion of qualified staff is growing. Many agricultural students go into teaching, the ancillary industries, research or advisory work where they have considerable opportunities to influence the attitudes and actions of farmers. The agricultural education system is therefore a very powerful means of influencing farmers on wildlife and landscape conservation matters. So far little attempt has been made to use it for this purpose, although the opportunities seem to exist.[30]

Specialist courses have been established for rural land use planning, recreation management on farms, and landscape construction, but there are no courses in wildlife conservation on farmland, reflecting the lack of demand for such qualifications within the industry. There are two agricultural courses (degree and HND) which study conservation and recreation needs in depth;[31] courses at this level will be useful for liaison or advisory staff but will do little to bridge the gap in language and information between farmers and conservationists. This problem can only be solved if landscape and wildlife conservation are taught as an integral part of all vocational agricultural courses. This could be achieved most effectively by the new Technician Education Council which will administer a national system of courses and awards in agriculture. The Council has pointed out the value of associating general studies with the technical and vocational content of courses,[32] but it has made no recommendations on conservation. Until a national policy is formulated, individual colleges could include some conservation education within existing courses, perhaps by developing the interest which some colleges have shown in preparing conservation plans for their farms and participating in local liaison groups.

Agricultural training (in skills for particular jobs) is the responsibility of the Agricultural Training Board. An industrial training scheme may not be the place to teach the theory of conservation, but it is important that farmworkers should learn the skills of conservation in routine jobs such as hedging, ditching and spraying. The Board, in consultation with FWAG, takes account of conservation needs when training workers in the use of sprays and chemicals. This could usefully be developed, to include in the agricultural training programme more specialized conservation techniques, such as those used by the British Trust for Conservation Volunteers.[33]

REVIEW

Agriculture is an important part of the national economy and can afford to support ancillary industries and finance powerful representative bodies; wildlife and landscape conservation have little economic justification and no direct effect upon living standards. The difference is illustrated by comparing the Agricultural Development and Advisory Service of MAFF, which has more than 5000 staff, with the Nature Conservancy Council, which has less than 500.

A complex pattern of influence has developed since 1969 when the conservation of landscape and wildlife on farmland first became a major public issue. The initiative came from outside the agricultural industry, from a conservation movement which was itself split into several different interest groups concerned with landscape or wildlife, in public or voluntary organizations, and at central or local level. All of these groups, trying both to change farmers' attitudes and to give them practical advice, had the choice of four different points of access to the industry: through the Ministry of Agriculture; through the organizations which represent farmers' interests; through the agricultural education and training system; and lastly by direct contact with the farmers themselves. In this situation, it is not surprising that the attempts to influence have been diverse and fragmented.

Most conservation agencies have realized the importance of the Ministry of Agriculture; not only does it have most influence over the farming industry through its fiscal control and its advisory services, but it is the only agricultural organization with a statutory executive duty to take account of wildlife and landscape conservation. None of the organizations concerned with wildlife or landscape conservation can match the power and influence of the Ministry of Agriculture. Thus the conservation organizations, especially the government agencies, have tried to make the best use of their limited resources by influencing the Ministry. Both the Nature Conservancy Council and the Countryside Commission have established conservation projects in co-operation with the Ministry, whose staff have participated in the Agricultural Habitat Liaison Group set up by the Nature Conservancy and also in the Countryside Commission's New Agricultural Landscapes Study. The opportunities for voluntary organizations to influence the Ministry of Agriculture are more limited, but the farming and wildlife conferences were a useful starting point and co-operation at a local level is now more evident, with the Ministry as members or organizers of local liaison groups. As a result of pressure from all the conservation interests, or in acknowledgement of its statutory duty, the Ministry has spent more time on conservation than have any of the other farming organizations. Advisory staff have received some training (but no specialist staff have been appointed); conservation advice has been introduced to some technical publications; and there has been consultation with conservation bodies.

But, in all, the efforts and the results are disappointing when they are related to the resources and power of the Ministry. It has been suggested that Ministry advisers can spread information on new farming techniques so quickly and efficiently that they exacerbate normal fluctuations in the supply of certain farm products.[34] If this is so, the advisory services, with adequate training and support, should be able to give information and advice on conservation with much more effect than has been achieved up to now. The conservation organizations, both public and voluntary, have neither the staff nor the resources to fill the gap in conservation advisory services, although they can continue to play an important role in research and development. For their initiatives to be successful, the Ministry of Agriculture must adopt a stronger conservation policy. Moreover, the activities of the Ministry are the key to greater involvement by other agricultural agencies, including the specialist press, radio and television, as well as those organizations which represent farmers.

The farmers' organizations have, when asked, been willing to co-operate with conservation groups although they could not be expected to change policies or provide technical advice in the same way as the Ministry of Agriculture. The support of the National Farmers' Union and the Country Landowners' Association has been ignored by some conservation groups (notably the Nature Conservancy), perhaps unwisely, for they have considerable political and practical influence over land managers. The NFU is the most powerful farming organization after the Ministry and through its local branches is in direct contact with four out of every five farmers; the CLA represents the owners of larger farms and estates, who are more likely to introduce conservation measures.

Few conservation organizations have attempted to influence the agricultural education and training system, despite its importance in shaping farmers' and farmworkers' attitudes. The absorption of conservation principles into the education system is a slow process, with a further delay (possibly of years) before results will be seen on the ground. This lack of immediate return may have discouraged conservation groups.

Links between individual farmers and conservation groups are rare. While most farmers have probably seen an advisory leaflet on conservation, circulated by the NFU some years ago, only a very small number will have attended a farming and wildlife conference or sought the advice of their County Conservation Trust; the majority are likely to have had no direct contact with any conservation organization. Only 1 farmer in 10 is a member of a conservation organization and only 18 of the 39 local conservation trusts are known to have made a special effort to recruit farmers.

In all, the progress made in convincing the agricultural industry of the need for conservation has been slow. The Ministry of Agriculture have not devoted sufficient resources to the problem; the conservation organizations have been unable to reach many farmers in a co-ordinated way; and the opportunities to influence education and training have been missed. The most promising development is the increasing contact between farming and conservation organizations at a local level as, for example, has been pioneered in the Countryside Commission management experiments in the uplands and in the urban fringe. Joint working of this kind is essential in the long term if conservation plans are to be prepared and implemented on ordinary farms.

Farmers' attitudes

It is impossible to assess what effect the various agencies of conservation influence have had on the day-to-day management of individual farms; there have been no 'before and after' surveys to use as a basis for comparison, but two studies do provide some indications of farmers' attitudes. The 1972 New Agricultural Landscapes Study revealed the views of some farmers on land-scape conservation, and in 1975 the Ministry of Agriculture carried out an interview survey of farmers' attitudes to wildlife conservation.[35] On the basis of these studies, certain general conclusions can be drawn.

Many farmers in the lowlands think that the evolution of the landscape should not be left entirely to them although there are differences in attitudes between livestock and arable areas. In livestock areas, where there has been comparatively little landscape change, farmers were more willing to accept responsibility for the landscape than were farmers of the arable eastern areas where recent landscape changes have been significant; most of these arable farmers thought that society should accept the new landscapes which emerge. Out of every 10 farmers interviewed by the Ministry of Agriculture 9 said that they were interested in allowing at least some types of wildlife (other than pests) to exist on their farms. The majority gave as their reason personal pleasure or a belief in the 'balance of nature', while less than a fifth were interested because of the sporting potential of their land. (These results conflict with the views of the New Agricultural Landscapes consultants who con-cluded that many lowland farmers were interested in shooting but few were interested in wildlife generally.) This apparent acceptance by so many farmers of both landscape and wildlife objectives may be misleading. It is known that a farmer's idea of a 'good' landscape does not necessarily meet the standards generally accepted by the public. In the wildlife survey the interviewers did not go on to explain what habitats would have to be provided for different types of wildlife, and the farmers perhaps did not think, or even did not know, what this would mean; one-quarter of the farmers in this survey admitted that they knew virtually nothing about wildlife, and the New Agricultural Landscapes Study found that many farmers did not recognize the wildlife value of a hedge.

Perhaps a more useful indicator of farmers' attitudes is their intention to alter wildlife habitats. Of all farmers interviewed by the Ministry of Agricul-ture, 13 per cent intended to reduce some of the 'non-farmed' areas of their land during the next 10 years; the areas most likely to be reduced were unimproved grazing, scrub, derelict buildings, quarries and marshy land or water—very few farmers intended to remove hedges or trees. A similar proportion of farmers (13 per cent) intended to improve existing wildlife habitats or to create new ones but they favoured particular habitat types. Woods and wetlands were most likely to be improved and, together with hedges, were the only wildlife habitats which farmers intended to create. The farmers with positive wildlife management intentions were not typical of farmers as a whole—they were more likely to have a personal interest in wildlife or game, to be members of conservation organizations and to have large farms. Both surveys show that farmers favour certain types of wildlife habitat; this is all the more significant for future conservation because the least favoured habitats are those which already occur least frequently on farmland.

Perhaps the most significant finding of all is that three farmers in four intend to make no changes in the area of wildlife habitat on their farms during the next 10 years.

CONCLUSIONS

Surveys have shown that the majority of farmers accept the principles of wildlife and landscape conservation but evidence on the ground suggests that these are not widely practised. Effective wildlife and landscape conservation on farms will require positive and co-ordinated action from the majority of farmers. Three developments are needed before voluntary action can be achieved on this scale: farmers must treat wildlife and landscape conservation as an integral part of every farm plan and of every management decision on the farm; they must be helped to recognize opportunities for conservation and be advised how best to use such opportunities; and they must understand the management of wildlife and landscape resources.

Farmers are not given enough help with the detailed planning of conservation on individual farms and the advice which is available has not been properly co-ordinated with the comprehensive agricultural advisory services which already exist. The integration of conservation and agricultural management decisions needs a more positive conservation element in all agricultural education courses, and the careful co-ordination of advice so that the farmer receives both conservation and agricultural advice from the same source. *All* agricultural advisers must be trained to help farmers recognize the conservation opportunities which arise during routine farm advisory work. Specialist conservation staff, with a good working knowledge of agriculture, are needed to help farmers make best use of these opportunities. Wildlife and landscape advice must be co-ordinated to avoid conflict (for example tree planting on unproductive areas of the farm might improve landscape but destroy valuable wetland or grassland habitats).

If the best use is to be made of opportunities for conservation, some schemes may have to be implemented jointly by several farmers. Special project officers could be used in areas where landscape and wildlife conservation are particularly important, acting as a link between farming and conservation interests, co-ordinating new schemes and dealing with a variety of problems such as help with labour and materials for conservation work. For long-term conservation management farmers will need detailed knowledge of wildlife and landscape resources and their staff may need specialist skills (for example, in hedge or pond management). Again this must come through agricultural education and training, but the voluntary conservation interests could help by stimulating farmers' interest.

Voluntary action by farmers on the scale required cannot be achieved until wildlife and landscape conservation become an integral part of agricultural education, training and advice. This demands the commitment of more resources within these services, an increase in the number of specialist conservation advisers, and the broader training of all advisers in both agriculture and conservation.

Appendix

CODES OF PRACTICE AND ADVISORY PUBLICATIONS

Listed below are some of the codes of practice and advisory publications used to encourage wildlife or landscape conservation on farmland; some are aimed at a wider audience than farmers and some refer to other problems also. The addresses are those of distributors; prices have *not* been included in this list.

Pesticides, A Code of Conduct
Joint Association of British Manufacturers of Agricultural Chemicals/Wildlife Education and Communications Committee, Alembic House, Albert Embankment, London SE1. (17pp)

Code of Practice for Ground Spraying (1968)
Ministry of Agriculture, Fisheries and Food (Publications), Room 203, Block C, Government Buildings, Tolcarne Drive, Pinner, Middlesex, HA5 2DT. (5pp)

Code of Practice for the Use of Herbicides on Weeds in Watercourses and Lakes (1975)
Ministry of Agriculture, Fisheries and Food (Publications), (address as above). (29pp)

Scrub Clearance . . . A Conservation Code
Society for the Promotion of Nature Conservation, The Green, Nettleham, Lincoln. (2pp)

The Straw-burning Code
National Farmers' Union, Agriculture House, Knightsbridge, London SW1X 7NJ. Published annually. (2pp)

Farming With Wildlife
Farming and Wildlife Advisory Group, Royal Society for the Protection of Birds, The Lodge, Sandy, Bedfordshire, SG19 2DL. (7pp)

Farming and Wildlife in Dorset
Dorset Naturalists' Trust, Hon Secretary, 58 Pearce Avenue, Parkstone, Poole, Dorset. (5pp)

Wildlife on Farmland (1973)
Publications Officer, The Nature Conservancy Council, Attingham Park, Shrewsbury, SY4 4TW. (5pp)

Tree Planting and Wildlife
Society for the Promotion of Nature Conservation, The Green, Nettleham, Lincoln. (4pp)

Tree Planting and Wildlife Conservation (1974)
Publications Officer, Nature Conservancy Council (address as above). (13pp)

  Examples of Trees and Shrubs which are Associated with Wildlife (1973) (1p)

  Suggestions for Trees and Shrubs (1973) (1p)

  Britain's Native Shrubs (1974) (2pp)

  Growing Native Trees and Shrubs to Form a Wildlife Area (1974) (3pp)
All: Farming and Wildlife Advisory Group, Royal Society for the Protection of Birds (address as above).

Hedges and Shelterbelts (1973)
Publications Officer, Nature Conservancy Council (address as above). (7pp)

Hedging, A Practical Conservation Handbook (1975)
British Trust for Conservation Volunteers, Zoological Gardens, Regents Park, London NW1 4RY. (117pp)

Replacement of Elm in the Countryside (1973)
Forestry Commission Leaflet 57, HMSO. (3pp)

Local Authority Tree-Planting Leaflets
Several county planning authorities have published advisory leaflets for tree planting on farmland.

Ponds and Ditches (1973)
Publications Officer, Nature Conservancy Council (address as above). (5pp)

Pesticides (1973)
Publications Officer, Nature Conservancy Council (address as above). (7pp)

Wildlife Conservation and Lichens (1975)
Devon Trust for Nature Conservation, 2 Pennsylvania Road, Exeter, EX4 6BQ. (16pp)

Wildfowl and Agriculture (1975)
Royal Society for the Protection of Birds (address as above). (15pp)

Predatory Mammals in Britain, A Code of Practice for Their Management (1973)
Council for Nature, Zoological Gardens, Regents Park, London SW1 4RT. Second edition. (56pp)

Predatory Birds in Britain
The Council for Nature (address as above) (64pp)

Focus on Bats, A Guide to Their Conservation and Control
Society for the Promotion of Nature Conservation (address as above). (5pp)

Save Our Pollinating Insects
Bee Research Association, Hill House, Chalfont St. Peter, Gerrards Cross, Buckinghamshire. (6pp)

The Maintenance of Field Monuments on Cultivated Land and Pasture
Department of the Environment, Directorate of Ancient Monuments (AP), 23 Savile Row, London W1E 7EZ (4pp)

Ministry of Agriculture, Fisheries and Food Publications
MAFF publishes several hundred agricultural advisory publications. The complete list is revised frequently and is published in two parts which may be obtained from the addresses below:

Government Publications, Sectional List 1, Agriculture and Food, HMSO. Free of charge from: Director of Publications (Section PM1C), HMSO, Atlantic House, Holborn Viaduct, London EC1P 1BN.

Agriculture Fisheries and Food, Catalogue of Departmental Publications, MAFF.
Free of charge from: Ministry of Agriculture, Fisheries and Food (Publications), Room 203, Block C, Government Buildings, Tolcarne Drive, Pinner, Middlesex HA5 2DT.

NOTES AND REFERENCES

1. Westmacott, R. and Worthington, T. (1974). *New Agricultural Landscapes*, Countryside Commission Publication No. 76.
2. References in the Countryside Act (1968) to the conservation of the natural beauty of an area include the conservation of its flora, fauna and geological and physiographical features; Countryside Act, Chapter 41.
3. Hughes, Cledwyn (1970), quoted in Barber, D. (ed) (1970). *Farming and Wildlife: a Study in Compromise*, Royal Society for the Protection of Birds and others, Sandy, England.
4. Staff members of ADAS for 1974/75 (Ministry of Agriculture, Fisheries and Food, 1976, personal communication).
5. For example: Ministry of Agriculture, Fisheries and Food (1969). *The Safe Use of Poisonous Chemicals*, Leaflet APS/1, London.
6. Government White Paper (1975). *Food from our own Resources*, Cmnd 6020, HMSO, London.
7. Darke, M. (1970). Quoted in The Countryside in 1970, *Proceedings of the Third Conference*, Royal Society of Arts, London.
8. Country Landowners' Association (undated), *Small Woods and Tree Planting on Farmland*, CLA, London.
9. Westmacott, R. and Worthington, T. (1974). *New Agricultural Landscapes*.
10. The Game Conservancy, Fordingbridge, Hampshire is an independent body which carries out research, publishes advisory booklets and provides training and advice on game management.
11. Nature Conservancy Council (1974). *Statement of Policies*, London.
12. Nature Conservancy Council (1975). *First Report: 1 November 1973–31 March 1975*. HMSO, London.
13. A recent survey has shown that 60 per cent of farmers are interested in having advice on wildlife conservation in the future; 26 per cent of farmers want only written advice but a further 26 per cent want both written advice and a visit by a wildlife specialist:
    Ministry of Agriculture, Fisheries and Food (1976). *Wildlife Conservation in Semi-natural Habitats on Farms, a Survey of Farmer Attitudes and intentions in England and Wales*, HMSO, London.
14. This film may be bought or hired from: The Films Officer, Royal Society for the Protection of Birds, The Lodge, Sandy, Beds.
15. The Farming and Wildlife Advisory Group, The Lodge, Sandy, Beds.
16. The Devon Trust for Nature Conservation deals with requests for advice from 20–30 farmers each year and for about half of these the Trust prepares a written conservation report. A small charge is made for advice partly to contribute to administrative costs but also because the Trust has found that farmers are more likely to implement the advice if they have paid for it.
    Elsewhere, after advice has been given, follow-up work by a trust can encourage implementation where voluntary labour is offered for maintenance or monitoring.
    Source: Author survey in 1975; information obtained from 24 of the 39 County Conservation Trusts in England and Wales.
17. British Trust for Conservation Volunteers (1975). *Hedging: A Practical Conservation Handbook*, BTCV, London.
18. The Countryside Commission is a statutory body with a wide range of responsibilities under the National Parks and Access to the Countryside Act, 1949 and the Countryside Act, 1968, covering England and Wales; there is a separate Countryside Commission for Scotland with responsibilities under the Countryside (Scotland) Act, 1967.

19. Westmacott, R. and Worthington, T. (1974). *New Agricultural Landscapes.*
20. Countryside Commission (1974). *New Agricultural Landscapes: A Discussion Paper*, Countryside Commission Publication No. 76A.
21. Countryside Commission (1976). *The Lake District Upland Management Experiment*, Countryside Commission Publication No. 93.
22. Countryside Commission (1974). Cited in note 20.
23. See note 20.
24. Council for the Protection of Rural England (1971). *Loss of Cover Through the Removal of Hedgerows and Trees*, CPRE, London.
    Council for the Protection of Rural England (1974). *Development Control—Package Buildings*, CPRE, London.
25. Council for the Protection of Rural England (1975). *Landscape—the Need for a Public Voice*, CPRE, London.
26. Essex County Council; personal communication.
27. Barber, D. (ed) (1970). *Farming and Wildlife: a Study in Compromise.*
28. Reports have been published on several farming and wildlife conferences including:
    Dorset Naturalists' Trust (1970). *Farming and Wildlife in Dorset, Report of a Study Conference*, DNT.
    Ratcliffe, A. J. B. (ed) (1972). *The Dinas Conference on Upland Farming, Forestry and Wildlife Conservation*, Ministry of Agriculture, Fisheries and Food, London.
    Barber, D. (1973). *The Chalkland Exercise on Chalkland Farming and Wildlife Conservation*, Ministry of Agriculture, Fisheries and Food, London.
    Mathias, J. and Jolliffe, W. (eds) (1974). *The Cowbyers Conference on Upland Farming, Forestry, Game Conservation and Wildlife Conservation*, Ministry of Agriculture, Fisheries and Food, Newcastle-upon-Tyne.
29. Royal Society for the Protection of Birds (1975). *Corner a Place for Wildlife*, RSPB, Newcastle-upon-Tyne.
30. The system offers opportunities to specialize and to adapt courses to particular local needs; many levels of course are available from short non-certificate courses through part-time, full-time or sandwich courses leading to City and Guilds qualifications, to degree and postgraduate courses. Up to University level, agricultural education is normally still separate from other technical education and many colleges enjoy a considerable degree of autonomy. In 1973 the Department of Education and Science organized a course for staff from agricultural colleges on the conservation of wildlife in relation to agriculture.
31. The University of London offers a BSc in Rural Environment Studies, aiming to produce graduates educated in the natural and social sciences and aware of contemporary environmental problems. *Wye College Prospectus*, 1974–76.
    Seale-Hayne College in Devon offers an HND course in Natural Resources and Rural Economy in response to a need for technologists educated on these issues. *Seale-Hayne College Prospectus*, 1974–75.
32. Technician Education Council (1974). *Policy Statement, June 1974.* TEC, London.
33. The British Trust for Conservation Volunteers Handbook on *Hedging* (see note 17) is one of a series of practical handbooks being prepared for the Trust.
34. Donaldson, J. G. S. and Frances, in association with Barber, D. (1972). *Farming in Britain Today*, Revised edition, Penguin Books, London.
35. Westmacott, R. and Worthington, T. (1974). *New Agricultural Landscapes.* Ministry of Agriculture, Fisheries and Food (1976). See note 13. The results of these surveys cannot be compared in detail. This assessment of farmers' attitudes draws on data from both studies; the gap in time between them does not, in the author's opinion, invalidate the comparisons.

Chapter 9

Incentives in conservation

R. J. LLOYD

The first part of this book has shown how the objectives and methods of modern farming often conflict with the needs of wildlife and landscape conservation. To retain on farmland features of conservation interest which now have little agricultural function, such as hedgerows, small woods and wetlands, a farmer incurs extra costs for little or no benefit to his enterprise. At a time of renewed emphasis upon economic efficiency, many farmers cannot afford these costs so that the features we value are either removed or managed in such a way that their conservation interest is lost. The case has been argued for farmers to be paid, at least in part, for the costs of conservation action on their land, or to allow others to undertake the work on the farmer's behalf. Many landowners may agree to action to benefit conservation interests as long as they do not have to take the responsibility for it.

The idea of public payment in cash, or in kind, for conservation management on farmland has wide support among farmers and landowners who would regard this as compensation for community benefits provided at their expense. But the argument has also received more general support: for example, in the report on 'Agriculture, Forestry and Land Management'[1] prepared for the Countryside in 1970 Conference, there was a recommendation that where a farmer is required to keep at least some of his land in a condition that is acceptable to amenity interests, at a cost to himself, he should be entitled to proper compensation and he should also receive incentives to consider the long-term renewal of the landscape.

The incentive approach is not new to British agriculture. Government intervention to promote increased output and to improve efficiency has for many years involved persuasive means rather than compulsion. Grants and subsidies in particular have been used to encourage efficient farming in a positive way. They have been applied in various forms since the 1930s and now cover a wide range of activities including land drainage, new buildings and fertilizer application.[2] The loss of many valued landscape and wildlife features in the farmed countryside can be attributed, at least partly, to the general availability of these incentives.

In contrast, grants, payments of compensation and other forms of assistance designed to promote conservation objectives in the farmed countryside have been used to a significant extent only during the last few years and the annual expenditure is probably still less than £1m per annum. Moreover, payments have often been made not to secure positive action but to prevent changes taking place. For example, compensation has been paid to farmers who have agreed not to plough or to improve their land for agriculture so that the interests of landscape and wildlife may be safeguarded.

The rest of this chapter examines the use of various forms of incentive to encourage landowners to adopt *voluntarily* those land management practices which also take into account the needs of conservation. Three types of incentive are recognized: *direct aid to landowners*, *management agreements* and *fiscal measures*, and each is discussed in turn.

DIRECT AID TO LANDOWNERS

Maintenance of the fabric of the countryside requires a continuous investment both in capital works, such as tree planting, and in management operations such as hedge laying. Although the declining visual and wildlife quality of the farmed countryside can be attributed mainly to the removal of existing features or to changes in management practices, an increasingly important factor is a lack of new investment. This is particularly significant in the case of farm trees, whether in hedges, parkland or elsewhere, where the number of new trees planted, or saplings retained in hedges, is now insufficient to maintain a continuing succession of trees.[3]

The case has been strongly argued for a substantial increase in the amount of tree planting in the countryside for landscape purposes,[4] and an obvious way to encourage this is by direct aid to landowners in the form of grants, free trees, or labour to undertake the necessary work. More local authorities are now adopting this approach, usually with financial assistance from the Countryside Commission, and the Commission can also provide grant aid direct to landowners.[5] But the effectiveness of these schemes in terms of landscape improvement has been limited so far.

A great many farmers, perhaps the majority, do not value trees in the landscape except where they have an agricultural function; and some may have a positive dislike of them.[6] In these circumstances a favourable and widespread response to aid for planting amenity trees will come only from those landowners already interested in trees and the experience of local authorities supports this conclusion.[7] Perhaps not unexpectedly, most of the interest in planting is found on the more visually attractive farms and estates where landscape deterioration, except as a consequence of elm disease, is a relatively minor problem. Yet the most urgent need for landscape improvement is in those areas largely denuded of hedges and trees and it is here that farmers tend to be particularly apathetic about amenity issues. The conclusion must be that directly aided planting schemes alone will never achieve the scale of new planting required in many areas for, as Westmacott and Worthington suggest, unless a landowner places a positive value on trees he will not regard a cash grant for tree planting as an incentive; neither is he likely to be prepared to give up land for planting by others.[4]

No one method of promoting tree planting will provide the panacaea. Nevertheless, while directly aided planting schemes alone may not be the complete answer to the maintenance or re-creation of attractive farm land-scapes, the approach could make a valuable contribution towards this goal. It could help to ensure the maintenance of good landscape in areas where landowners are sympathetic to landscape conservation but for economic or operational reasons (which are increasing constraints) cannot afford the time or the manpower to undertake new planting themselves. But to achieve a worth-while level of planting the scale of investment must be increased. Although it is rising, present expenditure is still minute compared with the need. In the financial year 1973/74 grant aid provided by central government for amenity tree-planting schemes in the countryside contributed some £300,000[8] towards a total expenditure of about £400,000 shared between local authorities and the private landowner. On the assumption that standard trees were planted at a total cost of materials (including fencing) and labour of about £4 a tree, this expenditure represents the planting of only 100,000 trees, a total which must be seen against a loss of almost one million *mature* elm trees alone between 1972 and 1973 solely as a result of Dutch elm disease.[9] It is true that planting is being undertaken by some landowners at their own expense and by voluntary bodies and that this is contributing to landscape renewal. In addition some local authorities are planting trees elsewhere in the farmed countryside, for example on smallholdings managed by them and along highways. Nevertheless, in most counties a substantial increase in the budget for incentive tree-planting schemes is needed. Even if the expenditure on tree planting reached £100,000 in each county, with rate support grant and assistance from the Countryside Commission (assuming their budget for tree planting could also be increased) the local contribution would only be £25,000—a very small proportion of the total expenditure of a county.

With the current exhortations to cut back on public expenditure, it is probably unrealistic to expect local authorities to allocate enough money to mount comprehensive tree-planting programmes. For this reason and since the problem of landscape renewal is more acute in some areas than others, it may be that local authorities should not be the main agents responsible for this work. It could be argued that national priorities should be determined and that implementation should be entrusted to a national agency such as the Forestry Commission or to an agency set up specifically for the purpose.

Where existing trees conflict with agricultural operations it might be possible to dissuade farmers from removing them by paying compensation to offset, at least in part, their economic cost or nuisance value. In the County of Hereford and Worcester the County Council is prepared to pay landowners £3 a tree for tellers retained in hedges[10] and a similar incentive is being offered by the Crown Estates Commissioners to their tenant farmers. But it seems probable that hedgerows and hedgerow trees will continue to be removed, for the reasons discussed in previous chapters. Providing grants for hedgerow tree planting or to retain tellers could therefore be wasted effort, except perhaps along roadsides where hedges provide less obstruction to farming operations. Only where public authorities have considerable influence over land management—as in the case of publicly owned land let to tenants—is there any firm evidence that hedgerow schemes could ever make a significant contribution to landscape maintenance. It is probably more realistic to think in terms of creating a new farm landscape in many areas rather than of fossilizing the existing pattern. Thus, except for replacing trees in roadside hedges, there is a good case for concentrating investment on planting clumps, tree belts and small woods on marginal land.

In areas where much new planting is required, a further incentive to farmer participation which local authorities could offer is their co-operation over the rerouting of public rights of way. Where there is an obvious conflict of interests, the needs of farming and of recreation would be better served if some footpaths could be rerouted to follow the line of new planting.

But all these approaches will fail if public authorities cannot do better at persuading farmers and landowners that the principle of tree planting is a good one. An essential prerequisite to any successful local authority tree-planting scheme is the local support of the NFU and the CLA. It is also important that farmers should respect the views of the local authority personnel involved and an understanding of farming problems is of obvious importance here. On an experimental basis, the Countryside Commission are sponsoring land management projects in the uplands[11] and in the urban fringe.[12] In both cases project officers with an agricultural background have been appointed whose role is to liaise with farmers and landowners, encouraging them to co-operate in schemes which maintain and improve the landscape (such as tree planting and rebuilding dry stone walls) and in schemes designed to improve the opportunities for informal recreation, which at the same time assist farmers by reducing disturbance (such as improvements to footpaths, repairs to stiles and bridges, and waymarking). Where requested, the work has been done through the project officers, often with volunteer labour. Any costs for materials have been paid out of public funds, the project officers having an allocation of money to spend at their discretion on small jobs. This provides the means to respond immediately to management problems. The practical results of the experiments, in terms of goodwill generated and jobs done, are encouraging and confirm the importance of a project officer on the ground, with local knowledge.

MANAGEMENT AGREEMENTS

A management agreement has been described as a formal written agreement between a public authority and an owner or occupier of land who thereby undertakes to manage the land in a specified manner to satisfy a particular public need, usually in return for some kind of consideration.[13] This is normally financial. Many management agreements contain covenants binding on the landowner. These are usually restrictive and prevent him from carrying out some activity: a covenant may for example stipulate that woodland may not be felled, or moorland ploughed, or the land built upon. Covenants of this kind are made for the benefit of adjacent land and are usually enforceable on successors in title.[14,15] Management agreements may also include positive covenants but at present these cannot normally be enforced on new owners and must be renegotiated.

Management agreements recognize formally, through the payment of a consideration, that land management measures undertaken by landowners for the public benefit cost money which can rarely be recovered in other ways. By this recognition, and because they are negotiated voluntarily, such agreements would seem in principle to be attractive to landowners. If management agreements could be negotiated widely and could cover the full range of conservation objectives and in particular positive management, the approach might provide a powerful method of achieving environmental goals in agricultural areas. The approach is already used by several government agencies to promote a number of different land management objectives in the fields of forestry, wildlife conservation, the protection of field monuments and access to private land, while the Countryside Commission have proposed an extension to the approach in the form of 'landscape agreements'.

The Woodland Dedication Schemes

At the end of the Second World War Britain's timber reserves were seriously depleted. To ensure a proper rehabilitation of felled woodland in private ownership and to promote new planting, the government introduced a Woodland Dedication Scheme in 1947. Under this scheme an owner agreed with the Forestry Commission under covenant to manage his woodland in perpetuity for the main purpose of timber production and in accordance with an agreed 'Plan of Operations'.[16] In return, the owner received a planting grant for every acre satisfactorily planted, followed by an annual grant for management and maintenance.[17] Where owners were prepared to manage their woodlands under an agreed plan of operations but were unwilling to enter into long-term agreements under covenant, an initial planting grant was available under the Approved Woodlands Scheme. In addition, for small areas of woodland, grants were available, without the condition of a comprehensive management plan, under the Small Woods Planting Grant.

The level of planting grant and maintenance payments under the Dedication Scheme was estimated to be about 25 per cent of the cost of establishing and maintaining commercial woodland under the best traditions of forest management, and rather less than 25 per cent under the Approved Woodlands Scheme (the actual cost to the State was however somewhat greater depending upon an owner's personal tax circumstances and reliefs). At this level of grant there can be little doubt that the main aim of the Schemes, to promote good woodland management, was realized, for by 1973 the total area of land covered by the Schemes (over 1·3 million acres) represented about 65 per cent of all productive woodland in private ownership.[18] The arrangements were clearly beneficial to both parties: the Forestry Commission was assisted in its task of promoting good forestry practice and an increasing reserve of timber; the landowner received a grant towards an enterprise which was profitable, particularly when his personal tax reliefs were taken into account. For the other types of management agreement now in operation the benefits to landowners are much less obvious and, in consequence, their use has been limited.

All these woodland management schemes have now been replaced by a single Dedication Scheme following a review of forestry policy.[19] Under the new Forestry Dedication Scheme (Basis III) a once-only grant is paid where agreements are made under covenant to manage woodlands to an approved plan which has been discussed not only between the landowner and the Forestry Commission but also with other public agencies.[20] Where the crop is predominantly hardwood an extra grant is payable in recognition of the long rotation period and also the desirability, for amenity reasons, of perpetuating broadleaved woods, particularly in the lowlands. Owners who have already dedicated their woodlands under the earlier arrangements continue to retain their rights and obligations; if they wish, however, they can transfer to the new scheme.

While the greater emphasis on amenity in the new Dedication Scheme is to be welcomed, the phasing out of the Small Woods Planting Grant may bring unfortunate landscape implications in predominantly agricultural areas. In contrast to grants under the Dedicated Woodlands and Approved Woodlands Schemes, this grant was available on a simple form of agreement and was taken up mainly by the small landowner and farmer rather than by the owner particularly interested in forestry. The absence of management controls may have been unsatisfactory for the Forestry Commission but it probably encouraged many farmers to take up the grant. It could well be that farmers will now be less willing to replace or plant new areas of woodland on their land. If such a conclusion is confirmed there is a case on landscape grounds for the restoration of the Small Woods Planting Grant, or a similar scheme. In its absence greater attention must be placed upon encouraging amenity planting by other means.

It is not possible to measure the full impact of the new Forestry Dedication Scheme since its introduction has coincided with a period of economic depression and major changes in taxation, in particular the replacement of Estate Duty (with its favourable provisions for forestry) by Capital Transfer Tax which it is thought will depress the level of investment in the industry at least for the next few years. In the longer term, however, if world timber prices rise as demand for timber exceeds supply, there may be economic potential for further increases in the area of afforested land; and if the need to maximize agricultural output is reduced, as has been suggested in Chapter 1, some of this new planting might take place in the lowlands with benefits to both timber production and amenity.

Management agreements for nature conservation

The Nature Conservancy Council may enter into 'Nature Reserve Agreements' which provide for the management of land in accordance with an agreed management policy which reflects nature conservation interests;[21] some 60 per cent (about 200,000 acres) of the total area of national nature reserves is in the form of these agreements. They are usually made for at least 21 years and may be binding on successors in title. Under the terms of an agreement the owner continues to carry out the general estate management of the land but in accordance with the agreed management policy which may include, for example, safeguarding the land against ploughing and afforestation, and against the introduction of alien plants and animals. An agreement is designed to ensure that land is managed to conserve wildlife and can be used for scientific research. Reserve powers of compulsory purchase are available where agreements are not honoured.[22] Compensation for restrictions on the normal rights of ownership and occupation of land is payable annually by the Nature Conservancy Council, the sum being agreed between the parties to the agreement. The Council may also contribute towards the costs of estate management, for example fencing, where this also benefits conservation.

Under Section 15 of the Countryside Act 1968, the Nature Conservancy Council have powers to negotiate management agreements over Sites of Special Scientific Interest, many of which include land in agricultural use. Indeed, the continuation of an appropriate agricultural practice is often essential to the maintenance of the scientific value of these sites. The agreements are similar to those for nature reserves although rather less formal and without reserve powers. In acknowledgement of the restrictions imposed upon land use and management (which may be binding on successors in title) an annual consideration is paid. In agricultural areas, the consideration can be taken to represent the additional return the landowner might be expected to make if he adopted more 'progressive' farming methods.

Most nature reserve agreements were negotiated during the 1950s and early 1960s when there were fewer pressures and opportunities for land exploitation. Since that period the rate of conclusion of new agreements has slowed down (Figure 16). It may also be significant that few Section 15 agreements for Sites of Special Scientific Interest have yet been made.[23] It seems likely that it is not the level of the consideration which is acting as a disincentive (there is considerable flexibility in this) but rather it is the long-term nature of the restrictions. Increasingly, owners are realizing that their land might be made to yield a higher return, either now or in the future, through the intensification of farming or through the development of new enterprises such as those based on

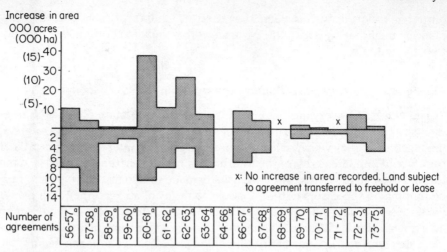

Figure 16. Nature reserve agreements. a. Oct.–Sep.; b. Sep.–Mar.; c. Apr.–Mar.; d. Nov.–Mar. (Source: Nature Conservancy Annual Reports 1956–57 to 1963–64. Natural Environment Research Council Annual Reports 1964–66 to 1972–73. Nature Conservancy Council, Annual Report 1973–75. London, HMSO)

sporting and other leisure activities. The presence of any long-term restrictions on land management could reduce this potential; it might also reduce land values. These arguments apply particularly to the management of large areas of land as nature reserves, but they also apply to the management of smaller areas of land either as reserves or under Section 15 agreements. Agricultural land values have risen dramatically in the last few years and many farmers will be reluctant to restrict agricultural operations, over even a small part of their farm, for this might reduce the capital value or potential earning power of the holding.

The access agreement

Access agreements, which may be binding on successors in title, are designed to secure access to private land for outdoor recreation. They are made by local planning authorities, with the approval of the Secretary of State for the Environment, and apply only to land defined as 'open country'.[24] Under the terms of an agreement landowners agree not only to allow public access over their land but also to manage the land in such a way that it will remain suitable for access, and it is through this provision that conservation objectives may also incidentally be achieved. Thus, an agreement may contain an undertaking from the landowner that he will not fence the land or convert any of it into 'excepted land'.[25] In return the local planning authority provides a 'consideration'[26] and can agree to supply any notices and other works which may be necessary for the implementation of the agreement. The authority may also make byelaws over the land and appoint wardens. By preventing the conversion of access land into excepted land, access agreements effectively prevent the ploughing up of permanent pastures, thereby aiding both wildlife and landscape conservation. The number, distribution and area of access agreements at 31 March 1975 are given in Table 20.

Table 20. Access agreements[a]

	Total	National parks[b]	Other land
Number of agreements	52	28	24
Area (ha)	31,265	25,675	5590

[a] At 31 March 1975.
[b] Over 80 per cent of the access land in the national parks is in the Peak District National Park, the national park under the most pressure from recreation.
Source: Figures derived from tables in Gibbs, R. S. and Whitby, M. C. (1975). *Local Authority Expenditure on Access Land*, Agricultural Adjustment Unit, University of Newcastle upon Tyne, Research Monograph No. 6.

In general, access agreements have been made only where there was already a substantial pressure for access and, in consequence, trespass was occurring. The main attraction of these agreements to landowners is unlikely to be financial (the consideration varies from nil to about £4/acre/year) but is the opportunity an agreement provides to regularize access and to control visitors through byelaws and wardening. There appears to be a reluctance amongst most landowners to allow the public on to their property and the conclusion must be that unless the level of consideration can be increased substantially to provide a real incentive there is little chance that access agreements will be negotiated on a large scale: and if access agreements cannot be negotiated then, at present, any incidental conservation benefits must also be lost.

The Field Monuments Acknowledgement Payment

The Secretary of State for the Environment may make payments to occupiers of land containing a 'scheduled' field monument if there is a danger that the monument will be damaged by agricultural or forestry activities.[27] These Field Monuments Acknowledgement Payments are made to occupiers who agree not to undertake damaging operations, in particular levelling, ploughing, cultivating or planting trees on the site of the monument.[28] In agricultural areas, the scheme applies only to land to be used for arable cropping and ley grassland and for tree planting, for here there is a particular risk of damage. While designed to protect field monuments, the scheme also serves wildlife conservation interests since many scheduled sites also include species-rich old grassland in otherwise intensively cultivated areas.

Several features of the Field Monuments Acknowledgement Payments Scheme contrast with access and nature reserve agreements. There is no pressure upon occupiers: the scheme is brought to their notice through the farming press and through Ministry of Agriculture publications such as *At the Farmers' Service*, a reference handbook used by most farmers. It is the occupier's responsibility to contact the Ancient Monuments Directorate of the Department of the Environment if he wishes to participate. Agreements are short-term, with occupiers committed only for one year at a time. Compared with the payments under access, nature reserve and Countryside Act Section 15 agreements, Field Monument Agreements are more generous in relation to the area of land involved. Even so, the success of the scheme has not matched expectations. By December 1975, just over three years after it was launched, less than 400 agreements had been made (this figure ought to be seen against an estimated 8000 monuments at risk in England, Scotland and Wales)[29] and the rate of conclusion of new agreements was disappointingly slow. However, once having entered an agreement almost all occupiers were willing to continue for a second year and the increased rates of payment from January 1976 have stimulated rather more interest.

Landscape agreements

Chapter 7 argued how urgent was the need to influence the conservation of landscape by encouraging the retention and proper management of important existing features and the creation of new landscapes. Management agreements covering forestry, wildlife conservation, public access and the protection of field monuments may contribute to the protection of valuable landscapes but the benefits can only be incidental as these agreements are not primarily directed towards landscape aims.[13] Existing agreement schemes are clearly insufficient to ensure the scale of landscape conservation now required and there is a case for empowering local authorities to enter into agreements which can relate specifically to landscape management. This idea has been developed by the Countryside Commission in their proposals for 'landscape agreements'.[13]

The Commission suggest that landscape agreements should contain not only negative restrictions preventing the destruction of valued landscapes but also positive clauses to ensure that features are properly managed: examples might be that an area of chalk downland should be kept free from scrub by grazing or that heather moorland should be burned in rotation. Positive clauses could also assist in the retention of important groups of trees or hedges. For example, an agreement might cover a parkland landscape to ensure the protection and phased replanting of the trees, or an historic hedge to ensure its proper maintenance through cutting and periodic laying. If the concept were interpreted widely, agreements of this kind might be used to promote a new, more functional but still pleasing landscape. Landowners could agree not to remove existing but inconvenient landscape features until replacement planting had begun.

The main value of landscape agreements would be the power they would give to local authorities to recompense landowners for retaining and managing for the public benefit those landscape features which are uneconomic in the context of modern farming practice. This concept was strongly supported by the National Park Policies Review Committee[30] and has now been endorsed by the government for these areas. New powers are required and the government are pledged to introduce the necessary legislation.[31] But the concept of landscape agreements is also relevant as a means of safeguarding special landscape features in the lowlands.[32] However, there remains the danger, which applies to all management agreements and to landscape agreements especially, that public money might be spent to prevent the loss of some feature which was not in fact threatened. Agreements must be used positively, not only to protect features for the immediate future but also to ensure their long-term management to the highest standards.

The potential of management agreements

Management agreements to promote conservation objectives in the countryside deserve to be exploited more extensively since they have some support among the farming community. But they will not provide the universal answer to countryside management problems as they have three obvious limitations. Firstly, the negotiation of long-term management agreements by public authorities involves a continuing financial commitment to service them, a commitment which could not be avoided during periods of restraint on expenditure. It is unrealistic to expect that public agencies will ever conclude agreements on a large scale (even where, in the case of local authorities, grant aid and rate support are available from central government) though they might do so in limited areas of special importance. Secondly, agreements are voluntary and, therefore, unless the consideration paid is financially attractive and more than compensates for restrictions imposed, they will not be popular with landowners. Yet the higher the consideration the more difficult it will be for public agencies to justify the expenditure. There will always be landowners who will not want to participate whatever the consideration and this is likely to be the case with absentee landlords (an increasing trend) who can derive little advantage from agreements in terms of, say, a more pleasant home environment. Finally, and perhaps most importantly, it is clear from operating the existing forms of agreement that there is a resistance amongst most landowners to long-term, legally binding commitments over land management. While owners might have more sympathy for short-term arrangements (and there is some evidence of this from the Field Monuments Scheme) their negotiation would increase the administrative work of public agencies at a time when they do not have the resources to accommodate it.

Perhaps the greatest potential of the management agreement approach lies in informal 'gentlemen's agreements', on the lines of those used in the land management experiments promoted by the Countryside Commission in the uplands and urban fringe discussed earlier in this chapter, where projects were agreed by a simple exchange of letters. Where a more formal agreement is required, the negotiation of annual agreements with the minimum of legal formality might prove to be most successful. The informal approach adopted in the Lake District Upland Management Experiment is undoubtedly popular with farmers who see no advantages in changing from a system that is already working well in their eyes to one which may prove burdensome in its restraints and responsibilities.[33]

FISCAL MEASURES

One way of encouraging landowners to adopt management practices which recognize the needs of conservation could be through the use of tax concessions. The advantage of this approach is that it might be capable of influencing the activities both of the absentee landlord, who does not normally benefit from the amenities of his estate but only from the financial return derived from it, and of those resident farmers who at present have little interest in conservation issues. As with compensation paid under management agreements, such concessions would be a formal expression of the cost to landowners of providing public conservation benefits. The approach would almost certainly find favour with them; it might also prove more acceptable to the Treasury than large increases in direct grants from government departments. In the present economic climate substantial increases in grant aid would be difficult to justify, whereas the concept of tax income foregone might be more readily accepted.

The government has gone some way in this direction with the introduction of exemptions of land of scenic, historic or scientific interest from Capital Transfer Tax on transfers at death where owners are prepared to manage their land for the public benefit.[34] This is a welcome concession which may ensure that the worst effects of the tax do not occur over at least some of the most important areas from the conservation viewpoint. Even so, the Capital Transfer Tax could still have serious implications for the landscape and its wildlife: estates may be fragmented and will probably need to be managed more intensively to maximize income in order to pay the tax. The proposed Wealth Tax will have similar effects and might, in the same way, require concessions.

Other concessions might also be considered. One possibility is tax allowances on expenditure undertaken for conservation purposes. The owner or tenant of land used for commercial forestry can claim tax relief on fencing costs but no such assistance is available for amenity planting. The smaller the area of land planted the greater the proportion of costs attributable to fencing and it is likely that these costs are a major deterrent to the creation of many small amenity plantations. More might therefore be achieved if fencing costs for amenity planting were also eligible for a tax allowance.

Another possibility might be exemptions from income tax on sales of timber from small woods. At present, the revenue from the sale of farm timber, whether from individual trees or from woodland, must generally be included as part of the farm receipts and therefore, as such, income tax is usually payable on receipts. The exception is shelterbelts, planted with no intention of felling at maturity, where the revenue from the sale of thinnings made in the interests of the proper management of the belt is not considered to be taxable income. Although forestry is unlikely, in the foreseeable future, to be competitive with agriculture on the better soils of lowland Britain, farmers might be more willing to maintain small plantations or to plant new areas if the sale of the produce were tax free. There may be a case on landscape grounds for making the income from the sale of timber from small managed plantations (say less than five acres) exempt from tax. To ensure that the plantations were properly managed to prevent indiscriminate felling, the concession would have to be confined to plantations dedicated to forestry under covenant and subject to an agreed management plan.

SUMMARY

This chapter has argued the case for incentives to encourage farmers and landowners to adopt voluntarily those management practices which safeguard and enhance conservation values. The most useful measures examined would appear to be:

1. An expansion of assistance by way of grants or labour to encourage the planting of clumps, tree belts and small woods on land marginal to agriculture.

2. The development of the concept of management agreements, both formal and informal, to promote positive land management in areas of special conservation importance and to recompense landowners for the extra costs incurred.

3. The use of selective tax concessions to promote objectives similar to the above and to encourage the better management of small woods.

NOTES AND REFERENCES

1. Third Countryside in 1970 Conference (1970). Report No. 1, *Agriculture, Forestry and Land Management.*
2. In 1974/75 £105m was spent on support for fertilizers and lime, and on grants for capital improvements. Source: Northern Ireland Office/Scottish Office/Welsh Office/Ministry of Agriculture, Fisheries and Food (1976). *Annual Review of Agriculture, 1976*, Cmnd 6392, HMSO, London.
3. See Chapter 3.
4. See, for example, Westmacott, R. and Worthington, T. (1974). *New Agricultural Landscapes*, Countryside Commission publication No. 76.

5. Local authorities have powers under Section 89 of the National Parks and Access to the Countryside Act 1949 to plant trees on private land with the agreement of the landowner. This planting, and amenity planting undertaken by the landowner directly, may be grant-aided by the Countryside Commission under Section 9 of the Local Government Act 1974. The Commission's policy towards grant-aiding tree planting is described in Countryside Commission (1977), *Grants for Amenity Tree Planting and Management*, Countryside Commission publication No. 103.

6. See Chapters 7 and 8.

7. The author discussed the operation of incentive tree-planting schemes with five County Councils with significant planting programmes. All reported that the response to their schemes had been 'patchy' and it was proving difficult to implement schemes in those parts of their counties most in need of landscape improvement.

8. Grants of 75 per cent payable by the Department of the Environment on the recommendation of the Countryside Commission. Source: House of Lords Debate on Forestry, speech by Earl Ferrers, *Hansard*, **356**(42), HMSO, London.

9. Figures derived from surveys into Dutch elm disease in 1972 and 1973. Source: Unpublished reports by the Forestry Commission's Research Station, Alice Holt Lodge.

10. Tellers are sapling trees growing in hedges which were often selected for growing on when hedge laying. With the almost universal adoption of mechanized hedge maintenance these saplings are now invariably cut off. The operation of this scheme is described in Hereford and Worcester County Council (1974). *Incentive Tree Planting Scheme*, an explanatory leaflet produced by the County Planning Department.

11. Countryside Commission (1976). *The Lake District Upland Management Experiment*, Countryside Commission publication No. 93.

12. Hall, A. (1976). *The Bollin Valley: A Study of Land Management in the Urban Fringe*, Countryside Commission publication No. 97.

13. Countryside Commission (1973). *Landscape Agreements*, Countryside Commission publication No. 61.

14. Where covenants are granted to a public authority (or to the National Trust) the authority (or the Trust) is deemed to be the owner of the adjacent land.

15. Details of the operation of covenants are given in Newsom, G. H. (1971). *Restrictive Covenants*, Sweet and Maxwell, London.

16. Only the commitment to dedicate the land to forestry runs with the land and the actual 'plan of operations' must be renegotiated with a new owner. Details of the preparation of the plan of operations are to be found in Forestry Commission (1974). *The Plan of Operations*, Forestry Commission Booklet No. 35.

17. Under the more usually adopted 'Basis II' provisions.

18. By March 1973, 3774 schemes involving over 1·13 million acres had been completed under the Dedication Scheme and 784 schemes involving over 170,000 acres had been completed under the Approved Woodlands Scheme. Source: Forestry Commission (1974). *Fifty-Third Annual Report and Accounts 1972–1973*, HMSO, London.

19. Ministry of Agriculture, Fisheries and Food/Welsh Office/Scottish Office (1972). *Forestry Policy*, HMSO, London.

20. The Forestry Commission must now consult with the Agricultural Departments to resolve possible conflicts between agriculture and forestry, and with planning authorities to ensure that due weight is given to amenity and other considerations in the schemes objectives. Details of the new Dedication Scheme are given in Forestry Commission (1974), *The New Dedication Scheme (Basis III)*; and Forestry Commission (1975), *Advice to Woodland Owners*.

21. National Parks and Access to the Countryside Act 1949, Section 16.
22. As note 21, Section 18.
23. By March 1975 only nine such agreements had been concluded. Source: Nature Conservancy Council (1975). *First Report* covering the period 1 November 1973 to 31 March 1975, HMSO, London.
24. Land which consists either wholly or predominantly of mountain, moor, heath, down, cliff or foreshore (National Parks and Access to the Countryside Act, Section 59(2) and, if in the countryside, woodland, rivers, canals, and other water areas and a strip of land on either side sufficient to allow picnicking and embarking or disembarking from a boat but excluding reservoirs owned or managed by statutory undertakers or river authorities and British Waterways Board canals (Countryside Act 1968, Section 16).
25. Land as described in Section 59(5) of the National Parks and Access to the Countryside Act. Usually this comprises agricultural land other than rough grazings—land which cannot be made the subject of an access agreement.
26. Prior to 1970 payment for access agreements generally took the form of a lump sum paid five years from the start of the agreement. This represented little more than compensation based on an assessment of the depreciation of the value of the land over the period as a consequence of the agreement. Since 1970 it has been acceptable for authorities to make annual payments which may be reviewed at five-year intervals. The level of payment is negotiated between the landowner and the district valuer, taking into account not only the diminution of the value of the land to the occupier, including damage to the land, but also, as far as this is possible, an estimate of the value of the land to the public.
27. Full details of the scheme are to be found in *Tax Free Payments for Protecting Ancient Monuments: a Scheme for Farmers and Timber Growers*, available from the Ancient Monuments Directorate of the Department of the Environment.
28. Payments vary with the area occupied by the features and in 1976 ranged from £20/acre/annum for the first acre of each monument, £10 for the next four acres, £4 for the next five acres and £2 for subsequent land.
29. Statistics provided by the Ancient Monuments Secretariat of the Department of the Environment, February 1976.
30. Department of the Environment (1974). *Report of the National Park Policies Review Committee* (The Sandlord Report), HMSO, London.
31. Department of the Environment/Welsh Office (1976). Ministerial conclusions on the Report of the National Park Policies Review Committee, DOE Circular 4/76 and Welsh Office Circular 7/76.
32. Countryside Commission (1974). *New Agricultural Landscapes: A Discussion Paper*, Countryside Commission publication No. 76a.
33. Rural Planning Services (1976). *A Study of the Hartsop Valley*. A Report to the Countryside Commission and the Lake District Special Planning Board. Countryside Commission publication No. 92.
34. The details of the operation of this concession were not known at the time of going to press.

Chapter 10

Statutory controls in conservation

R. J. LLOYD

Voluntary conservation action by those who manage agricultural land can be promoted in various ways: the previous two chapters have discussed, in detail, the roles of education and training; advisory and information services; codes of practice; financial incentives; and different forms of management agreement. But the evidence is that many farmers and landowners will not be influenced by these means of persuasion. More direct and enforceable methods of influencing farming activities through statutory procedures[1] will also be needed to protect features of outstanding conservation importance and to ensure that at least a minimum standard of conservation applies throughout the countryside. This chapter considers the use of some existing statutory controls over agricultural land management which are applied in the interests of wildlife and landscape conservation, and suggests how these might be made more effective. A case is also made for some additional controls.

Attitudes to control

Compared with most other industrialists, farmers (and also foresters) enjoy considerable freedom in the development and management of their land. They can introduce major landscape change and modify and destroy environmental values without reference to the control powers of local planning authorities,[2] for most agricultural (and forestry) operations are expressly excluded from the meaning of 'development' as defined under town and country planning legislation.[3]

The idea of greater public intervention in the farming industry would not be popular. It must be anticipated that additional controls in the interests of conservation would be strongly resisted by farmers and their representatives. Apart from the traditional view that agriculture is a special case in terms of planning and other statutory measures, farmers remain sceptical of bureaucracy and critical of those in local authorities and in central government agencies such as the Department of the Environment for failing to understand farming problems. The farming lobby is articulate and powerful on these issues.

The fact that landowners and farm managers may resent further interference in their affairs has important implications for the introduction of any new

189

controls. They may be more difficult to enforce and, because of them, farmers may become less responsive to the persuasive mechanisms designed to promote conservation objectives discussed in the previous two chapters. If they are to work at all, statutory controls will need to be used only where other mechanisms have failed. They must be seen to be fair, with provisions for compensation where they are applied selectively, and significant costs could result. Above all, they must be simple and relatively inexpensive to operate, without adding unduly to the administrative or financial burdens of land managers or public authorities.

TREES AND CONTROL

The maintenance of tree cover is a major contemporary conservation problem which several chapters in the earlier part of the book have discussed. Tree-felling is controlled under the Forestry Act 1967 where there are powers to regulate the felling of timber of commercial value, and under the Town and Country Planning Act 1971 which makes provision for tree preservation orders to be applied in the interests of amenity.

The felling licence

A licence is required from the Forestry Commission to fell growing trees but there are important exemptions. No licence is required to fell relatively small trees (of diameter not exceeding 3 inches at breast height); or fruit trees; or any trees in orchards, gardens, churchyards or public open spaces. Nor is a licence required to fell up to 825 cubic feet of timber in any quarter (of which 150 cubic feet may be sold).[4] The Commission have powers under the Forestry Act to modify these exemptions from felling control: for example, in 1972 all restrictions on felling were removed from elms affected by Dutch elm disease. There are also powers to reduce the amount of timber which may be felled without a licence, and all licences can be granted subject to conditions[5] which may, for example, require that felling should be followed by replanting.[6] Over land covered by a Forestry Dedication Agreement and where the felling is in accordance with a plan of operations approved by the Commission, a licence is usually automatic. Where a licence is refused, compensation is normally payable based on any depreciation in the value of the timber resulting from the refusal. There are penalties for felling without a licence: in 1977 these were a £10 fine or twice the value of the tree, whichever was the greater.

In its operation of the felling licence system, the Forestry Commission must take into account the interests of good forestry and their duty to promote adequate reserves of growing trees in Britain. They must also consider the interests of agriculture and amenity.[5,7] Although the Commission have always consulted the appropriate agricultural department where an application appears to affect agricultural interests, or the local planning authority in areas of known amenity value, some decisions (particularly those which have licensed felling without replanting) have been criticized on amenity grounds.

Consultation arrangements between the Forestry Commission and other interests have now been strengthened; agricultural departments, planning authorities and other interest groups are involved to ensure that land use, agricultural, amenity, recreation and nature conservation requirements are taken into account. Where differences of opinion still remain the Commission can invite the appropriate Regional Advisory Committee[8] to assist in reconciling views and as a last resort cases may be referred to the Minister of Agriculture for decision. The Commission have a statutory duty to consult the local planning authority over licence applications for trees covered by preservation orders, or else they refer applications to the authority for determination.[9]

The new arrangements whereby local planning authorities are consulted on all felling licence applications does give the authorities an opportunity to comment on the amenity implications of each case and to prevent felling where the Forestry Commission may be unwilling to withhold a licence or to impose replanting conditions. Local authorities can use their own powers to serve tree preservation orders or to buy the land in question.

In all, the felling licence system works well to protect the amenity interest of commercially productive woods, and these make up a major component of the rural landscape. Replanting can be secured where appropriate, and the system gives the Forestry Commission influence over the choice of species, recognizing the Commission's duty not only to promote good forestry practice but also their obligation to safeguard amenity. But in the case of unproductive woodlands and those up to about five acres in extent, a licence to fell is often issued without replanting conditions, particularly if the land is to be converted to agricultural uses. The Forestry Commission have no rigid policy regarding felling licence applications in predominantly agricultural areas and each case is judged on its merits, although where only a small area of woodland is involved their agreement to the conversion of land to agricultural use will usually be automatic unless the local planning authority raises strong amenity objections. For larger areas of woodland (where replanting conditions would normally be imposed) the Regional Land Commissioner of the Ministry of Agriculture is consulted and, if he supports the conversion, it is usually permitted.

The past policy of the Forestry Commission towards small and unproductive woodlands has undoubtedly led to their decline in predominantly agricultural areas. In the year ending March 1974, the Commission issued unconditional licences to clear-fell 959 hectares (2370 acres) on private estates.[10] While the loss of a single copse may not have serious consequences for the landscape (although it might have for wildlife), the cumulative effect of this loss of woodland is of greater concern. Moreover, no licence at all is required to fell up to 825 cubic feet of timber in any quarter—a considerable volume—estimated by Essex County Council to be the equivalent of ten fully mature oak trees.[11]

Thus, a landowner can fell up to 40 mature trees in the course of a year without applying for a felling licence which means, in effect, that unless they are covered by a tree preservation order single trees and groups of trees are unprotected.

These exemptions are the principal disadvantage of the felling licence system as a tool in landscape conservation. But it is straightforward to operate, since outside the permitted limits consent for felling must always be obtained. This is in marked contrast to tree preservation order procedures where, to be legally protected under the planning acts, trees must be made the subject of a specific order; this is a time-consuming and cumbersome process.

The tree preservation order

'In the interests of amenity', local planning authorities, through the use of tree preservation orders, have powers both to prohibit the felling of trees and to secure replanting where felling is permitted.[12] Under tree preservation order regulations,[13] the local planning authority must serve a copy of the order (and the grounds for making it) on the owners and occupiers of the affected land and on anyone else directly affected.[14] The order may be confirmed by the local authority after 42 days but if objections are raised the order cannot take effect until confirmed by the Secretary of State for the Environment. An order cannot apply to dead, dying or diseased trees but trees subject to an order which have to be removed subsequently must be replanted unless the local authority dispenses with this requirement. Where valued amenity trees are not subject to an existing tree preservation order but are threatened with damage or felling, local planning authorities may make provisional orders[15] which take effect immediately and remain in force until confirmed or rejected by the Secretary of State, or for six months, whichever occurs first.

Where an application is made to remove or lop trees subject to a tree preservation order and this is refused, or granted subject to conditions, local planning authorities may be liable to pay compensation. Compensation liability can arise in the case of commercial woodland where a tree preservation order reduces its value. It may also be payable where replanting is specified to replace protected trees which are felled, but this is not grant-aided by the Forestry Commission on the grounds that the form of planting demanded under the order is incompatible with commercial forestry requirements. Liability to pay compensation does not normally arise in the case of single trees and groups of amenity trees.

If a protected tree is cut down without permission or so damaged that the tree is likely to die, the fine can be up to £400 or twice the value of the tree, whichever is the greater amount. If an order is contravened in other ways the maximum fine can be £200 or, in the case of a continuing offence, £5 for each day on which the offence is continued. Where replacement of trees is required, the local planning authority do have powers of enforcement.

Tree preservation orders have been used in the countryside in various ways: to protect individual trees (for example, in hedgerows), groups of trees and areas of woodland. Orders have been applied to woods of amenity importance (other than those subject to a plan of operations agreed with the Forestry Commission[12]) where it is likely that replanting conditions would not be imposed as a condition of felling or where the character of the woodland would be adversely affected by any conversion from deciduous to coniferous species. A substantial number of woodlands covered by tree preservation orders have been scheduled by the Nature Conservancy Council as Sites of Special Scientific Interest, and some have been covered following specific requests from the Council, who are anxious that long-established deciduous woodland, which is of considerable scientific importance, should not be clear-felled or replaced by conifers. Once lost, the scientific value of old woodland cannot be replaced.

Tree preservation orders appear to be an effective means of protecting woodland trees against felling. Their use has been accepted by many landowners, probably because compensation may be paid where an order imposes costs. In contrast, the use of tree preservation orders to protect individual trees and groups of trees on farmland has been strongly opposed by farmers.[16] The effectiveness of tree preservation orders in the farmland situation is also limited for several reasons. Firstly, in terms of local authority staff resources, the application of orders to hedgerow trees and groups of trees is an extremely time-consuming process involving the recording of each individual tree of amenity importance and undertaking an extensive consultation process before an order can be confirmed. As Bedfordshire County Council[17] point out, to achieve really effective control they would need to assess the amenity value of all the trees in their area and place orders on those of value. Such a programme, if undertaken, would represent an enormous task. The Council also make the point that any programme of this sort would lead to a lot of unproductive work in that it would mean applying tree preservation orders in many cases where trees may not be under threat. Secondly, it is clearly not difficult to destroy protected trees 'accidentally', as shown by the findings of the New Agricultural Landscapes Study.[16] In this situation there are severe problems of enforcement. Thirdly, tree preservation orders are essentially negative and cannot ensure either the proper management of the trees being protected or of any replacements.

Perhaps the major limitation of tree preservation orders lies in their attempt to fossilize the farmed landscape by preventing the removal of existing trees, even where this may be particularly desirable on agricultural grounds. The insistence, in many cases, on replanting on the same site where trees subject to an order have to be felled has a similar effect. Such a restrictive policy is unrealistic in a situation of rapid change in the farmed countryside and the emphasis could be placed, with more effect, on establishing new landscape features 'in the right place'. If this general policy were adopted towards trees, farmers would probably be more co-operative in the protection of exceptional features of the existing rural fabric, even where the retention of these features is in conflict with agriculture.

Presenting the farmers' point of view at the Countryside in 1970 Conference, Darke[18] suggested that a tree preservation order converted a tree into an encumbrance. He believed that many farmers and foresters regarded the tree preservation order not as a conservation measure but as one which allowed the present generation of trees to die, providing no incentive to replant them. Evidence suggests that there is now an uneven age structure in hedgerow timber with the majority of trees being either mature or overmature and with few saplings to replace them.[19]

Changing existing procedures

For the felling licence system to make an effective contribution to the process of landscape management, at least two modifications seem to be desirable. Firstly, small-scale felling operations should be brought under control by reducing the quantity of timber which is presently exempt from felling restrictions (825 cubic feet). Secondly, where felling licences are conditional upon replanting then it should be made possible for the replacement trees to be planted on a new site, instead of on the felled land, to provide a measure of flexibility.

While tree preservation orders might be appropriate for woodlands of conservation importance, their application to individual trees and groups of trees in agricultural areas could be phased out in view of the difficulties of operating the system effectively and its doubtful value in promoting landscape conservation. Nevertheless, control over felling is vital in those areas of special scenic value, for example within the National Parks and Areas of Outstanding Natural Beauty, and in areas largely devoid of cover where it is essential to safeguard any remaining trees. This control would probably be best achieved not by tree preservation orders but through the felling licence system if the present exemptions were reduced or suspended altogether.

Since local planning authorities are the arbiters in many decisions affecting landscape conservation, it would seem sensible for them to issue felling licences rather than the Forestry Commission, except where commercial forestry interests are involved. This idea is supported by the County Planning Officers' Society[20] although they consider the task unrealistic at present because of the heavy burden it would impose upon local authorities.

If a licence to fell was refused by the local authority, it is envisaged that compensation would be payable where it could be shown that loss or damage was being incurred as a result of retaining the trees. It is also envisaged that compensation would be payable in the case of individual trees and groups of trees in contrast to the position with tree preservation orders. The extension of compensation in this way would remove one of the main objections of landowners to being 'ordered' to retain trees which conflict with agricultural requirements.

In most situations, it is anticipated that felling would be acceptable so long as replanting takes place. In many areas, farm layouts need to be rationalized on agricultural grounds and much farm timber is located in inconvenient positions. The location of replanting of a similar or larger area of trees elsewhere on the farm would be agreed between the landowner and the local authority. There would also seem to be a case for grant-aiding the replanting, although some part of the value of the timber felled should perhaps be taken into account in determining an appropriate level of grant. The flexibility built into this arrangement, together with the improved provision for compensation and the possibility of a grant towards new planting, might remove much of the opposition farmers have to restrictions over tree-felling. Contact between local authorities and landowners would also be established through which the question of further planting schemes could be raised.

It is probable that most of these changes in procedure could be achieved within the existing legislative framework, although the determination by local authorities of applications for felling licences under the Forestry Acts may require new powers, as would the proposed new compensation arrangements.

OTHER CONTROL PROCEDURES

Notification of intended changes

For some features of special value in the countryside, landowners are required to notify the appropriate authority of any major changes they intend to make. Some extension of this notification system could benefit conservation interests in two ways. Firstly, it might encourage landowners to think more carefully before deciding to remove or manage particular features differently. Secondly, where notification was given, the local authority (or another agency) would have an opportunity to prevent the loss of or damage to those features of national or local significance. Under such a system, the local planning authority might advertise notifications of change as is the case for proposed developments in urban conservation areas. If a planning authority failed to act on a notification within (say) six months, the landowner would then be free to act as he wished. If this system was applied only to outstanding features of wildlife, historic or landscape value, the additional work (and expense) both for landowners and for public authorities, should not be formidable and the system should stand a reasonable chance of acceptance.

The notification approach has been recommended strongly by the Council for the Protection of Rural England, who see it as the major element in a series of suggested measures designed to secure conservation objectives in countryside management.[21] But the Council argue that notification should apply to the majority of landscape features, including all hedges and walls. Such an extensive application of the procedure is probably unrealistic in terms of local authority processing at the present time and would without doubt be opposed strongly by the farming community.

The principle of notification of change already operates for certain operations affecting field monuments and, in some of the National Parks (for example Exmoor), over the ploughing of moorland and heath. These applications of the principle are considered below, with the possibilities for further applications to cover other special countryside features.

Field monuments

'Scheduled' field monuments[22] are given some protection under the Ancient Monuments Act of 1931[23] which requires landowners to give the Department of the Environment three months notice of any activities which will materially affect a scheduled monument. Failure to comply with this ruling can lead to fines of up to £100. The value of the procedure is that it provides an opportunity for either the Secretary of State for the Environment or a local authority to negotiate guardianship of the monument, or to purchase it (compulsorily if necessary) or, where appropriate, to make payments towards its maintenance. Alternatively, the Department of the Environment may negotiate a management agreement under the Field Monuments Acknowledgement Payments Scheme[24] or, as a last resort, serve a Preservation Order on the monument which prevents the owner from damaging it. Where it is inevitable that a monument must be lost the procedure provides time to mount a 'rescue operation'.

But the notification procedure covers only 'major disturbances'; in particular it excludes the ploughing and drainage of agricultural land. Yet, as discussed in Chapter 1, deep ploughing and drainage operations are now the greatest threat to field monuments. The case is strong, as recommended by the Walsh Committee,[25] for making it a statutory duty to give notice of any proposed deep cultivation, land drainage or other major agricultural works affecting scheduled monuments. Further, an increase in the statutory period of notice from three to six months, as the Committee also recommended, would allow authorities to assess the relative value of the monument and give more opportunities for negotiation and protection.

Sites of Special Scientific Interest

Sites of Special Scientific Interest are not at present included in a notification system. Landowners are in no way obliged to inform the Nature Conservancy Council of changes in land management which may substantially affect the wildlife value of these scheduled areas, and many SSSIs have been destroyed or seriously damaged, quite legally, as a result of agricultural operations. There is no reason why the conservation of Sites of Special Scientific Interest should be accorded any less attention than field monuments, and it is suggested that landowners should be obliged to give the Nature Conservancy Council adequate notice (say six months) of proposed changes in land management affecting scheduled sites. Minor management changes, which would have to be defined by the Council, might be excluded from the process. Under current powers, the notification procedure would give the Nature Conservancy Council the chance to prevent damage to the site by means of a nature reserve agreement or a Countryside Act Section 15 agreement or, if these failed, by land purchase.

The introduction of a notification procedure should help to safeguard these sites, but some further reserve power would also seem to be required. At present the Nature Conservancy Council have no compulsory powers over the management of SSSIs and they cannot ensure the protection of a site other than by purchase. The lack of reserve powers seems to be a serious weakness in the legislation which could usefully be amended to give the Council the power to prohibit the destruction of scheduled sites and to carry out essential work in cases where an owner refuses to enter into a management agreement. The concept of a 'Conservation Order' is discussed below.

Landscape features

In the national parks, the Secretary of State for the Environment may order the owner or occupier of land which consists primarily of moorland or heathland not to plough unless he has given six months written notice to the local planning authority.[26] Failure to comply with this ruling can lead to fines of up to £200. This system allows time for the authority to negotiate an access agreement, secure an access order, purchase the land, or persuade the occupier not to plough. The power has been used in the Exmoor National Park where it may have helped to arrest the steady loss of open moorland. However, the provision would be more useful if there were powers to negotiate landscape agreements and to impose landscape orders, concepts discussed in Chapter 9 and later in this chapter.

From a conservation viewpoint, notification of ploughing would be desirable not only to safeguard the moorland and heath of national parks but also the landscape of any area of countryside 'of critical amenity importance' where the essential character of the land is dependent upon permanent pasture and rough grazings, as with chalk downland and river meadows, for example. New powers enabling local planning authorities to order the notification of ploughing in such critical amenity areas would provide time to allow them to prevent the ploughing if they considered it to be in the national or local interest.

Notification could also be applied to trees and other landscape features. Earlier in this chapter modifications to the present arrangements for felling licences and tree preservation orders were discussed: it was suggested that a wider application of the felling licence system outside woodlands could be operated by local planning authorities. The notification of proposed felling might offer a workable alternative. Under such a procedure, landowners and occupiers, at least in areas of special landscape importance, might be obliged to notify the local planning authority of their intention to fell trees in all parishes without a comprehensive coverage of tree preservation orders. On receiving this notification of proposed felling, the local authority would examine the trees: if their retention was thought desirable on landscape grounds, then a provisional tree preservation order could be issued. Alternatively, the authority might negotiate a landscape agreement with the owner.

Other features of special importance not already safeguarded, for example hedgerows or walls of particular landscape, historic or wildlife value, might be 'listed' by the local planning authority. A landowner would then be required to notify intended changes which might affect the feature and where its retention was considered to be essential, a landscape agreement could be negotiated or a landscape order imposed.

Management orders

Chapter 9 discussed the use and value of management agreements. But there may be cases where it is in the public interest that an area of countryside should be managed in a particular way but the owner is unwilling to enter into such an agreement. In these circumstances, the imposition of a 'management order' could provide an alternative to purchasing the land, compulsorily or otherwise.

The power to impose a measure of this kind already exists in relation to access where the Secretary of State may confirm an access order, at the request of the local planning authority.[27] The provisions are those normally found in an access agreement, including the right to compensation, but such an order has rarely been used.[28] The Countryside Commission have suggested that the concept could be extended to include a landscape order, if their proposals for landscape agreements are accepted.[29] Such orders would prohibit the destruction of specified landscape features and enable a local authority to manage the land in ways which would have been specified under an agreement, including, for example, tree planting and maintenance.

The whole concept of management orders could be widened still further to cover scheduled sites of wildlife and historic importance; thus the Nature Conservancy Council could be given powers to prevent the destruction or mismanagement of wildlife areas by means of a 'conservation order', and the Department of the Environment could be similarly empowered to secure 'field monument orders'. A conservation order would allow the Nature Conservancy Council to impose nature reserve or Countryside Act Section 15 agreements on landowners, and to enter the land to carry out essential work. A field monuments order could likewise allow the Department of the Environment to impose arrangements similar to those which operate under the Field Monuments Acknowledgement Payments Scheme.

But the power to impose management orders would need to be used only as a last resort. While sanctions of this kind seem to be necessary, it would be counterproductive to destroy, by their introduction or operation, the goodwill already built up between landowners and public authorities on which the successful negotiation of voluntary management agreements depends. It is unlikely that powers of compulsory land purchase will be relinquished. However, for the farming community it is believed that the use of management orders could be a more acceptable reserve power to ensure the proper management of features of exceptional value, particularly if the local authorities were also obliged to buy the land in question, if requested by the landowner through a 'Purchase Notice'.[30]

Removal of woodland subject to planning permission

The Ramblers' Association and the Countryside Commission,[31] among several organizations, have argued that afforestation of bare ground should be brought under planning control. The conversion of agricultural land to forest could be considered a material change of land use and therefore one which should be subject to planning control. Perhaps the converse should also apply and the conversion of woodland to agricultural uses be similarly controlled. Such a system could be seen as an alternative to the earlier proposition that the determination of felling licence applications for non-commercial woodland should be transferred from the Forestry Commission to the local authorities. However, this arrangement would control only woodland clearance and not the felling of individual trees. Further, although the procedure might ensure that no woodland was clear-felled for conversion to agricultural use without the consent of the local planning authority, it could not prevent felling for replanting which might, in the case of old woodland, be just as damaging. Extra measures such as tree preservation orders would therefore still be required and thus limit the value of this proposal.

Preservation orders

In 1971, the Council for the Protection of Rural England suggested that the more important historic hedges should be 'listed' to prevent their removal or alteration without reference to the local planning authority.[32] The Council still believe that this concept should be pursued and indeed extended to cover downland and heath.[21] Yet, despite the importance of these features, a preservation order may be an inappropriate mechanism to ensure their survival. Hedges, downland and heathland need proper management and it is unlikely that a preservation order alone could ensure this unless it was coupled with a maintenance requirement upon either the landowner or the local authority. In many ways the proposed landscape agreement and landscape order would be a more appropriate mechanism to secure the retention and proper management of these landscape features.

Minimum area of cover

In areas where the majority of hedges, trees and other forms of cover have been removed, reducing the overall visual quality of the landscape and the number of wildlife habitats, there may be a case for defining a minimum area of cover which farmers should retain on their land. The idea, put forward by several farmers contacted in the New Agricultural Landscapes Study,[16] is an interesting one but a number of problems could be anticipated. It would be difficult to define what should be the minimum area of cover and many farmers would interpret the minimum as the desirable amount. Nor could a procedure such as this guarantee the retention of the most valuable components of existing cover or ensure that these are managed to maintain and enhance their landscape and wildlife value. Problems of enforcement would also be considerable. Although it is superficially attractive, the proposal is probably too crude and inflexible a measure to achieve the desired result of conserving or creating a rich and varied landscape.

SUMMARY

This chapter has examined a number of possible new measures and some modifications to the existing procedures for regulating change in the fabric of the farmed countryside. The most feasible and useful proposals would seem to be:

1. The existing felling licence system should be modified. In special landscape areas, the concessions on the need to obtain a licence for tree-felling should be reduced; licence applications for non-commercial woodland and individual trees should be determined by local planning authorities; compensation should be paid for any trees retained as a result of a refusal to grant a licence where this imposes costs; and the procedure should be used primarily to secure replanting after felling on sites more appropriate to modern agricultural needs.

2. The principle of notification of change should be extended to cover: the ploughing and drainage of agricultural land where this affects a field monument; changes in land management affecting Sites of Special Scientific Interest; and the ploughing of permanent pasture in any area which local planning authorities consider to be of 'critical amenity importance'.

3. Management orders should be introduced as reserve powers to ensure that land of outstanding landscape, wildlife or historic value is appropriately managed.

NOTES AND REFERENCES

1. A procedure which has the backing of legal sanctions.
2. Phillips, A. A. C. and Roberts, M. (1973). The Recreation and Amenity Value of the Countryside. *Journal of Agricultural Economics*, **24**(1), 85–102.

3. Section 22(2) of the Town and Country Planning Act 1971 states that the use of any land for the purposes of agriculture or forestry (including afforestation) and the use for any of those purposes of any building occupied together with the land so used shall not be taken to involve development of the land.
4. Forestry Act 1967, Section 9.
5. Forestry Act 1967, Section 10.
6. Forestry Act, 1967, Section 12.
7. Countryside Act 1968, Section 11.
8. The Regional Advisory Committees now comprise representatives from forestry, agricultural, planning and environmental interests. However, they appear to be heavily weighted in favour of growers and the timber industry and it remains to be seen whether amenity considerations will be given adequate attention. It is also questionable whether cases of dispute should be referred to the Minister of Agriculture for decision, rather than to the Secretary of State for the Environment.
9. Forestry Act 1967; Section 15.
10. Forestry Commission (1974). *Fifty-fourth Annual Report and Accounts of the Forestry Commission for the year ended 31 March 1974*, Table 18, HMSO, London.
11. Essex County Council (1972). *The Essex Countryside—A Landscape in Decline.*
12. Section 60 of the Town and Country Planning Act 1971 enables local planning authorities to make tree preservation orders which prohibit the cutting down, topping, lopping or wilful destruction of trees except with the consent of the local planning authority. In the case of dedicated woodland a tree preservation order can only be made if the Forestry Commission consent to the order and if there is not a plan of operations made under covenant operating over the land in question.
13. Town and Country Planning (Tree Preservation Order) Regulations 1969, SI 1969, No. 17.
14. Anyone entitled to work minerals on the land or to fell any of the affected trees.
15. Town and Country Planning Act 1971, Section 61.
16. Westmacott, R. and Worthington, T. (1974). *New Agricultural Landscapes*, Countryside Commission publication No. 76. See in particular Chapter 7.
17. Bedfordshire County Council (1973). *Forestry Aspect Report*, County Review, Consultation Draft.
18. Darke, M. (1970). Statement at Third Countryside in 1970 Conference.
19. This is discussed in Chapter 3.
20. County Councils Association (1971). *Felling of Trees in Connection with Agricultural Improvement*, a report by the County Planning Officers' Society.
21. Council for the Protection of Rural England (1975). *Landscape—The Need for a Public Voice.*
22. Monuments included in a list published under Section 12 of the Ancient Monuments Consolidation and Amendment Act, 1913.
23. Ancient Monuments Act 1931, Section 6.
24. The operation of these agreements has been discussed in Chapter 9.
25. Committee of Enquiry into the Arrangements for the Protection of Field Monuments.
26. Countryside Act 1968, Section 14.
27. National Parks and Access to the Countryside Act, Section 65.
28. By 1975, such an order had been used only twice. Gibbs, R. S. (1975). *Local Authority Expenditure on Access Land*, Agricultural Adjustment Unit, Newcastle upon Tyne, Research Monog. No. 6.
29. These have been discussed in Chapter 9.
30. Under planning law, an owner of land can serve a Purchase Notice on the local authority where planning permission is refused or granted subject to conditions so

that the land becomes incapable of reasonable beneficial use in its existing state. Such a procedure could be extended to situations where owners are not permitted to 'improve' rural land.

31. Ramblers' Association (1971). *Forestry: Time to Rethink*. Brief for the Countryside No. 3. Countryside Commission (1972). *Note on the Countryside Commission's Views on the Consultative Document on Forestry Policy published 28 June 1972.*
32. Council for the Protection of Rural England (1971). *Loss of Cover*. Report of Working Party.

Chapter 11

New farming enterprises

M. A. B. BODDINGTON AND C. J. BULL

Earlier chapters in this book have demonstrated the extent of the economic, social and political pressures upon agriculture and some of the environmental consequences of these. At the local level, the farmer is faced with increasing costs and relatively static prices for his produce. He is often forced to intensify production on a holding which cannot be expanded and devote all his resources to a single objective of making a living out of food production. Any concern he may have for conserving or enhancing amenity values over his land can have little practical expression; public access, often uncontrolled and undisciplined, is seen as an interference. Rather than direct these urban pressures to his own benefit, the farmer has erected barricades against them.

There is now growing pressure for the agricultural industry to pay greater attention to the requirements of an amenity-conscious public. Farmland must be productive of food; it must also provide an attractive landscape, and opportunities for access and recreation. An increasingly urbanized and mobile society demands a diversity of opportunities in the countryside. Yet visitors are often channelled to a limited number of areas which may suffer from overuse whilst surrounding agricultural landscapes increasingly reflect the requirements only of economic food production, with little regard for amenity.

However, there are signs of a change in farming attitudes. More farmers find that they can accommodate some of the new pressures by allowing controlled public access to their land. They can also reap other advantages by providing for public recreation and for sport in a positive way. Some farmers, especially in marginal agricultural areas like the urban fringe and the uplands, have realized that their enterprise must be diversified (and not only into recreation provision) if it is to survive.

This chapter examines the nature of some new farm-based enterprises which, incidentally or by design, may provide opportunities for the environmental protection and improvement of farmed land.

THE RANGE OF NEW FARM ENTERPRISES

Subsidiary farm enterprises may be defined as those which are largely supplementary to existing farm activities; their establishment and operation should not significantly affect the scale of farming operations already taking place.[1] In many instances they are atypical of traditional farming activities and cannot be seen as natural extensions within agriculture. They should not necessarily be regarded as total alternatives to farming but rather as complementary to existing activities.

A farmer may improve his income or capital position in a number of ways. He may introduce a new enterprise which is basically of an agricultural or horticultural nature but which yields high rates of return because there is an imbalance of supply and demand as is the case with viticulture or asparagus growing. He may take advantage of the grants and incentives which exist for new woodlands, or he may tap the cash flow generated by those who visit the countryside by providing accommodation or recreational attractions. Many subsidiary farm enterprises have been practised for a long time. Examples include forestry, traditional rural sports like fishing and shooting, and various kinds of farm tourism involving farmhouse accommodation, camping and caravanning.

An important feature of many subsidiary enterprises is the variety of benefits which may accrue indirectly from them. In areas where shooting is important, hedgerows, spinneys, copses, individual trees and woods are retained and managed as cover for a game crop which can be produced only if the correct environmental conditions are provided. Similarly, duck flighting requires the provision of ponds, and these could be created of a size to allow stocking with fish. They could also be used for boating or for irrigation, and may introduce valuable new habitats for wildlife which are attractive features in the landscape. A pond can thus benefit the interests of farming, sporting and conservation.

Amenity improvements may be a concomitant of many recreational enterprises. The development of a caravan site, suitably landscaped, may improve the visual amenity of an area, diversify ecological interest, and provide an incentive for shelterbelt planting. In addition, caravanners may support a farm shop, giving a market for farm produce and a boost to farm income.

A farmer who builds a new road, or improves an old one, to give access to a recreational enterprise may be carrying out a long overdue improvement which his farm business alone could never justify. The road not only serves the new venture but gives improved access for farming purposes. In these various ways, private and social benefits can result from a new enterprise.

The range of possible additional enterprises is extremely wide, but three main groups can be identified.[2]

(a) Non-recreational:
    such as, alternative agricultural and horticultural enterprises;
        timber production.
(b) Recreational:
    such as, accommodation for visitors;
        shooting and fishing facilities;
        picnic sites, wildlife parks and other day visitor attractions.

(c) Educational
 such as, farm open days;
  farm demonstration centres and museums;
  farm trails and nature reserves.

Appendix I describes the procedures involved in establishing enterprises of these kinds; Appendix II suggests a basic list of advisory sources.

AGRICULTURAL AND HORTICULTURAL ENTERPRISES

There are many enterprises which may be viewed as extensions of farming activities while providing a useful supplementary income. If properly executed, they may absorb the farmer in an interesting diversion from the main farm business, at the same time remunerating him well. They do not bring direct environmental benefits but they can diversify the agricultural landscape, provide new habitats for wildlife and support farming in marginal areas where traditional agricultural practices are failing to yield sufficient income.

A number of unusual crops offer opportunities for farmers to diversify and increase their incomes but almost all require special conditions of growth or marketing. Generally they cater for a relatively small, specialized market so that any substantial proportional increase in acreage can completely remove profitability. Asparagus is an example of such a crop. This has certain advantages in that it may yield very large returns per acre and requires only two or three consecutive months' labour in the spring when work on the farm may be relatively slack. Fine, sandy soils are required for the crop and heavy manuring and fertilizing is necessary. Generally, asparagus does not yield until the third year after planting, so that there is a considerable overhead to carry initially. Once cutting begins the harvesting operation is critical, for between mid-April and mid-June the crop must be cut and marketed every day. If the spears are left a day too long they may become unmarketable.

Like asparagus, rhubarb takes about two years to establish before first pulling. It may be planted in October or November, or late winter–early spring, and will be ready for first harvest in its second spring. Another similarity with asparagus is that it must be harvested quickly when yields are at a maximum, or they will drop away rapidly. Most of the British output goes to canneries in the east of England and growers should generally be situated close to one. About 6000 plants are needed per acre and these can cost up to £600. It is vital to acquire good stock since the rhubarb crop is beset by problems, chief amongst which is attack by virus. Once down a crop will yield for about five years.

Farmers in areas where spring is early may often take advantage of the good returns from daffodils. The crop yields a double harvest in early blooms, and bulbs later in the year. Daffodils tend to thrive best at higher altitudes where eelworms are not a nuisance. In common with the crops mentioned above, they require casual labour in picking times but this is not always available in the more elevated situations on the west coast where a suitably equable climate exists. Also, in common with asparagus and rhubarb, a guaranteed market outlet is most desirable. Bulbs are generally planted at a rate of about four tons to the acre in autumn. In the first spring they yield about 10,000 bunches and 20,000 bunches in the second spring. The bulbs are havested in the summer following the second spring and yield about six tons to the acre. The capital investment per acre may be £2000 or more.

After more than a decade of research into varieties which will grow in the British climate, grain maize is being planted on an increasing scale in southern England. The Maize Research Unit at Wye College (University of London) monitors a number of plots every year and records the progress of the crop in this country. Whilst the gross margins are not usually as high as those for winter wheat, performance is generally better than for other cereals. The crop has two major advantages: it provides a break from cereals and it spreads farming operations. Sowing is carried out in late April, when soil temperatures reach 50°F, and harvesting is generally between mid-October and mid-November. A special attachment is required for standard combine harvesters and this can cost anything from £200 to £2000. Drying can be a problem in a wet autumn and can cost about £5/ton.

The popularity of viticulture is rapidly increasing in England and Wales after an absence of some 800 years. Hugh Johnson recorded three vineyards in England in 1966.[3] In 1971 the *Farmers' Weekly* suggested that there were then some 70 vineyards averaging four to five acres each.[4] It was anticipated that by 1975 there would be some 1,000 to 10,000 acres in England. By 1975 the *Sunday Times* reported that there were 14 vineyards in Wales and 125 in England, with 400 members of the English Vineyards Association.[5]

The majority of vineyards in this country grow a Riesling type of vine which makes a light, white table wine. Various reports in the *Farmers' Weekly* suggest that capital requirements range from £500 to £2000/acre establishment costs, with gross returns after four years amounting to about £1600. Gross margins are of the order of £900 to £1000/acre. A vineyard, once established, should be productive for 20 to 25 years.

These are just a few of the wide variety of unusual crops which may be grown. Their environmental impact is equally diverse. The well-ordered and tended vineyard, typical of many European countries, introduces a new element in the British landscape which has its equivalents only in hop-gardens and orchards. Vineyards provide a habitat for many forms of wildlife—most of which however would be regarded as unwelcome by the commercial vinegrower. Similarly, fields of maize for grain produce large quantities of lush green vegetation late in the season when other cereals have been harvested. The six-foot-high crop, with its dense foliage, provides refuge for many birds, insects and mammals. Flowering crops like daffodils make a visual impact over a short period, although we have become accustomed to this phenomenon in the arable areas of eastern England with the growing popularity of oil seed rape. Asparagus and rhubarb have a similar short-term effect with early lush growth, but their residues can be unsightly for a time, although these are food for a range of wild species.

TIMBER PRODUCTION

The benefits from planting trees in association with agriculture may be substantial. Apart from financial benefits, there are a variety of other gains from planting trees, whether these stand alone, or in spinneys, copses or plantations. Most landscapes are improved by new cover (see Chapter 7), trees provide shelter and diverse habitats for wildlife[6] and woodland may temper the local climate by reducing the risk of frost. Woods and trees, especially of mixed species and ages, benefit game by providing a warmer and more sheltered environment and a range of food. Trees are also essential for many recreational enterprises such as camping and caravan sites, picnic areas and wildlife parks, as they provide seclusion and screening.

Financial aspects

The nature of timber production is such that it is impossible to quantify a financial return. Plantation rotations may be as long as 70 years and while there may be a small income from thinnings relatively early in the rotation, planting costs and timber prices change quite markedly from year to year. It is now generally accepted that individual trees, whether in hedges or elsewhere on the farm, are a nuisance in agricultural terms and are being removed for this reason (see Chapter 1). On the better soils, however, the growth rate of open-grown hardwoods is such that good-quality, saleable timber can be produced in shorter rotations and can provide a useful source of income on the farm.

On richer, wetter sites there is scope for small plantations of the rapid-growing 'hybrid' poplars grown on short rotations, often as little as 30 years. The hybrid black poplars *Populus x euramericana*, 'Serotina' and 'Robusta' are now commonly grown as timber trees in the lowlands as is the hybrid race of balsam poplar *Populus tricocarpa x tacamahaca*, 'TT32'. Other rapid-growing species may have potential for commercial production on a small scale. Of particular promise appear to be two species of southern beech, the roble beech (*Nothofagus obliqua*) and raoul (*Nothofagus procera*) which have growth rates up to five feet a year and produce valuable timber. They are also attractive as landscape trees.

The most important support the forest industry receives is in the form of tax incentives. There are concessions on capital gains and capital transfer taxes which are designed to ensure that planting and replanting continue smoothly and that trees are not felled prematurely to meet unplanned liabilities. On Income Tax, woodland owners may choose to be assessed either under Schedule B or Schedule D. When a woodland changes hands it is automatically assessed under Schedule B, but the new occupier can elect to have his woodlands assessed under D. The advantage of D is that losses on woodlands may be offset against other Schedule D income whilst the assumed profit from the occupation of land in its unimproved state may be assessed under Schedule B.[7] Expenditure on woodlands can thus be offset against taxable income.

Timber crops are exempt from Capital Gains Tax, although the exemption does not apply to the land upon which they grow. If woodlands are sold, roll-over relief is available providing the sale proceeds are reinvested in commercial woodlands. Estate duty has now been replaced by Capital Transfer Tax (C.T.T.) and many of the advantages that timber growers once enjoyed have been lost. The main concession is that deferment may be claimed for commercial woodlands and the ultimate realized value of the timber is charged to C.T.T. with no reference to the value of the timber at the date the death of the owner occurred. If a further death and transfer occur before the timber is felled the original liability is cancelled. However, *land* under trees is charged to C.T.T. immediately upon death regardless of the fact that the value cannot be realized without selling the crop. The difficulties surrounding forestry and C.T.T. are compounded by uncertainty about wealth taxes which may be introduced.[8] The government appear to have recognized these difficulties: an interdepartmental review was set up by the Treasury in July 1976 to review again the taxation and also the grant arrangements for the private forestry industry. (See Note 2 of the Postscript, p. 245.)

Direct support

As from 1 October 1974 a new forestry grant scheme has been in operation.[9] This applies to areas in excess of one hectare where the land has been dedicated to the production of timber. However, there are important secondary conditions attached to grants relating to amenity and recreation. The explanatory leaflet states that the woodlands concerned must be managed in accordance with a Plan of Operations designed to secure the objectives of sound forestry, effective integration with agriculture, environmental benefits and opportunities for recreation where appropriate; and that the landowner will, if and when requested by the local planning authority, enter into an access agreement consistent with the requirements of sound silviculture and nature conservation.[10]

The grants available differ as between softwoods and hardwoods. The basic grant for approved softwood plantings is £45/hectare. An additional £125/hectare is payable for approved planting with hardwoods (totalling £170/hectare) to establish a hardwood crop and to give a predominantly hardwood appearance to the landscape over the greater part of the woodland's life.[11]

Certain county councils are now grant-aiding the planting of individual trees and small areas of woodland (generally areas of less than one hectare). These schemes often have the support of the Countryside Commission (see Chapter 9) and are primarily concerned with amenity planting although the timber at maturity will have some commercial value.

RECREATIONAL AND EDUCATIONAL ENTERPRISES

Many of the enterprises so far discussed are not widely divergent from traditional farm activities. In this section we are concerned with enterprises that can truly be considered new since they often appear alien to accepted farm practices and they involve the farmer in a very different role from the one he has traditionally played.[12,13,14] Appendix III lists the many different kinds of enterprise which can be introduced, within the three major groups of tourist accommodation, provision for resource-based activities and provision for day-visitors. The rest of this chapter discusses the nature and implications of these enterprises.

Tourist accommodation

Accommodation for the tourist is the most widespread form of recreational enterprise associated with farming. The range includes farmhouse accommodation, self-catering accommodation, second homes, and caravan and camp sites. All are popular with farmers for a number of reasons. Great demand for tourist accommodation exists in the remoter areas of Britain where both the land quality and farm structure are often poor. It is in such regions that there is most need for additional farm income.[1] Accommodation for visitors gives scope for flexibility in the scale of operation. Farms can offer either simple bed and breakfast accommodation or sophisticated facilities with opportunities for a complete family holiday. Caravan sites can range from small unlicensed facilities, occupying a field corner, to extensive sites licensed for many vans. By providing accommodation, farmers can make use of unused resources, for example a half-filled farmhouse, empty cottages, or a piece of waste land. The new enterprises may involve organizational and managerial commitment, basic secretarial work and some expertise in catering, but no other special skills are needed beyond those of most farmers and their wives.

Evidence shows that tourist accommodation can yield good returns on capital. Davies, for example, calculated average rates of return for farmhouse accommodation, self-catering accommodation and caravan/camp sites of 26, 26 and 74 per cent respectively.[14] The amount will depend to a large extent on the scale of operation, with larger enterprises often showing higher rates of return on capital.[13] Even so, very small enterprises, although they produce small incomes, do this with little capital investment and operating expenditure. A small camping site, for example, will require no particular facilities, whereas a large caravan site will need, among other facilities, lavatories, shower rooms and the installation of sewage disposal equipment. In a survey of farm-based caravan sites in southeast England, four small sites involved no capital expenditure at all and yet produced returns of £11, £50, £75 and £100.[12] Appendix IV gives a range of costings for farm tourist enterprises.

Although farm tourism can bring financial gain to the farmer, the amenity benefits from such developments are less certain. Caravans and camping sites may damage the environment if they are not suitably sited and screened. More important, however, may be the role of subsidiary enterprises of this kind in helping farms, and thus the farmed landscape, to survive. Specifically, some of the extra income derived from farm tourism may be used to carry out visual improvements to land and buildings. Farm buildings which are falling into disrepair may be renovated to house visitors and this can both remove an eyesore and ensure the survival of traditional buildings which add variety to the landscape. Oast houses in Kent and barns in the Lake District and the Yorkshire Dales have been renovated to provide second homes or self-catering holiday accommodation. Farmers who are sensitive to public opinion (and a Wye College study suggests that many are[12]) may plant trees and shrubs to screen caravan sites. These are anyway generally small (five vans or less) and operate for only part of the year, often when the countryside itself is vegetated enough to absorb them. The means to increase the vegetative framework may be available through county council tree-planting schemes.

Resource-based activities

Resource-based activities, such as riding, shooting and fishing, depend upon the existence or creation of specific assets such as woodland, rides and water. Horse-riding enterprises, including pony-trekking, horses at livery and equestrian centres, are perhaps the most difficult to establish and operate, although they are very numerous.

All can be highly demanding in terms of land, buildings, capital, management and labour. Land is needed for exercising and riding the horses and also for grazing. Buildings are required for staff and visitors as well as for the horses; a study for the Countryside Commission found that buildings associated with equestrian centres were among some of the largest found on farms, involving costs of £12,000 and higher.[13] Although use can be made of old stables and cowsheds can be converted into stalls, costs can still be high. All farmers with horse-riding concerns in the Wye College study[12] had made use of such facilities, yet these enterprises still required the highest capital investment of all those examined. As well as buildings, the purchase of horses adds a further heavy demand on capital. Running costs can also be high: the most costly items are usually labour and feed. Horse-riding is one of the few recreational pursuits for which specialized knowledge is required and the provision of this can be costly if the farmer does not possess it himself.

Returns from farm-based horse-riding show marked variation. Although some enterprises studied have been unprofitable, the reasons for this are unclear. Some farmers have a distinct advantage when they have buildings which can easily be converted, where horses are already owned, or where the farmer or his wife have the necessary specialized knowledge. Environmental gains can accrue from the restoration of disused buildings and from the maintenance of bridle paths which would otherwise become overgrown.

Fishing, like horse-riding, can take a variety of forms depending upon whether it is river or lake, from bank or boat, or for coarse fish or game. It is one of the most popular sports in Britain and there seems to be a large demand for facilities. Provision is unlikely to encroach upon traditional farm practices and establishment costs need not be high. The cost and effort involved are primarily related to whether or not a farm possesses natural water areas. If it does an enterprise can be established with few costs.[12] If the fishing rights are leased to angling clubs who will take responsibility for operation, then even fewer costs are involved. On many farms the basic resource of open water is already present, requiring only to be modified: old ponds may need to be dredged and streams widened. It is only where artificial lakes need to be constructed that the capital requirements can be high. A study for the Countryside Commission estimates a cost of £3000 for a five-acre lake.[13] Once the water area is established, the only other major costs are those of stocking and restocking with fish (about £200 to stock a five-acre lake with trout) and the purchase of boats if required. The returns from fishing, in relation to its quality and the size of water area, seem to be particularly good. The same water areas can also be used for farming purposes such as irrigation, and possibly for boating. In addition, they provide habitats for waterfowl which, apart from their conservation value, can be the base for a shooting enterprise. All this may be gained from a previously unproductive resource. Economic uses of these kinds may be the only way to safeguard remaining farm wetlands (see Chapter 4).

Three main types of shooting can be developed on farms: rough shooting (for pigeons and rabbits), quality shooting for pheasant, duck and hare, and (less commonly) clay pigeon shooting. The amount of revenue that a farmer can expect is dependent upon the quality of the shoot and the size of the farm; pheasant, duck and hare shooting are generally more remunerative than rough shooting. The quality of the shoot is further improved if a varied habitat for wildlife is available including feed crops and water areas. Table 21 outlines financial data for a number of shooting concerns ranging from a rough shoot

Table 21. Financial data for seven farm-based shooting enterprises

Farm number	1	2	3	4 (£s)	5	6	7
Capital costs	–	–	–	–	–	75	–
Operating costs	–	–	20	–	–	–	2571
Revenue	48	50	60[a]	130	230	700	3400
Total net cash returns	48	50	40	130	230	700	892
Type of shoot	R	R	Ph	Ph	Ph	Ph/D	Ph/D

Notes: R = Rough shooting; Ph = Pheasant shooting; D = Duck shooting.
[a] Farmer belongs to the shooting syndicate: were he not he could expect to receive a greater revenue.
Source: Bull, C. J. and Wibberley, G. P. (1976). *Farm Based Recreation in South East England*. Studies in Rural Land Use, Report No 12, Wye College (University of London).

over 89 acres to a duck and pheasant shoot over 1500 acres. The most significant aspect of the figures is that only one enterprise involved any substantial expenditure. Rough shooting need not involve any expense for the farmer and, in addition to the income, the farm will benefit from a reduction in vermin. Provision for better quality shooting can be expensive however, especially if a gamekeeper is employed and young pheasants reared. Here, costs can be avoided if the shooting is let to a syndicate. If the farmer provides a high-quality shoot, he may charge commensurately (as in Case 7).

Shooting, like fishing, can bring other advantages to the farm, the most important being the use of unproductive land and the creation of a more varied environment. Scrub woodland found on many farms can be ideal cover for game; marshy areas can attract wild duck or may be converted into lakes.

Day-visitor enterprises

There are many day-visitor enterprises which can be established on farms: they include informal recreation facilities (country parks, picnic sites and coastal car parks); enterprises providing special attractions, such as wildlife parks; sporting facilities like golf courses; and farmhouse catering. All are amply discussed in a report to the Countryside Commission.[13]

It is the more informal kinds of recreation provision, such as country parks, farm and wildlife parks, rather than the formal sports facilities, which offer the greatest opportunities for achieving direct and indirect environmental benefits, while perhaps at the same time improving farm incomes, offsetting farm losses, or reducing damage by formalizing public access over private land. All offer a means of diversifying the landscape and retaining or introducing habitats and animals which may be disappearing as a result of modern agricultural practices. Nineteen private country parks,[15] grant-aided since the Countryside Act, have so far been established, and a number of these are subsidiary farm enterprises.

Facilities of the informal kind need not involve buildings or new capital although some are fairly demanding of land, management and labour. Unlike sports facilities, which can be managed by clubs, most informal recreation enterprises do not offer scope for controlling the numbers of visitors by membership or booking arrangements. The number of visitors to expect on any particular day will not be known and this generates considerable organizational problems. It is not normally possible to establish a regular clientele and publicity is required. Although the overheads may be high, income per visitor is often low: the entry charge to picnic sites, wildlife and other country parks, for example, is generally between 10 and 50p. Large numbers of visitors (50,000 a year has been suggested) are necessary to produce worthwhile margins.[16]

Educational and interpretive enterprises

Perhaps the most important of all the enterprises which may be linked to farming are those which attempt to encourage urban visitors to learn about the countryside. The gap in understanding has widened between increasingly mobile urban populations and those who live and work in the countryside. The townsman is accused of using the countryside unsympathetically while the farmer is seen to resent this intrusion upon his traditional preserve. Farm interpretation is an attempt to bridge this gap; unfortunately, it offers one of the least profitable means of grafting on a subsidiary farm enterprise.

Farm interpretation aims to increase the visitor's understanding of farming and its relevance to him.[17] Understanding brings greater enjoyment and, it is hoped, a greater appreciation of farmers' problems and the need to use the countryside wisely. Through their contact with the public, farmers may also learn more of the urban dweller's concern for conservation.

All the farm-based recreational and tourist enterprises so far discussed have some educational or interpretive value, albeit incidental. Apart from these, however, there are a number of activities and facilities, such as farm open days, farm trails, exhibition farms, farm parks and rural museums which are designed either specifically or in part to interpret farming to the public. To be commercially successful these enterprises must put across farming in an enjoyable way: interpretation alone is not generally a financial success without the provision of some recreational attraction.

A Dartington Amenity Research Trust report on farm open days gives exhaustive detail on this type of facility.[18] They are usually special events, held on one or two days in the summer, involving considerable organization. They must be well-advertised. Few open days yield a profit, but this is not generally their main objective. Farm trails are open all the year, most often with printed guides or notice boards providing the interpretive element. Again, there is little opportunity to make a commercial success of such facilities.

Interpretation may be provided as an adjunct to other farm recreational enterprises, especially at farm parks or exhibition farms. Special features, such as viewing galleries in milking parlours, may be created and interpretational displays can be arranged, but these must generally be supported by more profitable facilities. Some dedicated farmers have established special relationships with schools and encourage classes to visit their farms. This invariably means producing special educational packs to assist in briefing teachers and pupils in advance of the visit or keeping children in touch with what is happening on the farm throughout the year after the visit has been made.

CONCLUSION

This survey of the broad range of new enterprises which can be associated with farming is not intended to be exhaustive, nor is it an operational manual for their development (see Appendixes I and II). It seeks only to show that opportunities exist to enhance farm income and farm capital, and to harness new markets. At the same time public understanding and enjoyment of the countryside can be increased and substantial environmental improvements made.

Appendix I

ESTABLISHING A SUBSIDIARY ENTERPRISE

In setting up any new enterprise there are certain procedures which it is prudent to follow, including the listing of objectives and resources, identifying uses, recognizing constraints and evaluating alternatives.

Listing objectives

In deciding the optimal use of any set of resources the question must first be asked 'optimal for what?' Traditionally it has been assumed that the most important objective of any entrepreneur is to maximize profit. But there are other objectives which may be important and have little or nothing to do with making money. Most people seek to maximize satisfaction. In order to do this, a farmer may wish, for example, to preserve and enhance the countryside he owns or manages, encourage wildlife on his land, and pursue a number of goals which are not necessarily compatible with making the maximum profit.

When contemplating a new enterprise, it will almost always be the case that a financial break-even situation or better will be required, but the farmer must also list those other objectives which go to make up his satisfaction. New enterprises grow out of a hobby. A farmer may enjoy riding or shooting but may not be able to support the expenditure involved entirely for his own pleasure, or he may wish to improve quality or spread his overheads and the only way to do so is to create an enterprise from his hobby. There are circumstances in which a farming couple decide to take in guests during the summer because their family has grown up and left home. They have spare bedrooms in their house and they seek company for part of the year.

Listing resources

Generally, the larger the farm the greater the possibility for diversifying, in the fullest sense, the range of activities which may be introduced. Resources are

215

not confined solely to the more obvious assets of the farm itself. The list could, for example, cover:

> farm buildings and other structures, including the farmhouse and farm cottages;
> tracks, roads, trails, footpaths;
> woodlands;
> scrub and marginal areas;
> vegetational framework;
> wildlife assets;
> landform;
> manpower;
> capital;
> management;
> skills;
> equipment.

Many of these resources may have little or no agricultural function, and may be transferred to other uses with no loss to the farm. There may be redundant farm buildings which could ideally be converted either into self-catering holiday accommodation or into a museum to house agricultural machinery. Other important resources to be considered are the location of the farm in relation to roads and population centres, the level of regional activity in tourism and recreation, and the quality of the local landscape. A farm with good access, in a National Park and with spare buildings, may be well-placed for exploiting the tourist market. A farm close to a large urban area may be ideally located to develop recreational enterprises, a farm shop or facilities for interpretation.

Identifying uses

Even when alternative farming uses have been considered, it may be that a particular piece of marginal land or outdated buildings offer no feasible means of continued agricultural use. It will usually be appropriate to list all the possible alternative non-agricultural uses before selecting the best enterprise for the circumstances.

Recognizing constraints

Constraints arise from personal attitudes, resource limitations and external considerations. A farmer who does not want large numbers of visitors will not favour some recreational activities; if he is against blood sports he will be unlikely to develop a shooting or fishing enterprise on his farm.

Resource constraints flow directly from the listing of objectives and capital resources. A farmer should have a good idea of the amount of capital available to him and the more limited this is the more he will have to envisage either very small enterprises or highly profitable ones which will yield sufficient return on capital employed to justify raising a substantial loan. A major constraint, often overlooked, is management time and effort. Any new enterprise will demand a more than proportional amount of managerial effort, relative to the proportion of other resources taken up. This may severely detract from existing farm business efficiency, but it may be possible to make use of an underutilized resource, such as the farmer's wife who can make a contribution to the management of such enterprises as farmhouse and self-catering accommodation, farm catering or produce stalls.

The final element in the list of constraints is one on which the farmer will generally need to seek advice, in particular on the question of planning permission. It is well worth discussing any proposals informally with local authority representatives at an early stage. Such discussions will reveal the authority's attitude to such problems as traffic generation and management, impact on landscape and conflicts with other groups such as neighbouring landowners, naturalists, ramblers and others whose interests might be affected. Some new enterprises require no planning permission and may be developed without reference to outside bodies. For example, a shoot may be created, a very small caravan site (certificated location) set up, or a farmhouse opened for accommodation without planning permission. Many subsidiary enterprises fall under the 28-day rule whereby land may be used temporarily (not more than 28 days in any one year) for certain activities without application being made for planning permission. This rule would apply, for example, to temporary car parks, caravan rallies, shows and exhibitions and farm open days.

Evaluation of proposals

Each alternative enterprise must be examined in the light of objectives previously set. In many respects the farmer will be able to assess for himself the extent to which a proposed activity will fulfil these. It may be necessary, however, to call in specialist advice to evaluate the short list, especially in terms of likely financial performance if this is an important element. A farmer may also require design and landscaping expertise. Where grants are to be applied for it is necessary to have a plan and estimate of costs to ensure that a realistic sum is put forward. In this respect the experience of one farmer is relevant; he assessed the total capital cost of a barn conversion for self-catering holiday flats at £20,000. In the event the total cost was £40,000, but the grant was paid only on the original estimate.

In the case of a major investment in an alternative enterprise it will be appropriate to prepare a complete business plan. This should show the anticipated cash flow over a reasonable time horizon in the project life and a range of internal rates of return under a number of assumptions about changes in levels of demand. Calculations of this nature take account of the incidence of taxation and the availability of grants and are often necessary if outside finance is to be sought.

Appendix II

SOURCES OF ADVICE

It has been stressed that consultations should be held at an early stage with the local planning authority and with other groups who may have strong interests in any proposal which affects the use of land. There are other bodies, official and otherwise, which specialize in countryside matters. Many of them will provide advice and assistance at a low or nominal cost and may provide grants or loans to support certain developments.

The Countryside Commission and the Countryside Commission for Scotland provide general and specific advice on a wide range of opportunities for informal recreation in the countryside. They may support, through grant aid, certain developments such as country parks and picnic sites. They are also concerned with advice on the conservation and enhancement of the landscape and with increasing the urban visitor's understanding and appreciation of rural areas.

The Tourist Boards are primarily concerned with encouraging the provision of tourist accommodation. They may assist farmers financially, in the Development Areas, with the provision of farmhouse accommodation or self-catering holiday units. They also support other facilities which are expected to encourage tourism in these areas, and may publicize recreation attractions throughout the country. Leaflets are available on the role of the Boards and their fields of interest.

Organizations ordinarily associated with agriculture are becoming more interested in tourism and recreation and are acquiring expertise to offer to farmers. The Agricultural Development and Advisory Service of the Ministry of Agriculture Fisheries and Food, the National Farmers' Union and the Country Landowners' Association are all able to offer the farmer advice and to recommend other organizations capable of detailed planning and feasibility work. Cannington Farm Institute in Somerset is building up a data bank for farmers who wish to develop tourist and recreation enterprises. A comprehensive information and advisory service will be based on the Institute in future. Farmers wishing to develop the sporting potential of their estate can contact the Game Conservancy at Fordingbridge.

Forestry advice is available from the Forestry Commission and a number of private forestry firms undertake planting schemes and manage woodlands for individual farmers and estate owners. Details are available from the Timber Growers' Organization.

Finally, there are now a number of private consultancy firms which provide comprehensive services in recreation, tourism and the broader aspects of land use, including some of the larger land agent's firms with a leisure department, and certain architects and landscape architects whose offices can offer comprehensive advice on recreational development.

Appendix III

RECREATION AND TOURIST ENTERPRISES WHICH CAN BE LOCATED ON A FARM

(Source: Appendix 2 in: Dartington Amenity Research Trust/Rural Planning Services (1974). *Farm Recreation and Tourism in England and Wales*, Countryside Commission Publication No. 83, and DART publication No. 18.)

A. Tourist Accommodation
1. In the farmhouse: bed and breakfast; farm guesthouse; farmhouse holiday; farm auto-holiday.
2. Self-catering accommodation in converted farm buildings, cottages, chalets.
3. Second homes, including redundant farm buildings (leased or sold) and long-let caravans.
4. Camping sites.
5. Caravan sites: transit/touring/static.
6. Specialized holidays: i.e. accommodation plus an activity (field studies, sketching etc.).

B. Resource-based activities
7. Riding, pony-trekking, equestrian centres.
8. Fishing, swimming, boating, boat moorings.
9. Game: rough shooting, pigeon shooting, pheasant and duck shooting, clay-pigeons.

C. Day-visitor enterprises
10. Informal recreation: car parks, picnic sites, country parks.
11. Access for caving, climbing etc.
12. Special attractions:
    Rare breeds, wildlife parks, museums of farm machinery etc.;
    Sporting facilities: squash, tennis, swimming pool, sauna, golf-driving range, golf course, grass-skiing, plastic ski slopes etc.;
    Wildlife hides.
13. Farm catering: teas, meals etc.
14. Farm produce:
    farm-gate sales to public;
    homeground wheat;
    self-picking of fruit and vegetables.

15. Indoor activities and events: barn dances, concerts, plays etc.
16. One-day/occasional events:
    (a) Related to farming—hedge-laying, ploughing matches.
    (b) Unrelated to farming—traction-engine rallies, motor-cycle scrambling, archery, clay pigeon shooting, autocross, pop concerts.
17. Educational visits: farm open days, farm trails, school visits, demonstration farms etc.

Appendix IV

COSTS AND RETURNS FOR SOME FARM TOURISM ENTERPRISES

(Source: based on figures originally published in Dartington Amenity Research Trust/Rural Planning Services (1974). *Farm Recreation and Tourism in England and Wales*, Countryside Commission Publication, No. 83, and DART publication No. 18.)

Farmhouse accommodation	*Capacity*	
	2 rooms 3 people £	4 rooms 6 people £
Establishment cost		
Cost of furnishing bedrooms at £100 each	200	400
Wash-hand basins	100	200
Cost of furnishing lounge/dining rooms	200	300
Miscellaneous at £10/head	30	60
	530	960
Annual income		
Average bed, breakfast and evening meal charges £3·50/head Assume two-thirds usage over season of 150 nights	1050	2100
Annual expenditure		
Labour	—	300
Heating and lighting	50	100
Food	400	750
Management time	50	100
Repairs and maintenance at 20%	100	200
Advertising	20	20
	620	1470
Margin	430	630
Margin if charges were:		
increased by 10%	535	840
decreased by 10%	325	420
Days spent by farmer's wife	100	150

Note: no charge has been made for the labour of the farmer's wife so that the margin shown represents the amount by which the net farm income is increased. The margin is the amount of money the farmer's wife can put in her pocket for her endeavours.

Self-catering cottages/flats

	(1) Single cottage: holiday lets only £	(2) 5 units converted £
Establishment costs		
Cost of building conversion/ modernization	5000	15,000
Architect's fees at 12%	350	1800
Furnishing	300	2500
	5650	19,300
Annual income		
Winter—4 weeks at average: £20 per week	80	400
Summer—30 weeks at average: £28 per week	840	3650
	920	4050
Annual running cost		
Repairs/maintenance	80	400
Rates	70	200
Heating and electricity	80	350
Advertising	50	75
Clerical and domestic work	—	200
Insurance	60	100
	340	1325
Margin	580	2725
Margin if charges were:		
increased by 10%	670	3130
decreased by 10%	490	2320
Days spent by farmer's wife	15	65

Self-catering holiday cabin

	Single unit £
Establishment cost	
Cabin—200 sq ft	
(Dimensions 20 ft × 10 ft)	1500
Connecting services, furnishings	
and equipment	500
	2000
Annual income	
26 weeks at £26 average	676
Annual expenditure	
Insurance	10
Repairs and replacements	30
Rates	20
Advertising	50
Rent 0·5 acre at £20/acre	10
Annual charge on chalet	
cost—10 years at 15% on £1500	300
	420
Margin	256

Margin if charges were:	
increased by 10%	323
decreased by 10%	189

Days spent by farmer's wife	15

Static caravan site

	5 vans $\frac{1}{2}$ acre £	10 vans 1 acre £
Establishment costs		
Clearing and preparing site	50	100
Toilet facilities	300	450
Access provision	200	200
Other expenditure	200	200
	750	950
Annual income		
Caravan site rent at £100 p.a. /unit	500	1000
Annual running costs		
Rent at £20/acre	10	20
Rates	75	120
Insurance	40	80
Maintenance	25	50
	150	270
Margin	350	730
Margin if charges were:		
increased by 10%	400	830
decreased by 10%	300	630
Days spent by farmer/ farmer's wife	5–10	5–10

Note: in the case of the vans being owned by the farmer, then the vans are likely to cost between £1000 to £1200 each (accommodating 4–6 people) and associated facilities may cost in the region of a further £50 to £100. The gross annual income from such a van would probably be of the order of £675 (an average of 26 weeks at £26 per week), whilst the annual margin can be expected to be of the order of £350 to £400. This figure includes an allowance for depreciation.

Small touring caravan site

Capable of accommodating five caravans at a time
Open for eight months a year

Alternative occupancy levels (1 unit = 1 caravan/night)	300 units/ season £	400 units/ season £	600 units/ season £	900 units/ season £
Establishment costs				
Sanitation point installation				
Laying on of water				
Access improvement				
Miscellaneous				
	350	350	350	350
Annual income				
80p/unit/night	240	320	480	720
Annual running costs				
Rent 0·5 acres at £20/acre				
Grass cutting				
Insurance				
Miscellaneous				
	55	55	55	55
Margin	185	265	425	665
Margin if charges were:				
increased by 10%	209	297	473	737
decreased by 10%	161	233	377	593
Days spent by farmer's wife	20	25	40	50

Camping site

	50 tents 2 acres £
Establishment cost	
Installation of water and electricity	1000
Toilet block	3000
	4000
Annual income	
Two-thirds usage over season of 150 nights at 50p/night, say	2500
Annual expenditure	
Rent at £120/acre	40
Rates	100
Labour (part-time for season)	500
Advertising	50
Maintenance	200
	890
Margin	1610
Margin if charges were:	
increased by 10%	1860
decreased by 10%	1360
Days spent by:	
farmer	40
farmer's wife	40

NOTES AND REFERENCES

1. Burton, T. L. (1967). *Outdoor Recreation Enterprises in Problem Rural Areas*, Studies in Rural Land Use, Report No. 9, Wye College (University of London).
2. The classification of enterprises is necessarily arbitrary and the boundaries between the suggested groups are blurred.
3. Johnson, Hugh (1966). *Wine*, Nelson, London.
4. Turff, R. (1971). 'Three English Vine Growers', *Farmers' Weekly*, 27 August 1971.
5. Robertson, Andrew (1975). *'Baccus backs Britain'*, *Sunday Times*, 2 November 1975.
6. See Steele, R. C. (1975). *Forestry Management and Nature Conservation*. This paper, presented at a Conference on Forestry Management organized by the Royal Society of Arts, provides a more exhaustive discussion of nature conservation in woodlands.
7. The new owner of woodlands has ten years in which to decide whether to have that wood assessed under Schedule D. A woodland manager will generally have some woodland under Schedule D and some under Schedule B. Normally, woodlands which are profitable will be under Schedule B whilst those making a loss will be under Schedule D so that profits may be balanced against losses. It is not often that such an ideal state is achieved since it is not possible to switch freely from D to B.
8. The evaluation of the impact of new and potential tax measures on forestry is a continuing debate. See, for example, Campbell, J. (1974), Private Investment in Forestry, *Scottish Forestry*, **28**, 174–191; Campbell, J. (1975), Can Private Forestry Survive High Capital Taxation? *Quarterly Journal of Forestry*, **69**(4), 195–201; and Lynch, T. D. (1974), *Forestry Management and Taxation*, a paper presented to a Conference on Forestry Management, Royal Society of Arts, 25 November 1974.
9. Forestry Commission (1974). *The New Dedication Scheme (Basis III)*. The operation of the previous schemes is outlined in Chapter 9.
10. Forestry Commission (1974), p. 2, para. 4.
11. Forestry Commission (1974), p. 3, para. 6. Grants were revised at 1 October 1977. See Note 2 of Postscript, p. 245.
12. Bull, C. J. and Wibberley, G. P. (1976). *Farm Based Recreation in South East England*, Studies in Rural Land Use, Report No. 12, Wye College (University of London).
13. Dartington Amenity Research Trust/Rural Planning Services Ltd (1974). *Farm Recreation and Tourism in England and Wales*, Countryside Commission publication No. 83 and DART publication No. 18.
14. Davies, E. T. (1973). *Tourism on Devon Farms: A Physical and Economic Appraisal*, Agricultural Economics Unit, University of Exeter, Report No. 188.
15. October 1976.
16. DART/RPS (1974). *Farm Recreation and Tourism in England and Wales*, Chapter 5, Section C.
17. Aldridge, D. (1975). *Principles of Countryside Interpretation and Interpretive Planning*, HMSO, Edinburgh (for the Countryside Commission for Scotland).
18. Dartington Amenity Research Trust (1974). *Farm Open Days*, a report of an experiment undertaken by the Countryside Commission. Countryside Commission publication No. 77, DART publication No. 14.

Chapter 12

The prospects for action

J. DAVIDSON

The idea of conserving those natural resources which have no direct economic value may seem inappropriate in periods of economic stress. The conservation of wildlife and landscape has always been most active at prosperous times, in prosperous places and among prosperous people. For Britain in the later seventies, it is not an auspicious time to be questioning the expansion of a major economic activity like agriculture: there is continuing uncertainty about the costs and supply of food products from abroad and pressure to intensify the output at home.[1] Farmers face rising input costs for materials, energy and wages as well as new taxes. In circumstances such as these, suggestions for the modification of some established farming practices, which do little or nothing to improve agricultural productivity even though they may limit the further loss of amenity values from the countryside, must seem to some frivolous and impracticable. But it is also possible to be profoundly pessimistic about the rate at which environmental values are declining, and to see in the future no prospect for compromise.

In this book we have tried to be realistic: to find out where the ecological effects of modern agriculture matter most and, in particular, to explore those means of conservation which seem to be politically and economically feasible at the present time.

ECOLOGICAL PROBLEMS

Part I of this book provides evidence of the nature and scale of the effects of changing agricultural practice for a number of important wildlife habitats. Some of the work discussed is still inconclusive as experience of new farming systems has often been short, the research effort has been small, and the measurements themselves are frequently difficult to make. Real uncertainty about the future pervades discussion about almost every habitat.

Yet it is clear that, for a number of species at least, the position is less worrying than many ecologists once feared. The early devastating effects of pesticide spraying, particularly with organochlorine derivatives, have not persisted and recoveries have been made in the species most noticeably affected. Paradoxically, economic stringency has brought some conservation

231

benefits. Increasing costs have caused farmers to curtail the frequency and extent of crop spraying, especially aerial operations, thus reducing the risk from spray drift to wildlife in hedge and woodland habitats. Most highway authorities have likewise ceased to treat road verges with herbicides except where this is essential to maintain visibility.

But there is no cause for complacency. There is abundant evidence to show that a rapid decline is taking place in many of the most important natural and semi-natural habitats, especially in the lowlands, including hedgerows and small woodlands, downland, meadows, rough grazing and heath and most of the micro-wetland habitats of farmland such as ponds, ditches and marshy areas. A major cause for concern is the rate at which agricultural drainage is progressing since this contributes not only to the loss of wetlands of all kinds, but also to the die back of many trees as the water table falls. The generation of new wildlife habitats, for example along motorways and following sand and gravel extraction, does not compensate for the losses.

All these findings are symptoms of the more general and growing ecological problem of fragmentation. Changes in the regional farming pattern and in many agricultural practices over the last two decades have contributed to a disintegration of the *network* of habitats. Some habitats and some species have been virtually extinguished over this period: chalk grassland, sandy heaths, coppice woodland, for example, have all lost their economic values and have often been replaced by more productive vegetation. The few remaining areas survive only where they have special protection as nature reserves or public open spaces, or where they are inaccessible to agricultural machinery. But less obvious and more insidiously dangerous is the fragmentation of common habitats which, like hedges and small woods, are the home of many plant and animal species at some time in their life cycle and often at the crucial breeding period. We do not yet know the precise role of habitats such as hedgerows and wetlands in supporting the wildlife stock over a wide area of the farmed countryside.

The widespread removal of cover in eastern England has become a familiar and well-documented story. But the potential for major change now lies also in the pastoral areas of south and west Britain at a time when Dutch elm disease has drastically reduced tree cover, and the other main tree species of the farmed landscape (oak and ash) are failing to replace themselves. Hedgerow trees in many areas are disappearing at a faster rate than the hedges in which they stand. Much of the lowland landscape, and its complement of wildlife, is quite simply decaying.

Habitat destruction and modification is not just a lowland problem. Here the changes may have been more rapid and more noticeable, but there have been losses in the uplands as pastures continue to be enclosed and improved by draining, reseeding, burning and other means. Here, as in the lowlands, deleterious ecological changes are taking place as a result both of the intensification and the decline of agricultural activity, particularly in relation to grazing.

THE AGRICULTURAL FUTURE

There is much uncertainty about the way British farming will develop. Alternative agricultural futures will affect environmental values very differently and will require flexibility in the kind of response environmental planners should make.

Expansion

The official outlook, expressed in 'Food from our own Resources',[1] is one of expansion, with agricultural productivity rising steadily to bring greater self-sufficiency in temperate foods. Chapter 1 argues that there seem to be few technical constraints upon such a goal; indeed self-sufficiency might be achieved by the end of the century if the rate of growth in output of the early 1970s can be maintained.

The environmental consequences of expansion, despite the optimism of the White Paper, could be severe. All the habitat losses identified in the earlier chapters of this book would continue, perhaps at an accelerating rate, with the conversion of more non-agricultural land to productive farming and further improvement of the poorer hill land. It is not easy to predict the individual effects of further technical developments in mechanization, in agricultural chemicals and in the methods of intensive livestock rearing, but a whole range of *new* environmental problems might be generated.

Beresford, however, is more sceptical of the potential for agricultural expansion.[2] He has argued that British farmers lack sufficient capital, skilled men and, most of all, the confidence necessary to respond to a further call for expansion at this point in time. Memories of recent losses in the beef and dairy industries, continued inflation and high interest rates, and the uncertainties of new taxes on land, together with the implications of changing Common Market agricultural policies may discourage farmers from investment and long-term improvement of their enterprises. In the short term, the combined effect of all these pressures on working farmers means that many will be in no position to consider amenity values when the survival of their livelihood is threatened. The environmental consequences of an agricultural industry in which there is reduced confidence could be at least as harsh as those which will follow from a successful expansion programme.

Alternative futures

It is possible to suggest a more fundamental change in British farm policy. A continuation of the pattern of hot dry summers experienced in 1975 and 1976 will force changes in crop-growing and especially in livestock-rearing, quite apart from any conscious redirection of our agricultural programme of the kind proposed by Mellanby.[3] He argues persuasively that the supposed conflict between a better fed nation and a richer, more beautiful countryside is a false one. It is, he suggests, both feasible and desirable to increase self-sufficiency in foodstuffs and at the same time bring about a substantial and permanent improvement in conditions for wildlife and in the quality of the farmed landscape.

This plan rests upon an overall reduction in the numbers of livestock, particularly those, like broiler fowl and intensively reared calves and pigs, which depend upon imported feed. There would be much greater production of grain and vegetables for direct home consumption (at present more than half of all our homegrown grain is fed to livestock while bread grains are imported). As a consequence of these changes in production, the national diet would need to be adjusted. It would become, over the long term, less dependent on meat (some of which is superfluous, if not damaging, nutritionally) to be replaced by extra vegetables—especially potatoes—and grain products, including protein substitutes.

Mellanby envisages that agricultural output will continue to increase with technical developments in breeding, in the use of chemicals and with food augmented by the produce from gardens and allotments. This, together with the increased efficiency in production from a readjustment in the kind and amount of livestock reared, will remove the pressure to farm every piece of land intensively. Likewise, the threat of more industrialized farm buildings to house more animals will be reduced, along with the risk of increased pollution from their effluent. Hedges, woods and wetlands can be safeguarded. Most grasslands would continue to be improved for direct grazing, mainly by dairy herds, but some old grasslands would need to be grazed only to the level necessary to maintain their floristic interest. Environmentally, therefore, the proposals offer a rather different future from the one which might follow a more zealous expansion programme along the lines of the recent White Paper.[4,5]

But there are problems in the Mellanby plan, some of which may have been underestimated. Dietary adjustment may take some time to achieve, even with extensive propaganda, for most British housewives and their families not only enjoy a varied and meaty diet but they are used to fairly quick and simple methods of food preparation which Mellanby's suggested diet could not offer. Nor will British farmers and their representatives be easily or rapidly persuaded, let alone the meat wholesalers, butchers, food-processing industries, transport services and others for whom the proposals have direct implications. The wider investment, employment and land use effects have not been fully investigated.

Other agricultural futures have been suggested, based upon a substantially greater use of industrially produced foods, or upon a return to traditional methods of labour-intensive crop and animal husbandry. Neither are particularly realistic, certainly in the short term. The environmental implications of a return to subsistence farming on smallholdings, in terms of the extra housing and servicing required in rural areas, are likely to be as undesirable as those of the current expansion programme.[6]

In all, the future of British agriculture seems uncertain. Over the longer term, we may see some change towards a more environmentally satisfactory system of farming of the kind Mellanby suggests, less likely to suffer from fluctuations in the world food, raw material and energy markets, and better able to adjust to the vagaries of the British climate. Over the short term, the most likely course seems to be one of expansion, and it is possible, as Wibberley notes, to be pessimistic or optimistic about the outcome.[5] Chapter 1 argues that even without the change in diet suggested by Mellanby, an 85 per cent or greater level of self-sufficiency in temperate foods can be achieved by the end of the century with a lower rate of growth in productivity than was occurring in the early 1970s or is now planned ($1\frac{1}{2}$ rather than $2\frac{1}{2}$ per cent as suggested in the White Paper). This should make us cautious about the need to farm so intensively and more concerned to ensure that long-term environmental values are not sacrificed unnecessarily.

IMPLEMENTATION OF CONSERVATION POLICIES

The second part of this book is concerned with some of the alternative means of redressing the damaging effects of modern agricultural practice, especially over the short term. In *strategic* terms, three main kinds of action seem to be required. First, some, if not all, of the best remaining natural and semi-natural habitats associated with farmland must be *protected* from further change which might reduce or destroy their wildlife and amenity values. Such is the case with old grasslands and patches of heath in the lowlands, water meadows, primary woodland and ancient hedgerows, and other features of archaeological or historic importance. In the uplands, the rate at which heather moor is being reclaimed must be reduced. Some semi-natural habitats are now so rare that only special measures of protection, probably involving ownership or management by public or voluntary conservation bodies, will be needed. It is in these areas that conservation will be the primary objective, although it is desirable that as much productive use as it is possible to combine with this aim should take place: for example, by the grazing of heath and grassland, and the selective cropping of timber from amenity woodlands. Other purposes such as public recreation, education and sport may be perfectly compatible in some areas.

The second requirement is for *remedial* action. Many habitats, and particularly the micro-habitats of agricultural land, have already been greatly modified by recent farming practice; yet some of their value for conservation could be restored by changing the way in which they are managed: by, for example, altering the timing and intensity of chemical spraying, especially of wetlands; by trimming hedgerows more carefully to allow some saplings to grow up; by following a rotational pattern of hedge management; and by taking more care of newly planted trees. Public as well as private land managers are involved here, for poor management of much land in public ownership—along highways, waterways, railways and on defence lands—also contributes to the scenic and ecological poverty of some rural areas.

Finally, if farmland in future, particularly in the lowlands, is to continue to offer the ecological richness and scenic diversity with which we are familiar and on which so many countryside activities depend, then *creative* action must also take place to introduce new elements to a rapidly decaying landscape. Chapters 9 and 11 discuss the possibilities of creating new cover on scales which range from field corner planting to extensive new woodlands.

This may be the strategy, but the most effective *tactics* of action are less clearly defined, since they involve difficult questions about the need for new controls; the availability of funds for essentially non-productive uses of land; the worth of private and public trusteeship; and the nature of attitudes to the environment. An issue on which there is much conflict is the degree to which conservation should be a partnership with agriculture, particularly on the better land. Conservationists themselves are divided in the solutions they offer, from those who seek a greater segregation from agriculture, with the designation of many more nature reserves (available only for scientific protection and research) to those who argue for more multiple use of land—a phrase now so vague and so widely interpreted as to be almost worthless, for few activities can happily co-exist on the same land at the same time. Alone, both extremes are unrealistic.

Some new reserves are obviously needed; they are probably the only way of achieving long-term protection of rare habitats. Local authorities could be more enthusiastic about using their powers to designate Local Nature Reserves.[7] Better means of protecting the values of other scheduled sites of conservation importance are also required: Chapter 10 discusses the problems of Sites of Special Scientific Interest. But for many habitats and species, reserves and other forms of special designation would need to be impossibly large or numerous to provide sufficient protection against the damaging effects of widespread modern agricultural practices. High land values and interest rates will limit the public acquisition of new reserves, especially on the better grades of agricultural land; and as Chapter 9 argues, landowners are not encouraged, in the present economic climate, to commit themselves to long-term management agreements.

There is scope for some extension of the idea of multiple land use: wetlands can be used for economic gain; small hardwoods can provide marketable timber; chalk grasslands open to the public can be grazed; shelterbelts provide cover for a number of species; and rough upland pastures can be used by sheep and people with better regimes of visitor management and estate improvements, for example to footpaths and boundaries. This type of 'area management', pioneered in the Countryside Commission's Upland Management Experiment, and subsequently developed on the urban fringe of Manchester and London, is particularly appropriate to marginal agricultural environments.[8] Here too, farmers may graft on to their business those subsidiary enterprises, in recreation or afforestation, which incidentally bring about conservation benefits (see Chapter 11).

Conservation and intensive farming

None of the approaches so far discussed will be enough since they will have little effect over the bulk of the agricultural landscape; and in the prosperous farming zones on the better land scarcely any effect at all. It is in these areas that Westmacott and Worthington found the greatest loss of wildlife and landscape values and forecast the most dramatic future change.[9] They suggest that enough public and private land is available, which is unproductive or otherwise unused, to build up the basic cover for new agricultural landscapes and new wildlife habitats. But further study suggests that their optimism may not be justified. It is possible to argue that the disparate areas are far too small for an adequate replacement of what is being lost, and that the solutions Westmacott and Worthington offer accept too easily the continued destruction of the elements of an enclosure landscape.[10] Nor is there any real evidence yet that enough effective tools of implementation are available.[11]

Two questions on implementation are particularly significant. First, how far is it possible, and desirable, to influence farmers on the better land to adopt conservation practices which yield little or no benefit to them? Secondly, how far is it necessary to *remove* from agricultural use (and more particularly from the possibility of further agricultural expansion) those remaining vestiges of old landscapes and habitats which could form the basis of a new network of cover?

The means of persuasion

The notion of supporting farmers (not only with cash, but also with information, advice, labour and materials) is attractive: it has the appeal of using to the full all the accumulated skills and experience of those who own and manage land, of building upon feelings of trusteeship, of retaining individualism and originality, and of safeguarding the countryside from the advance of bureaucracy. Chapter 8 discusses a wide range of persuasive measures. It is difficult to assess how effective these may be for many are of recent introduction, but even optimists acknowledge that there have been few direct practical gains for conservation other than among the minority of farmers already committed. But this does not invalidate the contribution of persuasive methods, particularly in agricultural education, to the development of a more fundamental sympathy for conservation in the longer term, and a return to the acceptance of the responsibilities for trusteeship that traditionally go with land ownership. In the short term, there is a need for more, and more accessible, practical advice for farmers about conservation methods, augmenting the valuable work of public agencies such as the Nature Conservancy Council and the Countryside Commission and of voluntary groups like the British Trust for Conservation Volunteers and the Farming and Wildlife Advisory Group.

The use of financial incentives, associated for example, with management agreements and tree planting schemes (see Chapter 9) may bring more direct benefit to some areas. More could be done to demonstrate and persuade farmers of the economic values of small hardwood plantations, especially of fast growing species which can provide an almost immediate landscape effect. Chestnut coppice, game-rearing and wetland management for grazing can also be profitable, while at the same time providing environmental gains.

But for the immediate future, the effects of all these approaches will be limited and confined to the less prosperous agricultural areas *unless* there can be a much greater integration of conservation objectives with agricultural policies which are formulated at national level and reflected locally in the discharge of grants and advice from the Ministry of Agriculture to individual farmers.

Farmers will not be persuaded by financial incentives to conserve wildlife and landscape features unless the grants or compensation they receive are more than equal to existing incentives to improve their enterprise and its productivity. What is needed is the introduction of *selectivity* to the award of agricultural grants for such operations as ploughing, draining, and hill land improvement; so that in certain areas, grants can be withheld while farmers receive conservation payments on the basis of an agreed plan which adequately reflects extra costs and lost revenues. In some areas, even where there are no grounds for restricting grants for improvement, their award should be subject to (and reflect the costs of) a management plan which recognizes conservation needs.

The case for greater public control

Many agricultural activities which are scenically and ecologically damaging take place without grants and outside the scope for monitoring that a modification of the grant system would allow. Even if a much increased emphasis were placed upon conservation matters in the local advisory work of MAFF officers, the problem of uncertainty would not be resolved. Landscape and wildlife are too valuable to be left entirely to the whim of private voluntary action, which in the short term is bound to be patchy. A failsafe system of legal sanctions is needed to protect the non-farming interests in land. Chapter 10 suggests some modifications to existing control measures to improve their effectiveness, for example in the conservation of trees, and discusses the possibilities of 'notification of intended change', for activities such as ploughing, draining and hedge removal in certain areas.

The introduction of all these measures presupposes a substantial change in the attitudes, objectives and functions of the Ministry of Agriculture, and in its staff, reflecting a much better linkage of conservation and agricultural policies in the same way that the Ministry has adjusted to EEC demands for greater recognition of the socio-economic problems in farming. The idea is not novel: Chapter 7 discusses the various arrangements for integration which are practised elsewhere in Europe. Other Ministries (for example those concerned with Defence and Energy) would also need to implement more effectively the spirit of Section 11 of the Countryside Act, which requires all government departments and public bodies 'in the exercise of their functions' to 'have regard to the desirability of conserving the natural beauty and amenity of the countryside'.[12]

It is possible to argue for more fundamental changes in the structure of government; Wibberley, for example, suggests a new super-ministry concerned with rural affairs.[13] Tinker argues for an executive agency at national level to be responsible for landscape renewal and wildlife conservation outside designated areas, based upon some modification of the roles of the Countryside Commission, Nature Conservancy Council and Forestry Commission.[14]

It may be that the scale of environmental renewal required in parts of the countryside can only be achieved by employing more doctrinaire methods of landscape reconstruction in the style of Dutch and West German practice. In these countries, public agencies take certain proportions of land in schemes of agricultural improvement for landscape and wildlife management. Programmes of farm consolidation designed to increase productivity by farm amalgamations, field enlargement, drainage, and road improvements are undertaken by the State for groups of landowners with their consent, and landscape management is an integral part of these programmes.[15] Although the principle of consolidation is inappropriate for Britain, where the restructuring of farms has already taken place, there is a need in many areas to superimpose a new landscape and wildlife framework on to a modernized pattern of land holdings. The amount of land required for amenity purposes would be small, probably never more than 2 or 3 per cent of the land areas, and the trend towards self-sufficiency in temperate agricultural produce suggests that small losses of productive land to achieve this total could be justified.

But there would be problems. British resource agencies have neither the experience nor the equipment to own and manage land in small and scattered parcels. Such a notion goes against current pressures for the devolution of executive responsibilities.

Local conservation—co-ordination of interests

No one method of conservation offers the panacea: all the measures, from persuasion to public ownership, will be needed, especially on the better land. The crucial problem is how to implement conservation policies locally. The kind of conservation this book is about it not achieved by the definition of national aims, by planning designations or structure plan statements; it relies

upon almost daily co-ordination of the estate management decisions of public
and private landowner's over tracts of countryside.

There is no obvious choice of group suited to the task of co-ordinating the
interests of farming with those of conserving wildlife and landscape. The
national agencies such as the Ministry of Agriculture, Nature Conservancy
Council, Countryside Commission and Forestry Commission have more
limited remits in executive action or advice and research; some have no local
representation. Although there is much enthusiasm and expertise among
voluntary groups, the means of guiding it towards practical local action remain
elusive. MAFF advisers, whom farmers are familiar with and have confidence
in, are not always adequately trained in conservation matters, nor do they give
them sufficient weight in advice. In theory, it is the local planning authorities
who have the overview of interest in land which spans more than one ownership
for both district and county councils are empowered to be concerned about
environmental management. But most lack the staff who are able to liaise well
with farmers.

Some way must be found of harnessing the efforts of all these groups in the
preparation and implementation of local environmental plans. Experience in
management experiments in the Lake District and the Bollin Valley and
elsewhere suggest that success depends heavily upon local attitudes, but also
upon the negotiating skills of a specialist 'project officer' who can co-ordinate
the varied interests.[16] Amenity interests themselves will not always be aligned:
a richer ecological environment may be, visually, a very untidy one; a pleasing
landscape is not automatically the best for wildlife.

Local environmental schemes

One possibility is for local planning authorities, probably at District level and
employing a specialist liaison officer, to prepare local environmental schemes
for those areas where a comprehensive approach is needed.

The Ministry of Agriculture, Highway Authorities and other statutory and
voluntary bodies would be involved in the preparation of a scheme. The liaison
officer would need to work with all these groups and, with his detailed local
knowledge and contact with land occupiers, he could prepare a first draft on the
basis of land identified as marginal to agriculture, and highway land, taking into
account existing landscape, wildlife, archaeological and historic features of
interest. Where a satisfactory scheme could not be devised solely on the basis of
land marginal to agriculture and highway land, some productive farming land
may have to be used. It is likely that in many areas a satisfactory environmental
scheme could be agreed with little extra land of this kind.

Local environmental schemes of this type could provide the key instrument
for matching national aims with local needs. The Ministry of Agriculture could
be required to take account of their content in the giving of advice and grant to
farmers, for example, towards farm improvement or drainage operations.

Schemes could not only provide the framework for practical action by farmers, but also by local authorities (in tree planting, designation of local nature reserves, negotiation of access or acquisition of amenity land), and by local representatives of central government agencies; for example, the Forestry Commission in the operation of the felling licence system, and the Countryside Commission and Nature Conservancy Council in their advisory and grant-aid work. Voluntary conservation bodies would probably welcome a framework of this kind to guide their activities.

A programme of local environmental schemes will generate new costs, not so much for preparation as for implementation. It might be appropriate that the central government contribution to the programme should come from the vote of the Ministry of Agriculture. The Ministry already contribute towards any increased costs of erecting buildings which also need to satisfy amenity requirements, and this principle might be extended to ensure that all farm improvements are environmentally acceptable.[17] A rolling programme of tree planting with an expenditure of £1m could make a major impact on the landscape of the farmed countryside. Yet such a level of expenditure would represent less than 1 per cent of the level of public support for agricultural improvement which in the year 1974/75 was about £105m.[18]

CONCLUSIONS

There is a clear need for change at two levels. First, in *national* attitudes and in the organization of government, landscape and wildlife must be seen as legitimate interests in land together with food production, taking precedence in some areas, even on the better land. Secondly, there must be a new emphasis upon *local* implementation; the means are there for positive action in protecting and creating varied, rich and satisfying environments.

The present landscape and its wildlife will not wait for the national economic climate to improve, nor for a new fashion among farmers for amenity management. The problem is not lack of money or lack of means but public and private apathy.

NOTES AND REFERENCES

1. Ministry of Agriculture, Fisheries and Food (1975). *Food From Our Own Resources*, Cmnd 6020, HMSO, London.
2. Beresford, T. (1975). Food from our own resources. *The Countryman*, Winter 1975/76, 101–107.
3. Mellanby, K. (1975). *Can Britain Feed Itself?*, Merlin Press.
4. See note 1.
5. Wibberley, G. P. (1975). Changing landscape: the threats and the remedies. *The Countryman*, Winter 1975/76, 36–42.
6. Anderson, M. A. (1975). Land planning implications of increased food supplies. *The Planner*, **61**(10), 381–383.

7. As designated under Section 21 of the *National Parks and Access to the Countryside Act*, 1949.
8. Countryside Commission (1976). *The Lake District Upland Management Experiment*, Countryside Commission Publication No. 93. Hall, A. (1976). *The Bollin Valley*: *a Study of Land Management in the Urban Fringe*, Countryside Commission Publication No. 97. For a discussion of the notion of 'Area Management' see also: Countryside Review Committee (1976). *The Countryside—Problems and Policies, A Discussion Paper*, HMSO, London.
9. Westmacott, R. and Worthington, T. (1974). *New Agricultural Landscapes*, Countryside Commission Publication No. 76.
10. Council for the Protection of Rural England (1975). *Landscape—the Need for a Public Voice*.
11. MacEwen, M. (1976). The Unknown Future; in MacEwen, M. (ed.) *Future Landscapes*, Chatto and Windus, London.
12. Section 11, *Countryside Act, 1968*. See also: Phillips, A. A. C. (1976), Too Much Planning—or Too Little? in MacEwen, M. (ed.) *Future Landscapes*, Chatto and Windus, London.
13. Wibberley, G. P. (1975). See note 5. The role of the main agencies which exercise some advisory or executive responsibilities in the field of countryside policy are being examined by the Countryside Review Committee, chaired by the Department of the Environment.
14. Tinker, J. (1974). The End of the English Landscape. *New Scientist*, **64** (926), 5 December.
15. In the past the consolidation process often did considerable damage by removing the natural cover of trees and shrubs, in much the same way that damage has been done to the British countryside as a result of agricultural changes here. In recent years, however, increasing attention has been directed to making consolidation schemes more environmentally satisfactory and in some countries the provision of generous landscaping is now written into the legal framework. For example, in Holland, where over 130,000 acres of land a year are subject to consolidation schemes, a landscape plan is now a condition for any project carried out under land consolidation legislation. These landscape plans involve the preservation of valuable landscape and wildlife features from the existing countryside fabric, but, more significantly, they also involve the creation of new landscape elements often to the extent of 3 per cent of the land area. In addition, the plans are designed to maximize benefits for recreation and the new landscape components frequently form the locus for footpaths and bridleways.
16. See Note 8.
17. Grant can be paid on the total cost of an eligible improvement including any increased costs due to amenity considerations, although subject to an overriding consideration that the total cost is not unreasonably high in relation to the agricultural benefit derived from it. The provision covers both those cases where a more expensive building is required as a result of a planning condition, and where the farmer is willing to incur the expense voluntarily. Source: Ministry of Housing and Local Government/Ministry of Agriculture, Fisheries and Food/Welsh Office/Council of Industrial Design/Countryside Commission (1969), *Farm Buildings and the Countryside*, HMSO, London.
18. Payments for fertilizers, lime, farm capital and other improvements, and additional payments for improvements in the uplands. Source: Northern Ireland Office/Scottish Office/Welsh Office/ Ministry of Agriculture, Fisheries and Food (1976), *Annual Review of Agriculture 1976*, Cmnd 6392, HMSO, London.

Postscript

Since this book was first written, a number of relevant reports have been produced and three are particularly significant.

Following on from their publication of *New Agricultural Landscapes* the Countryside Commission held a series of regional conferences to discuss the conclusions and implications of the study with many interests. Drawing upon these and written comments received, the Commission set out their recommendations in January 1977.[1]

The emphasis for action in the lowlands is placed upon stopping the unnecessary clearance of existing features of landscape value and upon much more new planting of trees and shrubs both on public and private land, and especially in eastern England which has suffered the most rapid landscape change in recent years.

By way of support, the Commission propose to make use of their own grant-aid powers, and those of the Forestry Commission, to promote the planting of many more small woods and smaller areas of trees on farmland. In Chapter 9 a case was made for the reintroduction of a Small Woods Planting Grant; in April 1977 a new Forestry Commission grant for small woods was announced which will apply to planting schemes as little as $\frac{1}{4}$ hectare with an emphasis on broadleaved trees.[2] This should do much to encourage the creation of new cover in the countryside.

Along with new planting, the Commission suggest various ways in which the clearance of features of landscape value could be reduced and those that remain could be better managed. These rely on persuasive means including, for example, the improvement of advisory services, tax concessions and management agreements. The Commission also place considerable emphasis upon codes of practice. They have invited the Secretary of State for the Environment to draw up management guidelines for all government departments (and the nationalized industries) that hold and manage land. They also suggest that the farming organizations and local authority associations should produce codes of practice for land management.

Finally, the Commission reaffirm their belief in persuasion by example. They have demonstrated practically (in the Upland Management and Bollin Valley Experiments) how it is possible to achieve greater harmony between rival interests in the management of tracts of countryside. The Demonstration Farms Project will show the financial and other implications of landscape conservation at a farm scale. Combining these approaches, the Commission now hope to demonstrate the viability of all their proposals in new projects (not unlike the ideas we discuss in Chapter 12) whereby landscape improvement can be promoted over large areas of good farmland in the lowlands.

The Nature Conservancy Council have published a parallel study and policy document on modern agriculture and wildlife conservation.[3] As for landscape, the threats are seen to derive from the intensification of farming on the better land, and especially from the reclamation of land to agricultural use. Problems also lie in the fragmentation of habitats as well as in their removal and modification. The solutions are more than ones of maintaining and creating new cover; it is the integrity of the remaining semi-natural areas on farmland that needs to be safeguarded.

Outlining the elements of their national conservation strategy, the Nature Conservancy Council confirm the importance of National Nature Reserves, but recognize the present inadequacies of conservation measures outside these and other reserve sites, particularly on Sites of Special Scientific Interest (we discuss the limitations of this designation in Chapter 10). The Council call for more formal consultation over decisions about the management of SSSIs and for more incentives for owners to take conservation action (including exemptions from Capital Transfer Tax and more money for management agreements).

For the wider countryside, the Nature Conservancy Council argue, as do the Countryside Commission, for more accessible and directly usable advice on conservation (discussed here in Chapter 8) and for better management of public land. They call for greater co-operation between government agencies on issues such as incentive payments and conservation services and suggest that specially trained 'Rural Advisers' might be the way to maintain direct contact with landowners and other interest groups.

Over all is the call for a national strategy for rural land use to guide local decision-making about the priorities in management objectives over different tracts of countryside. It is clear that the Nature Conservancy Council want all future increases in agricultural productivity to take place by the *intensification* of production over existing agricultural land rather than by the further *reclamation* of unused or under-used land.

But a report by the Centre for Agricultural Strategy is not optimistic about the possibility of increasing productivity substantially in this way.[4] A figure of only 1–1·5 per cent is suggested as realistic for the future annual growth of agricultural output. Nor will this be achieved unless the unnecessary transfer of land out of farming can be reduced. Planning practice is roundly blamed for failing to take sufficient account of food production needs in decisions on urban development. The report calls for greater participation of agriculturalists in the planning process and, again, a national land use strategy seems to be sought, setting out national land needs for food production against which land allocation decisions can be checked.

In all, the CAS report is rather more pessimistic about future agricultural productivity, and the prospects for British self-sufficiency in temperate foods, than are the conclusions of Chapter 1 of this book. It argues that there is 'little room for manoeuvre' in the competition for land. Short of major developments in agricultural technology, only the more radical approaches to food production (discussed in Chapter 12) seem to offer a way out of these problems.

NOTES AND REFERENCES

1. Countryside Commission (1977). *New Agricultural Landscapes: Issues, Objectives and Action.* Countryside Commission Publication 102.
2. *Hansard*, March 31 1977, Columns 720–721.
   The rate of grant under the Small Woods Scheme is £300 per hectare for areas of 0·25 hectares to less than 3 hectares and £250 per hectare from 3 hectares up to 10 hectares. The Forestry Commission have also introduced (from 1 October 1977) new rates of grant under the Dedication Scheme (Basis III) which will now apply only to areas over 10 hectares. These are:
   Basic grant for approved softwood planting £100 per hectare.
   Additional grant for establishing a broad-leaved crop £125 per hectare (total grant £225 per hectare).
   Management grant £3 per hectare per annum.
3. Nature Conservancy Council (1977). *Conservation and Agriculture.* Published by NCC.
4. Centre for Agricultural Strategy (1976). *Land for Agriculture.* CAS, University of Reading.

Index